PATENTING IN THE
BIOLOGICAL SCIENCES

PATENTING IN THE BIOLOGICAL SCIENCES

A Practical Guide for Research Scientists in
Biotechnology and the Pharmaceutical and
Agrochemical Industries

R. S. CRESPI
British Technology Group
London, U.K.

A Wiley–Interscience Publication

JOHN WILEY & SONS
Chichester · New York · Brisbane · Toronto · Singapore

Copyright © 1982 by John Wiley & Sons Ltd.

All rights reserved.

No part of this book may be reproduced by any means, nor
transmitted, nor translated into a machine language without
the written permission of the publisher.

Library of Congress Cataloging in Publication Data:

Crespi, R. S.
  Patenting in the biological sciences.
  'A Wiley–Interscience publication.'
  Includes index.
  1. Patent laws and legislation. 2. Biology—
Patents. 3. Life sciences—Patents. I. Title.
K1505.C73   346.04'86   81-19771

ISBN 0 471 10151 6   342.6486   AACR2

British Library Cataloguing in Publication Data:

Crespi, R. S.
  Patenting in the biological sciences.
  1. Patent laws and legislation
  2. Biology—Patents
  I. Title
  342.64' 86   K1505

ISBN 0 471 10151 6

Typeset by Pintail Studios Ltd, Ringwood, Hampshire.
Printed in the United States of America.

Contents

Chapter 1

Introduction to the Patent System

The object of this work is to introduce research workers in the biological sciences to the subject of patents so that they may communicate more readily with those professionally engaged in the law and practice of patents. This communication will most often be with patent agents and attorneys, sometimes with patent counsel, and occasionally with patent office examiners, higher officials of boards of appeal, and judges in patent courts.

The need for an introductory manual of this kind arises from the experience of the writer that in the biological field the descriptive writing and interpretation of patent specifications and other documents used in patent procedures involve problems of an acute and special kind which flow from the very nature of the subject matter which the draftsman must characterize and define. These problems stem from the inherent complexity of biological entities, and frequently from the relative inadequacy of the data available at the time valuable discoveries are first made. Biological inventions are often difficult to fit into the simple framework of nineteenth century physics and chemistry which supports some of our basic concepts of patent law. The purpose of the writer is not to make patent specialists out of microbiologists and other biological scientists but to illustrate the fact that the writing of any patent and the creation of a patent situation requires the combined skills of the inventor and the patent draftsman and tactician. I shall in general refer to the research worker as an 'inventor' although there are some who still feel uncomfortable with this term because of past connotations. The more academically inclined researchers, and these can be found in industry too, prefer to think of themselves as good scientists proceeding according to the accepted canons of science but we shall see that invention and good plain science are not the same thing.

The patent system does not appeal to every inventive mind. Some inventors are naturally drawn to it and welcome the discipline it imposes on them in the development of their ideas towards a practical commercial end. For others the rules of the game are tedious and inhibitory and are not justified by the results the system offers. Our object here is to study and clarify these rules so that the final choice of the inventor or entrepreneur who supports the inventor can be made in more accurate knowledge of the options available.

Before attempting to describe the system in any detail it is first necessary to place patents in the broader context of forms of industrial property and from that point to go on to consider the classical arguments justifying the existence of the patent system and then to subject these to criticism from the point of view of the research worker. In looking at the merits and demerits of the patent system we must be careful to ask what it can be reasonably expected to provide for the inventor and businessman and what cannot be fairly demanded of it.

THE NATURE OF INDUSTRIAL PROPERTY AND ITS VARIOUS FORMS

Industrial property is a general term covering new ideas, designs, processes, products, devices and apparatus in a form in which the law will grant a property right and offer the author, designer, or inventor a measure of legal protection against imitation and copying. Like other forms of property it can be bought and sold or licensed to use.

Industrial property covers patents, designs and trade-marks. When we add to these the related concept of copyright the broader term intellectual property is sometimes used (this covers artistic copyright as well as industrial copyright).

A property right must be publicly proclaimed and therefore the scope of the right must be published. An alternative to seeking a public right is to keep the idea secret and exploit it privately, and so we also have the concept of a trade secret which is outside the statute law of industrial property. Trade secrets usually come under the common law of fiduciary relationships. They are of considerable significance in some fields of technology where a policy of trade secrecy may be successful and must always be considered as a possible alternative to seeking protection by means of industrial property.

Patents

These are rights granted in respect of inventions capable of industrial application, mainly processes, products and apparatus. Patents offer the widest form of protection in which the attempt is made to cover as many applications as possible of the fundamental principle of the invention. It is a common belief that possession of a patent conveys the right and freedom to use the invention but this is not so. The patent right is divorced from the positive right of making or doing anything and has instead a negative character, being a right of exclusion. Freedom to use the invention by the patentee himself may be affected by other laws and other patent rights which impinge on this activity.

Designs

These are a lesser form of protection than the patent and are concerned primarily with features of shape and ornamentation applied to articles. They are of little interest to the biological scientist.

Trade-marks

A trade-mark is a mark used by a manufacturer or trader to distinguish his goods from similar goods of other firms. It may be a word or sign or a combination of these which is used to indicate the origin of the product carrying the mark and a connection in the course of trade between the product and its originators. Trade-marks do not protect ideas or particular kinds of goods as such. They are nevertheless of enormous commercial value once a reputation and public demand for the goods has been established.

The rights conferred by patents, designs and trade-marks are not automatic but involve action to register them and therefore a registration system is established by statute law in all these fields.

Copyright

Copyright differs from patents and other forms of industrial property in that the legal rights arise spontaneously when the work is created and no registration system is necessary. In this respect it is a simpler system and offers many attractions. However, it suffers from the limitation that copyright protects only against actual copying whereas other forms of industrial property protect against independent duplication of ideas and efforts as well as actual copying.

Plant Varieties

Inventions in the field of microbiology are mainly dealt with by means of the patent system. For higher forms of plant life it is possible to obtain plant patents in some territories, e.g. USA, but new plant varieties are more often the subject of separate legislation. The protection granted under plant variety rights is restricted to the commercial exploitation of the reproductive material of the plant.

JUSTIFICATION OF THE PATENT SYSTEM

The basis of a patent is a bargain made between the inventor and the state whereby the state grants for a limited period a right to exclude others from the enjoyment of the use of the invention without the consent of the patentee. In return the inventor makes a full disclosure of the invention in a detailed written specification which is published in due course and made available for public use freely after the limited period has come to an end. The process by which patent protection is applied for and granted is handled by a special government department office, frequently known as the 'Industrial Property Office' or the 'Patent Office', and it is governed by specific rules laid down by statute and by regulations established for its practical operation. Each country will have its own national industrial property law and practice and the legal effect of the patent will be limited to the territory over which the particular state has jurisdiction. International systems of patent law also exist and will be discussed later.

Can such a system be justified? Should not all new ideas be freely communicated and freely available so that all may benefit from them without hindrance or restriction? The classical answer to this question which attempts to justify the system is threefold.

1. Patent protection encourages disclosure as against secrecy.
2. Patent protection encourages investment in research.
3. Patent protection encourages investment in production and marketing of new products.

Thus the system is justified on the grounds of greater dissemination of information and knowledge and the possibility of obtaining a reward for those who take the risks of innovation.

In modern times the classical answer has been expanded by emphasizing that the patent system provides a framework in which industrial competition is carried on fairly and in accordance with the law and in which technology transfer can be regularized between industrial firms in technologically developed countries and also between the developed world and the developing countries.

Economists have found it very difficult to discover data on which to test the basic hypothesis justifying some system of patent protection but it appears to most people to have a high intrinsic probability of being true and of reflecting human nature accurately.

THE ATTITUDE OF THE RESEARCH WORKER

A patent cannot prevent *bona fide* research but is only exercised in practice against actions of a commercial nature. The patent system therefore does not inhibit the carrying on of research activities. If a research group working for an industrial concern discovers that a particular patent held by a competitive firm presents an obstacle to its own commercial developments they may either seek evidence to invalidate the patent or research into ways of avoiding the patent or build up through their own research and patent holdings a position of strength from which to negotiate a licence from the competitor. This stimulant to research into new and alternative ways of solving technological problems is frequently argued to be another healthy result of the patent system.

In asking whether the patent system is helpful to research and development we must not fall into the trap of thinking that the system itself is designed to provide a reward. Textbooks on patent law invariably stress the negative character of the patent. From the patentee's viewpoint, the single purpose of a patent is to set up a prohibited area from which competitors are excluded other than by the express consent of the patent owner. Possession of a valid and strong patent gives its owner nothing more than the opportunity to exploit the invention in a privileged manner and to obtain commercial benefits and other positive rewards by his own actions. A similar confusion can arise in the debate as to whether greater importance is to be attached to patent rights or to know-how. These two items are essentially complementary and are in no way to be compared. Thus, although it is a fundamental requirement that a patent specification contain a sufficient disclosure to enable the reader to carry out the process or to make the product described it is asking too much to expect it to contain the fullness of teaching which would enable a third party to set up manufacture without the necessity for a substantial amount of development work of his own. When a patentee or a licensee begins operations for the practical industrial exploitation of any invention it is of course the know-how element which is of prime importance in getting anything off the ground. The possession of patent rights or the right to a licence comes into its own at the later stage when competitors and imitators appear on the scene and the rights can then be invoked to control unlicensed competition, if their mere existence has not already been of itself sufficient to inhibit the competitor or imitator.

How does the inventor react to the system? The first irritant is the need to be reticent about the nature of the discovery before steps can be taken to protect the invention. The modern patent law with respect to the requirement of novelty imposes a strict imperative against premature publication by an inventor and it is difficult for many inventors to accept this temporary curbing of their natural desire to publicize their discovery as much and as soon as possible. The second demand the system imposes on the inventor is that he will have done sufficient work on his invention to enable a specification to be written which has a sufficient content of practical teaching to be of use to the reader to justify the grant of rights. In a scientific paper an author may be content to disclose an experimentally justified idea or hypothesis leaving it to others to explore its many ramifications. The more seminal the original contribution the more the scientific community will acclaim it as a landmark in the development of scientific thought. But in a patent specification the author is now the inventor and the inventor's purpose is to protect and not solely to stimulate; the stimulatory function is more to be seen in the theory that the grant of protective rights will induce competitors and others to seek alternative routes to the same result and even to improved results. The objective of descriptive writing in a patent is to ensure that the many forms in which the basic idea is capable of exploitation are well covered. Protection of the full breadth of the inventive possibilities is not granted automatically but must be worked for. These two factors cause many inventors to conclude that there is a conflict between patenting and early publication and that the latter course is the much easier way to recognition. For them, meeting the demands of the patent system is far too onerous as in the case of the inventors who defended themselves in the following terms:

'We chose to publish rather than patent because of the complexity of specifying the idea on paper that would provide anything like comprehensive cover. We talked about the idea for a couple of days and every hour produced at least one idea embodying such a principle after which time the office was full of waste paper'.

This was not particularly good reasoning on the part of the inventors because it would be the duty of a competent patent agent, after a sufficiently full discussion with them, to encapsulate the principle of the invention in a broad patent claim which would embrace every one of these hourly manifestations of the basic idea.

The next irritant for the inventor is the challenge to his self-esteem that he has to endure from the patent office examiner whose responsibility it is to consider whether patent protection is merited. The inventor's reaction to this is often to be non-plussed at the objections raised by the examiner based on prior publications of very dubious scientific validity. If the inventor is the first to make something of practical utility he will have a sense of frustration with a system which denies him protection because of a collection of scattered references in the literature which really have made no effective contribution to the art. Patent practitioners feel much the same way about this as inventors and strive hard to overcome the difficulties raised by patent office examiners. It has been stated to be the function of an attorney 'to analyse, organize and present a body of data in a fashion so as to convince someone to follow a course of action desired by the attorney's client' and this is what he should be doing on the inventor's behalf to overcome the objections raised. However, patent law has to use some criterion for judging whether to grant or refuse patents and those charged with the duty of implementing the law must consider the public interest also. An inventor may be an applicant for a patent on one day but he may find himself on another day assisting someone to oppose the grant of a patent to another inventor, and his attitude to what is justly patentable can vary from one position to the other. The main criterion for patentability is novelty and originality and the examiner is entitled to construct a picture of what is effectively already part of prior knowledge for the purposes of this debate. If his picture is distorted and his arguments untenable it is for the attorney and inventor together to demolish them.

Inventors are sometimes reluctant to commit the time and effort asked of them to assist the patent agent in coping with official objections from the patent office. They may take the view that having disclosed a new invention and having provided the data little more should be asked of them especially when the objections raised seem unfair or ill-informed. This viewpoint is dangerous and can result in the patent agent making unaided decisions about what can be reasonably defended and what may have to be dropped from the scope of the original claim. It is much the better policy for inventors to show interest in the official dissection of their ideas and results and collaborate when required in the prosecution of a patent application designed directly or indirectly for their benefit. The patent agent will often gain much force in his argumentation from the insight the inventor can bring upon the relevance and interpretation of prior published work, be it the technical literature or patent specifications.

BRIEF SURVEY OF PATENTS SYSTEMS

It is the intention of this writer to address the inventor at large and not to stay rigidly within the confines of any one particular national system of patent law. The patent systems of the world have in the past been organized on a national territorial basis and until the emergence in recent years of the regional law of the European patent it was necessary to study each national law separately. However, certain groupings into type are possible and it is possible to identify the following.

British Law

The older UK Patents Act of 1949 provided the model for Britain and the countries of the British Commonwealth. This system was characterized by a liberal and sympathetic approach to the applicant for protection. In assessing the claim for patent rights the examination for novelty was based mainly on what knowledge was previously publicly available in the territory concerned. Great emphasis was placed on the literal wording of a patent in determining the extent of its protective scope but the courts also took into account the equitable doctrine of equivalence in regard to what was less crucial to the invention in their view. The inventor also had the possibility of writing his specification first in a provisional manner to lay the foundation of his claim and then to present a more complete version within one further year from the date of the provisional specification. This still survives in Australia, New Zealand and other Commonwealth territories but the UK itself has, since 1977, become untypical of this group because of its closer commitment to Europe and European ideas of patent law. Canada was always an exception to this group, its law and practice being more like that of the USA.

United States Law

The US patent system has many highly attractive features and in the technological literature of that country more tribute is paid to it as an ingredient of national progress than is accorded to their own systems by writers in other countries. Compared to these other laws the US system is unique; it is probably a more elaborate construction of the human mind than any other system and has the richest development of case law on most of its facets. On the debit side its method of assessing patentable novelty and level of inventiveness is far from satisfactory to the applicant and this judgment is not peculiar to the foreigner. It can take many years and the outlay of much expenditure before success is obtained. Once this consummation is achieved, however, it is to the credit of the system that the full term of 17 years protection is enjoyed from that time onward unlike most other systems where much of the full term has 'run out' before the patent is actually granted. Hitherto, the enjoyment of this full term has been without further cost but the US have recently introduced a system of renewal fees (other countries have always had them) to meet the high cost of administration in the US Patent Office. Bearing in mind the size of the US market, a US patent with claims of reasonable scope is still good value for money in spite of the above criticism. The US system is unfortunately subject to varying climatic conditions especially in the higher courts where anti-patent and pro-patent philosophies fluctuate.

German Law

The German law can perhaps be taken as a prototype of the laws of some other European countries, e.g. Austria, Holland and Scandinavia but this is only a very rough assessment. It is near to the truth as regards the drafting of the patent specification and the very exacting test for inventive merit applied by the patent offices of these countries. But the German courts are outstandingly liberal in not confining the protection to the literal wording of the patent where they are convinced a good invention is present. Of course it takes a lot to convince them on the question of level of inventiveness. Within the Dutch Patent Office it is very difficult to convince anyone that a patentable invention has been made.

It can often take an unconscionable time to obtain a German patent and competitors will readily oppose the application so that by the time the issue is settled there is little life left in the patent.

Euro-Latin Patent Systems

France, Italy, Spain and Portugal have had broadly similar patent laws and the actual practice of obtaining patents in these territories has been largely a matter of form without critical investigation. In this last respect the same can be said for Belgium, Luxembourg and to some extent for Switzerland. Consequently in most of these territories the precise value and scope of a patent would always be uncertain until litigation took place and the court was required to decide what sort of patent it would sustain in the particular case before it.

Japanese Law

Japan does not typify a group of far-eastern patent laws but is sufficiently important itself to justify special mention. It presents special problems especially to applicants from the broad stream of Western civilization and cannot be approached in ways familiar to them in their own jurisdiction. One relies almost entirely on having a good Japanese patent attorney with whom one can communicate reliably. The Japanese Patent Office is difficult to convince and the prosecution of a patent application tends to be protracted and almost always on paper. Interviews are sometimes granted and can be very effective but cannot be obtained easily and certainly not as of right. Japanese patents are valuable pieces of property and although Japanese industry will actively oppose the grant of patents the industry with which this book is concerned will respect patents when granted, and will enter into firm and reliable licensing arrangements with patent holders.

European Patent Law

The European patent convention, signed in 1973 and now ratified by the great majority of the 16 signatory states, came into operation in June 1978. It is a body of substantive law and procedure by means of which a single patent application and a centralized process of examination through the European Patent Office will result in protection effective throughout as many of the contracting states as are designated by the applicant when the European application is filed. Though prosecuted as a single application it in fact matures, if and when granted, into a bundle of separate national patents in the designated territories. The Community Patent Convention, not yet in operation, will provide for a Community patent obtained by the same route through the European Patent Office but having a unitary nature for the EEC as a whole. The European patent system is developing its own special character which will exist alongside the individual national systems and provide an alternative route to protection which may in some circumstances be preferred to that of the separate national routes.

All these systems of patent law provide material for the chapters which follow and reference will be made to selected statutory provisions and case law to exemplify the patenting of inventions in biologically-oriented synthetic chemistry, biochemistry, microbiology and other subjects embraced under a broad interpretation of 'the biological sciences' as understood by the writer. Extracts from particular national laws will be given either in the text where convenient for the discussion or in appendices at the end of the book.

Chapter 2

The Patent Disclosure and Structure of the Patent Specification

The content of the patent specification is of crucial importance in considering any patent situation. Because the vast majority of disputes about patents revolve around the way the specification has been drafted this topic must be the first to be addressed in some detail. In return for the legal protection given the patentee must provide a written description of the invention which is sufficiently clear and effective to enable a person of ordinary skill in the art concerned to practise the invention from its teaching. All the essential information must be included to enable the reader to achieve the results promised by the patentee. Omission of any such essential resulting in a defective disclosure means that the inventor has not fulfilled his side of the bargain. In such a case the patent application can be refused by the patent office or the patent later revoked by the patent office or by a court of law.

The structure of the patent specification falls into two distinct parts. The first is the disclosure itself which can be regarded as the technical description of the invention. Because the specification is addressed to the notional 'person skilled in the art' the draftsman can employ the technical language of, for example, the engineer, physicist, or chemist without explaining what particular terms and expressions mean unless he is using words in a special sense or coining special terms to convey new concepts to the reader. It has been said that the specification is its own dictionary and the draftsman may rely on this up to a point with confidence. The wise draftsman will realize that the ultimate addressee of the specification may be a judge in a court of law and he will therefore try to be as clear as possible without using too much technical shorthand. The draftsman will receive bonus marks from the judge if he has attempted to introduce literary merit into his description but as in all technical or other writing simple language is preferable to the tortuous style. The draftsman of US Patent No. 3,158,528 introduced his invention in this way:

'Despite the presently extensive and ever expanding suitability of synthetic resins in satisfying the infinite variety of structural demands which are raised by our present system of rapidly developing technology, certain extensive and significant areas still resist the utilization of such materials'.

He evidently meant to say that plastics cannot be used for everything. The judge will soon lose patience with this sort of language.

The second part of the specification consists of the patent claims and these must be viewed as the essentially legal part of the document because their purpose is to describe and define the scope of the protection which the applicant is seeking. A patent claim is a verbal formula defining the process, product or apparatus in such a way as to make clear to the public the area of technology that the applicant wishes to reserve for his own exclusive use and which cannot be entered by third parties without his permission. It is usual to present a set of claims varying in scope from the first (main) claim to the narrowest.

THE TECHNICAL DESCRIPTION

Over a long period there has evolved a form of technical disclosure which has become widely acceptable to patent office examining authorities over the world. This format is not prescribed by law but has become customary and there is a strong preference to continue its use. For example in United States patent practice it is now common to present the descriptive matter under the following series of typical headings:

Field of the invention: indicating in a general way the technological field and the broad nature of the invention.

Background of the invention: a section indicating the technological problem to be solved and including a brief description of previous proposals and earlier inventions in the field and the disadvantages they may have.

Objects of the invention: indicating the nature of the improvements that the invention seeks to provide.

Summary of the invention: this is a statement summarizing and distilling the essential elements of the invention in broad terms and is often

14

an advance presentation of the terminology which will be used in the main claim of the patent.

Detailed description of the invention and/or description of the drawings: these sections will include the experimental data given by way of example in describing the methodology of the invention and the apparatus used, if any. The data for incorporation in these sections will commonly be equivalent to the 'materials and methods' section of a scientific paper although it is more usual to present this information in chronological order of operating steps such that it could be carried out routinely by a technician. If the invention is a piece of equipment its structure and method of operation will be described.

The claims section: to be discussed below.

An example showing this format is US Patent No. 3,869,349 entitled *Method for the enzymatic hydrolysis of cholesterol esters* (granted in March 1975). The 'Field of the invention' section refers to the enzymatic method for hydrolysing cholesterol esters in aqueous solutions containing free cholesterol such as blood serum and this is amplified in the 'Background' section by outlining the clinical estimation of total cholesterol first by the conventional chemical assay method and secondly by the more recently introduced enzymatic assay based on the use of cholesterol oxidase. It notes the need for the cumbersome technique of chemical pre-saponification of the bound cholesterol to deliver its free cholesterol content to the enzyme. The 'Object' of course is to provide a simplified and improved method for the hydrolysis step. The 'Summary of the invention' which then follows signals what the applicant intends to claim and introduces the reader to the idea of using a mixture of a lipase having esterase activity and a protease to release free cholesterol.

The 'detailed description' section is an extensive discussion of the method used and includes recommended quantities of the enzymes and preferred temperature conditions. The units of enzyme activity are defined and microbial sources of the lipase are mentioned as well as commercially available enzyme preparations. In discussing the proteases and their sources the draftsman points out that the protease is only necessary where the fluid being processed contains protein, notably blood serum, and indeed in the experimental section which follows there is one specific example where only the lipase is present. This is an illustration of the occasional presence, to which we shall refer later, of gratuitous information in the specification. After further generalized

United States Patent [19]

Goodhue et al.

[11] **3,869,349**

[45] **Mar. 4, 1975**

[54] **METHOD FOR THE ENZYMATIC HYDROLYSIS OF CHOLESTEROL ESTERS**

[75] Inventors: **Charles T. Goodhue; Hugh A. Risley,** both of Rochester, N.Y.

[73] Assignee: **Eastman Kodak Company,** Rochester, N.Y.

[22] Filed: **Mar. 25, 1974**

[21] Appl. No.: **454,659**

[52] **U.S. Cl.** .... **195/103.5 R,** 195/62
[51] **Int. Cl.** **G01n 31/14**
[58] **Field of Search** .... 195/103.5 R, 4, 30

[56] **References Cited**
FOREIGN PATENTS OR APPLICATIONS
2,224,132   11/1973   Germany

OTHER PUBLICATIONS
J. Hyun et al., "The J. of Biol. Chem.," 244, No. 7, pp 1937–1945, 1969.

Primary Examiner—Alvin E. Tanenholtz
Assistant Examiner—C. A. Fan
Attorney, Agent, or Firm—A. L. Girard

[57]   **ABSTRACT**

A totally enzymatic method for the hydrolysis of cholesterol esters using a lipase having cholesterol esterase activity and a protease and a method for quantitative determination of total cholesterol in compositions containing both free and esterified cholesterol comprising enzymatically hydrolyzing the cholesterol esters with a lipase having cholesterol esterase activity and a protease and determining total cholesterol by gas-liquid chromatography or some other suitable technique are described.

10 Claims, 1 Drawing Figure

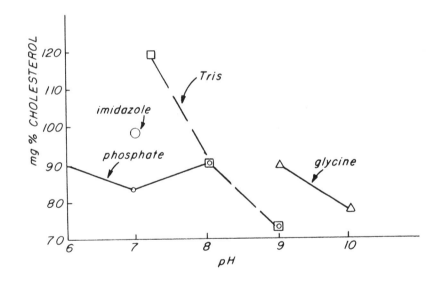

16

1

METHOD FOR THE ENZYMATIC HYDROLYSIS OF CHOLESTEROL ESTERS

FIELD OF THE INVENTION

This invention relates to an enzymatic method for hydrolyzing cholesterol esters in complex aqueous solutions which may contain both free and esterified cholesterol, for example, blood serum and in particular to a process comprising enzymatically hydrolyzing cholesterol esters using a lipase having cholesterol esterase activity and a protease.

BACKGROUND OF THE INVENTION

The most common clinical estimations of cholesterol in blood serum are for "total cholesterol." This value is a measure of cholesterol and cholesterol esters present in the serum and anything else such as cholesterol precursors that respond indiscriminately to the usual tests which are based on reactions involving "free" cholesterol and require prior conversion of cholesterol esters to "free" cholesterol.

In a well-known conventional procedure, serum is extracted with an organic solvent, the extract is saponified with alcoholic KOH and the liberated cholesterol is isolated and assayed. These methods require the handling of corrosive chemicals and are tedious, time-consuming, and not readily automated.

German, Offenlegungsschrift No. 2,246,695 published Mar. 29, 1973, describes an enzymatic assay for free cholesterol using a cholesterol oxidase, however, this technique requires hydrolysis of the blood serum cholesterol esters using the cumbersome techniques of the prior art prior to application of the enzymatic assay.

G. Bucolo, and H. David, *Clin. Chem.*, 19 476 (1973) describe a lipase-protease system for hydrolyzing serum triglycerides; however, it is specifically stated that cholesterol esters are not hydrolyzed in this system.

OBJECTS OF THE INVENTION

It is therefore an object of the present invention to provide a simplified and improved technique for hydrolyzing cholesterol esters.

It is another object of the present invention to provide a reproducible enzymatic process for the quantitative hydrolysis of cholesterol esters in blood serum, useful as an initial step in the quantitative determination of total cholesterol in blood serum.

SUMMARY OF THE INVENTION

The foregoing objects are accomplished by an improved process for hydrolyzing cholesterol esters which comprises treating a sample of an aqueous solution containing cholesterol esters, for example blood serum, with a mixture of a lipase having esterase activity and a protease to release free cholesterol. Subsequently, the free cholesterol can be assayed using any suitable technique including gas-liquid chromatography, cholesterol oxidase assay, or any of a number of other well known techniques for the assay of "free" cholesterol.

DETAILED DESCRIPTION OF THE INVENTION

According to a preferred embodiment of the present invention, hydrolysis of cholesterol esters in complex aqueous solutions (referred to hereinafter generally as blood serum) is achieved by treating the blood serum with a mixture comprising per ml of serum from about

2

20 to about 50 mg of a lipase having cholesterol esterase activity and from about 5 to about 50 mg of a protease at a temperature of from about 25° to about 55°C and a pH of from about 6.5 to about 9.5 for about 5 to about 15 minutes, preferably with agitation and in an inert atmosphere. When the foregoing concentrations of lipase and protease are utilized, the lipase should contain at least about 30 international units per mg and the protease at least about 10 units per mg. One unit of lipase is defined as the amount of the enzyme which will liberate 1 micro mole of fatty acid in a given time at a given pH and temperature using a substrate containing esterified fatty acid. For the preferred lipase materials described hereinbelow the conditions are 1 minute at pH 7 and 37°C with olive oil as substrate. One unit of protease will hydrolyze casein to produce color equivalent to 1 micro mole (181 μg) tyrosine per minute at pH 7.5 and a temperature of 37°C. (Color per Folin-Ciocalteu Reagent). It should, of course, be clear that as the level of enzyme activity per unit by weight of preparation increases or decreases, so also will the quantity of enzyme preparation added vary. Most preferably, the ratio of lipase to protease on an activity basis should range from about 3 to about 10 and at least about 1000 units of lipase should be used per ml of serum. Relative lipase activity to esterase activity is usually about 10 to about 50.

Generally speaking and in accordance with illustrative embodiments of our invention, we contact an aqueous medium containing the cholesterol ester, preferably blood serum, which contains both esterified and free cholesterol, with a mixture of a lipase which demonstrates cholesterol esterase activity as defined in Example 3 and a protease. The lipase may be of plant or animal origin, but we prefer and find best a microbial lipase such as the lipase from *Candida cylindracca*. Lipases from *Chromobacterium viscosum*, variant *paralipolyticum*, crude or purified, the lipase from *Rhizopus delemar*, purified, for example as noted in Fukumoto et al, *J. Gen. Appli. Microbiol*, 10, 257–265 (1964), and lipases having similar activity, which are those described in the aforementioned Bucolo and Davis publication, do not demonstrate the required cholesterol esterase activity. Specifically preferred commercial lipase preparations include wheat germ lipase supplied by Miles Laboratories of Elkhart, Ind., Lipase 3000 supplied by Wilson Laboratories, Chicago, Ill., Steapsin supplied by Sigma Chemical Co., St. Louis, Mo., (both of the last two enzymes are pancreatic enzymes) and Lipase M (from *Candida cylindracca*) supplied by Enzyme Development Corporation, New York, N.Y. Screening of lipases for this purpose to determine their cholesterol esterase activity may be accomplished using the technique described in Example (3) below. Using this technique, any lipase which demonstrates a cholesterol esterase activity which releases above about 25 mg% cholesterol in the screening procedure of Example 3 should be considered useful in the successful practice of the present invention.

Proteases in general may be used in the successful practice of this invention. These include by way of example, chymotrypsin, *Streptomyces griseus* protease (commercially available under the registered trademark "Pronase"), *Aspergillus oryzae* protease, *Bacillus subtilis* protease, elastas, papain and bromelain. Mixtures of such enzymes, of course, may also be employed, at times, with advantageous results as demonstrated in the examples below.

The protease utilized as described above, is only necessary where the cholesterol ester is present in a protein containing solution the most notable and important of which is, of course, blood serum. In the case where a simple non protenaceous solution is being assayed, it is possible, as demonstrated in Example 3 below, to obtain ester hydrolysis using only the lipase. As also demonstrated by the Examples, however, in a protein containing solution such as serum, the presence of the protease is essential to useful results.

As will be further elaborated below, the free cholesterol liberated by the action of the foregoing enzyme mixture may be assayed in a number of ways. According to a preferred embodiment of the instant invention, this assay is performed using gas-liquid chromatography.

According to a preferred embodiment of this "free" cholesterol assay technique, an aliquot generally from about 0.5 to about 5 ml of the hydrolyzed aqueous composition to be tested, hereinafter blood serum, is mixed with from about 0.5 to about 2 ml of heptane or some other suitable organic solvent, for example, isooctane. containing from about 25 mg to about 50 mg weight percent octacosane or some other organic suitable for use as an internal standard. The heptane may, of course, be replaced with any other solvents suitable for gas-liquid chromatography, for example, isooctane. The solvent mixture is then extracted with water according to conventional techniques, preferably using from about 3 to about 10 ml of water per ml of solvent solution. The water extracted solvent solution is then reacted with a silylating agent, for example, (N,O-bis(-trimethylsilyl) trifluoroacetanide with 1% trimethyl-chlorosilane or a mixture of equal volumes of trime-thylchlorosilane and 1,1,1,3,3,3,-hexamethyldisilazane for a period of from about 2 to about 15 minutes. The silylated solvent solution is then passed through a conventional gas-liquid chromatograph to determine the total cholesterol in the sample under examination. This method for determining cholesterol concentration is an adaptation of the technique described in detail in J. L. Driscoll, D. Aubuchon, M. Descoteaux and R. F. Martin, Anal. Chem., 43, 1196 (1971).

One of the most significant advantages of the instant enzymatic hydrolysis technique involves the requirement for dilution of blood serum for hydrolysis and assay. Surprisingly, using the techniques described herein, undiluted serum is hydrolyzed as rapidly and readily as diluted serum. This is quite surprising in view of the uniform requirements for serum dilution described in the prior art.

The following examples serve to illustrate particular embodiments of the present invention.

"Validate," a reconstituted serum standard produced by the Warner-Lambert Company, was used in the examples below. The total cholesterol content of "Validate" (lot 2560121) was checked by saponifying an aliquot according to the method of Driscoll et al, and analyzing the heptane extract by both glc and the Liebermann-Burchard method. Values of 160 and 162 mg% respectively were obtained. These are well within the range of values quoted by the supplier (148–192 mg%).

EXAMPLE 1 HYDROLYSIS OF CHOLESTEROL ESTER IN SERUM

A mixture of 1 ml "Validate" (a serum cholesterol standard sold by Warner-Lambert and containing 148–192 mg% cholesterol), 40 mg Lipase M, 40 mg papain, 8 mg α-chymotrypsin, and 0.1 M tris buffer to 3 ml total volume (pH 7.2) is incubated in a 25 ml flask under nitrogen at 50°C and 250 rpm for 10 min.

The hydrolysis is performed in an atmosphere of nitrogen in order to minimize artifacts introduced by autooxidation of cholesterol and its esters; of course, proper correction for such autooxidation factors will permit hydrolysis to be performed in a normal atmosphere.

EXAMPLE 2

QUANTITATIVE ESTIMATION OF TOTAL CHOLESTEROL BY GAS-LIQUID CHROMATOGRAPHY (GLC)

One ml samples of serum or reconstituted serum standards ("Validate," Warner-Lambert) containing up to 150 mg% cholesterol are mixed with 5 ml ethanol and shaken 3 minutes with 1 ml heptane containing 50 mg% octacosane. Five ml of water is added and the mixture is shaken again for 3 minutes. When the layers separate, equal portions of the heptane layer and N,O-bis(trimethylsilyl) trifluoroacetamide with 1% trimethylchlorosilane are mixed. After 5 minutes reaction 1 μl samples are injected into a Hewlett Packard F and M 810 chromatograph with a single stainless steel column (1/8 inch × 4 feet) packed with 3% SE30 on ov 1. Gas flow rate 20 ml/min, oven temperature 250°C, injection port 260°C, flame detector 265°C, range 10², attenuation × 1, chart speed ½ inch/min. Octacosane retention time is about 1 min. Cholesterol retention time is about 2½ min. Runs are complete in about 4 min. Under these conditions the amount of cholesterol in the sample is proportional to the peak height ratios of cholesterol to octacosane. This method is adapted from Driscoll et al referred to above.

EXAMPLE 3

SCREENING OF LIPASES FOR CHOLESTEROL ESTERASE ACTIVITY

Tests were conducted with cholesteryl linoleate as the substrate because it is the major ester component of human serum and because it gives relatively stable emulsions compared to saturated esters such as the palmitate.

A solution of 200 mg redistilled cholesteryl linoleate in 5 ml ethyl ether was mixed with rapid stirring into 100 ml boiling water containing 430 mg sodium cholate. Five ml of this suspension was added to a solution of 50 mg of lipase preparation in 5 ml 0.1 M phosphate, pH 7.0. This mixture was incubated 2 hours at 37°C, 400 rpm under N_2. Cholesterol esters remaining after this treatment were determined by the hydroxylamine method of J. Vonhoeffmayr and R. Fried, Z. Klin. Chem. u Klin., Biochem., 8, 134 (1970) which involves quantitative conversion of esters to hydroxamic acids. The results are shown in Table 1.

5

Table 1

Hydroxylamine Assay with
Cholesteryl Linoleate Suspension

Enzyme	Cholesterol released (mg%)
Lipase (Miles)	30
Lipase 3000 (Wilson)	42
Wheat Germ Lipase (Miles)	59
Steapsin (Sigma)	59
Lipase M (Enzyme Development Corp.)	68

All of the enzymes show esterase activity. However, Lipase M is preferred because of its significantly greater esterase activity and also because it is a relatively inexpensive commercial enzyme. As purchased, the preparation is about 80% lactose, so on a protein basis its activity is about five times its activity on a weight basis.

EXAMPLE 4

ACTIVITY OF LIPASE WITH SERUM CHOLESTEROL ESTERS

Mixtures containing 40 mg. of lipase in 1 ml "Validate" were incubated 10 min. at 50°C under nitrogen in 25 ml flasks at 250 rpm. The mixture was extracted and cholesterol was estimated as in Example 2. The enzymes tested and the results are given in Table II.

Table II

Esterase Activity with Serum as Substrate

Enzyme	Cholesterol (mg%)
None	23
Lipase 3000	26
Lipase M	36

Lipase M and lipase 3000 while exhibiting considerable esterase activity on cholesteryl linoleate emulsions show very little activity with serum esters.

EXAMPLE 5

ESTERASE ACTIVITY OF LIPASE-PROTEASE COMBINATIONS ON SERUM CHOLESTEROL ESTERS

Combinations of Lipase M and various proteases were tested in the same manner as in Example 4. Proteases, except for α-chymotrypsin, were added directly to serum at 40 mg per ml; α-chymotrypsin was added at 8 mg per ml. The amount of cholesterol (mg%) released by each combination is shown in Table III.

Table III

Enzymes	Cholesterol (mg%)
None	23
Lipase M	36
α-Chymotrypsin (Sigma, Type II, 3X crystallized)	37
Lipase M + α-Chymotrypsin	129
Papain (Sigma, Grade-Crude Type II)	29
Lipase M + papain	115
Lipase M + α-chymotrypsin + papain	114

It is seen that in the presence of proteases such as α-chymotrypsin or papain the cholesterol esterase ac-

6

tivity of Lipase M was enhanced nearly four fold. The proteases themselves may have a slight esterase activity but their major effect probably is to increase the availability of cholesterol esters to the lipase by breaking up ester-lipoprotein complexes in serum. Most cholesterol esters in serum are bound to lipoproteins.

Thus, for Lipase M to be optimally effective on serum cholesterol esters, a protease must also be present.

EXAMPLE 6

A series of commercially prepared proteases were tested for their ability to enhance esterase activity of Lipase M in serum. Protease was added directly to serum in the amounts shown in Table IV. Lipase M concentration was 40 mg per ml serum. Otherwise assay and conditions are the same as in Example 4. The results are contained in Table IV.

Table IV

	Protease	Amount added (mg/ml)	Cholesterol (mg%)
1.	Aspergillus oryzae (Sigma Type II)	20	118
		40	123
		80	145
2.	Streptomyces griseus (Sigma Type VI)	5	147
		10	144
		20	140
3.	Bacillus subtilis (Sigma Type VIII)	5	140
		10	118
		20	135
4.	Bromelain (Sigma Grade II)	5	114
		10	127
		20	132
5.	Protease 30 (Rohm and Haas)	20	80
		80	127
			161
6.	Pronase (Calbiochem, Grade A)	5	133
7.	Subtilisin BPN (Sigma Type VII)	5	87
8.	Protease, bacterial (Calbiochem, Grade B)	10	142
9.	Lipase M		36

All of the proteases tested appear to enhance the activity of Lipase M somewhat more than α-chymotrypsin and papain. However, it is difficult to compare the activities of these proteases on the basis of units given by suppliers since several different assays are used. In general, the enzymes judged less pure were used in higher amounts.

The effect of pH value on the esterase activity was tested with different buffers and enzymes as described in Examples 7 and 8 below.

EXAMPLE 7

Four different buffers were tested in a system containing three enzymes. Each sample consists of 1 ml "Validate," 40 mg Lipase M, 40 mg papain, 8 mg α-chymotrypsin and 0.1 M buffer to 3 ml total volume. The mixtures were incubated and tested as in Example 4. The results are depicted in FIG. 1.

7

The measurement of pH optimum in this assay with serum as a substrate may be somewhat ambiguous because two enzymes (lipase and protease) are necessary. It is possible that the pH optimum of each enzyme may not coincide. In this study tris buffer (tris(hydroxymethyl)aminomethane) at pH 7.2 was superior.

EXAMPLE 8

Studies with tris buffer were conducted on combinations of Lipase M with the series of proteases described in Example 6. The amount of each protease used was that which gave the best result in the experiment shown in Table IV. Three pH values between 7 and 9 were tested. The assay was the same as described in Example 6 except that time was reduced to 5 minutes so that it

8

Most of these proteases show an optimum within the three values tested. The best results were obtained with bromelain at pH 8.1, Calbiochem bacterial protease at pH values from 8 to 9, *A. oryzae* protease at pH 8.1 and α-chymotrypsin at pH 7.2.

EXAMPLE 9

Undiluted serum (1 ml "Validate") was incubated with 40 mg Lipase M, protease in amounts indicated in Table VI, and 12.1 mg of "Trisma Base" or Tris buffer at pH 7.2. The incubations were run at 50°C for 10 min. under nitrogen and at 250 rpm. Cholesterol was analyzed as before by glc. The results are shown in Table VI.

Table VI

Hydrolysis of Cholesterol Esters in Undiluted Serum with Lipase M and Various Proteases

	Protease	Amt (mg)	No Additions		"Trizma Base"[a]		Tris Buffer pH 7.2[b]	
			pH Range	Cholesterol (mg%)	pH Range	Cholesterol (mg%)	pH Range	Cholesterol (mg%)
1	B. subtilis	5	7.10–6.89[c]	104	8.61–7.85	84	6.98–6.64	208[d]
2	Protease (Calbiochem)	5	7.03–6.52	116	8.52–7.71	100	7.01–6.82	206
3	A. oryzae	80	6.90–6.27	90	7.60–7.25	103	6.72–6.70	174
4	Bromelain	20	6.78–6.56	119	8.25–7.93	52	6.82–6.45	165
5	α-Chymotrypsin	8	7.08–6.93	91	8.65–8.19	51	7.00–6.94	162
6	Pronase	5	6.82–6.66	134	8.72–7.99	64	7.01–6.89	160
7	S. griseus	5	6.88–6.48	96	8.60–7.94	63	6.89–6.68	119

[a]"Trizma Base" (Sigma) powder was added directly to serum
[b]Tris-HCl buffer, pH 7.2 freeze dried, then added as powder directly to serum
[c]pH value at start of incubation and pH value at end
[d]Some values higher than 160 mg% occasionally obtained from same lot of "Validate" calibrated at 160 mg%

would be expected to find cholesterol values well below 160 mg%, the maximum available in the "Validate" substrate.

Each incubation mixture contained 0.5 ml "Validate," 0.5 ml 0.2M tris buffer at pH shown, 40 mg lipase M and the protease in the amounts shown. Incubation was for 5 minutes under N₂ at 50°C, 250 rpm. Samples were analyzed by glc as in Example 2. The results are indicated in Table V.

Table V

	Protease	Amt (mg)	Cholesterol mg%		
			pH 7.2	pH 8.1	pH 9.0
1	A. oryzae	80	66	86	72
2	Thermolysin (Calbiochem, Grade A)	10	58	74	52
3	Bromelain	20	66	100	72
4	B. subtilis	5	54	65	70
5	S. griseus	5	56	58	30
6	Pronase	5	67	74	40
7	Subtilisin	5	56	66	56
8	α-chymotrypsin	8	84	56	22
9	Protease, bacterial (Calbiochem)	10	86	100	102

Although according to a preferred embodiment of the present invention quantitative estimation of total cholesterol is achieved using gas-liquid chromatography, any of the well known conventional techniques for the analysis of total "free" cholesterol (after cholesterol ester hydrolysis has been achieved) may be used. These include the Pearson, Stern and McGarack, Carr and Drecker, and Zak methods described at pages 355–361 of *Fundamentals of Clinical Chemistry*, TIETZ, N. W., W. B. SAUNDERS CO. (1970) as well as the well known Lieberman-Burchard technique and the cholesterol oxidase method described in German Offenlegungschrifft No. 2,246,695 referred to hereinabove which is incorporated herein by reference insofar as it describes a technique for quantitatively determining total free cholesterol by treating a cholesterol solution with cholesterol oxidase and measuring the quantity of one or more of the products of this oxidation. Furthermore, hydrolysis as described herein may be used as an integral part of a single solution assay using cholesterol oxidase as is described in concurrently filed U.S. Pat. application Ser. No. 454,622 filed Mar. 25, 1974, in the names of Goodhue, Risley and Snoke entitled "Method and Composition for Blood Serum Cholesterol Analysis," which is incorporated herein by reference insofar as it describes another useful application of the novel hydrolysis described herein.

9

10

While the invention has been described in detail with particular reference to preferred embodiments thereof, it will be understood that variations and modifications can be effected within the spirit and scope of the invention.

What we claim is:

1. In a process of assaying an aqueous proteinaceous liquid containing cholesterol esters for total cholesterol content in which said ester is hydrolyzed to liberate all of said cholesterol followed by determining the amount of cholesterol, the improvement comprising effecting said hydrolysis by treating said aqueous proteinaceous liquid with both a lipase having cholesterol esterase activity and a protease.

2. The improved method of claim 1 wherein said lipase having cholesterol esterase activity releases at least 25 mg% cholesterol (in 2 hours at 37°C under nitrogen) when 50 mg of a preparation of said lipase in 5 ml 0.1 M phosphate buffer, pH 7.0, is used to treat a dispersion of cholesteryl linoleate prepared by dispersing 200 mg cholesteryl linoleate in 5 ml of ethyl ether and 100 ml boiling water containing 430 mg of sodium cholate.

3. The improved method of claim 1 wherein said aqueous liquid is serum and said treating step is accomplished with a mixture comprising from about 600 to about 1500 units of said lipase having cholesterol ester-ase activity and from about 50 to about 500 units of said protease per ml of serum.

4. The method of clain 1 wherein said treatment is carried out at a temperature of between about 25° and 55°C and at a pH of between about 6.5 and about 9.5.

5. The improved method of claim 1 wherein said lipase having esterase activity is a microbial lipase.

6. The improved method of claim 5 wherein said microbial lipase is the lipase from *Candida cylindracca*.

7. The improved method of claim 1 wherein said lipase is selected from the group consisting of wheat germ lipase, pancreatic lipases and the lipase from *Candida cylindracca*.

8. The improved method of claim 1 wherein said protease is selected from the group consisting of α-chymotrypsin, papain, bromelain, *Bacillus subtilis* protease, *Aspergillus oryzae* protease, *Streptomyces griseus* protease and mixtures thereof.

9. The improved method of claim 8 wherein said lipase is selected from the group consisting of wheat germ lipase, pancreatic lipases and the lipase from *Candida cylindracca*.

10. The method of claim 9 wherein said treatment is carried out at a temperature of between about 25 and 55°C and at a pH of between about 6.5 and about 9.5.

* * * * *

description of how the method is carried out nine examples are given which contain practical details and actual test results. These are described as 'particular embodiments of the present invention'. In this specification one figure of drawings is given showing the variation of enzyme activity with four different buffers covering a range of pH. All the claims are in terms of a process or method. Claim 1, which is the broadest claim, reads:

'In a process of assaying an aqueous proteinaceous liquid containing cholesterol esters for total cholesterol content in which said ester is hydrolysed to liberate all of said cholesterol followed by determining the amount of cholesterol, the improvement comprising effecting said hydrolysis by treating said aqueous proteinaceous liquid with both a lipase having cholesterol esterase activity and a protease'.

Another example of the section by section approach is found in an earlier US patent taken out in 1961 before the format described previously and used for US Patent No. 3,869,349 became the stereotype. This is US Patent No. 3,013,947 entitled *Antibiotic production* and is concerned with the production of an antifungal antibiotic named lagosin by cultivation of a species of *Streptomyces*. Lagosin is believed to be identical with pentamycin obtained previously by culture of *Streptomyces penticus* and the improvement being patented here resides in the use of a new strain isolated from a Nigerian soil sample and named as *Streptomyces roseo-luteus*. The applicants have deposited samples of their new strain with the US culture collection NRRL, Peoria, and also with the British collection NCIB, and the accession numbers are quoted.

Although perhaps identical with the known pentamycin, the lagosin structure had not at the time been determined and so a section follows on 'The characteristics and properties of lagosin' in which melting point, specific rotation, colour reactions and solubilities are given. A suggested empirical formula follows and detailed ultraviolet and infrared spectral data are provided, including a drawing of the *u.v.* absorption spectrum. The microbiological spectrum is then listed and mammalian toxicity figures given.

The description continues with 'The characteristics of *Streptomyces roseo-luteus*' including growth on various media and its morphology and classification in a particular group of Bergey's Manual. Then follow the most important descriptive sections on 'Cultivation' and 'Isolation and

22

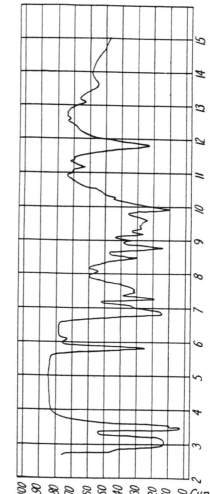

INVENTORS
CHRISTINE JOY BESSELL
WINSTON KENNAY ANSLOW
AILEEN MARION MORTIMER
DEREK LAWRENCE FLETCHER
ALAN RHODES
BY
Bacon & Thomas Attorneys

United States Patent Office

3,013,947
Patented Dec. 19, 1961

1

3,013,947
ANTIBIOTIC PRODUCTION
Christine Joy Bessell, Stoke Poges, Winston Kennay Anslow, Slough, Aileen Marion Mortimer, Selly Oak, Birmingham, Derek Lawrence Fletcher, Stoke Poges, and Alan Rhodes, Bracknell, England, assignors to Glaxo Laboratories Limited, Greenford, England, a British company
Filed June 14, 1960, Ser. No. 36,058
12 Claims. (Cl. 195—80)

This invention is concerned with the production of an important antifungal antibiotic which we have designated "lagosin." The antibiotic lagosin is believed to be identical with the antibiotic designated Pentamycin which is described in the Journal of Antibiotics, Series A, 1958, pages 26–29. Pentamycin is described as being produced by the culture of *Streptomyces penticus*. For convenience the antibiotic with which this invention is concerned will continue herein to be termed "lagosin."

We have found that lagosin may be obtained in advantageous manner by the aerobic cultivation of an organism newly discovered by us which we have identified as belonging to the genus Streptomyces. This organism, which is isolated from a soil sample taken in Nigeria has been designated *Streptomyces roseo-luteus* by which name it will be referred to hereinafter. Cultures of the organism *Streptomyces roseo-luteus* have been deposited in the collection of the North Regional Research Laboratory, Peoria, Illinois, United States of America, where it has been assigned the number NRRL 2776. It has also been deposited in the National Collection of Industrial Bacteria at the National Chemical Laboratory, Teddington, England, where it has been assigned the number N.C.I.B. 8984. The use of the new organism enables lagosin to be produced in good yield and in an economic manner.

Since the structure of lagosin is at present undetermined it is first necessary to describe its characteristics. Some characteristics are described in the literature above referred to but for completeness we now set out the full characteristics we have observed.

THE CHARACTERISTICS AND PROPERTIES OF LAGOSIN

Lagosin is a very pale yellow in colour and crystallizes in soft needles from methanol, M.P. (uncorrected), 230–240° C. (dec.). The substance has a specific rotation of $[\alpha]_D^{20} = -160°$ (c.. 0.2 in MeOH). It gives a bluish-violet colour with cold, concentrated sulphuric acid, which colour is stable for 24 hours. Lagosin is sparingly soluble in water, slightly soluble in methanol, ethanol, butanol; readily soluble in dimethylformamide, glacial acetic acid and pyridine. It is insoluble in chloroform trichloroethylene, ether and petroleum ethers.

Microanalysis of lagosin gives C, 61.25%; H, 9.12%; N, nil. On hydrogenation lagosin gives a derivative, M.P. 156–7°, $[\alpha]_D^{20} + 3.5°$ (c., 1.98 in MeOH), crystallographic determination of molecular weight, 810±15, which indicates the empirical formula for lagosin to be $C_{41}H_{66-70}O_{14}$ and for the hydrogenation product, $C_{41}H_{78-80}O_{14}$. $C_{41}H_{68}O_{14}$ requires C, 62.73%; H, 8.73%.

We have established a standard of activity for lagosin by assigning to an early partially pure isolate an activity of 1000 units/mgm. Crystalline lagosin in the purest form obtained by us has an activity on this scale of 4950 units/mgm. *Saccharomyces cerevisiae* NCTC4614 was used as standard test organism and assays are conducted by the agar cup plate method.

A solution of lagosin in methanol exhibits an ultraviolet absorption spectrum similar to the polyene antibiotics filipin (Whitfield, Brock, Ammann, Gottlieb and Carter, J. Amer. Chem. Soc. (1955), 77, 4799) and fungichromin (Tytell, McCarthy, Fisher, Bolhofer and

2

Charney, Antibiotics Annual, 1954–55, p. 716), with three characteristic maxima of

$$E_{1\,cm.}^{1\%}\ 1475\ \text{at}\ 357\ m\mu$$

1490 at 339 mμ, and 927 at 323 mμ; a shoulder appears at 308 mμ.

A nujol-mull of lagosin gives a characteristic infra-red absorption spectrum, shown in the accompanying drawing, which is similar to that given by filipin and by fungichromin; strong absorption bands are shown at 3580 (2.79μ), 3360 (2.98μ), 2900 (3.45μ), 2840 (3.52μ), 1716 (5.83μ), 1462 (6.84μ), 1374 (7.28μ), 1138 (8.79μ), 1040 (9.61μ), 1008 (9.93μ) and 846 cm.$^{-1}$ (11.82μ), medium absorption bands at 1340 (7.46μ), 1326 (7.54μ), 1178 (8.48μ), 1088 (9.19μ), 1068 (9.36μ), and 722 cm.$^{-1}$ (13.85μ), and weak absorption bands at 1645 (6.08μ), 1238 (8.08μ), 1110 (9.01μ), 975 (10.26μ), 896 (11.16μ), 805 (12.42μ) and 764 cm.$^{-1}$ (13.09μ). Lagosin is differentiated from filipin by the fact that the bands at 1178 (8.48μ), 1088 (9.19μ) and 1040 cm.$^{-1}$ (9.61μ) are about 25% weaker and the band at 1068 cm.$^{-1}$ (9.36μ) about 50% stronger than the corresponding bands in the filipin spectrum. It is differentiated from fungichromin by the absence of the band at 1587 cm.$^{-1}$ (6.30μ) shown by fungichromin and by possessing a band at 1326 cm.$^{-1}$ (7.54μ) not shown by fungichromin.

Lagosin appears to be distinguished from fungichromin and filipin by a number of characteristic differences. Thus, lagosin has an empirical formula of $C_{41}H_{66-70}O_{14}$ whereas fungichromin has an empirical formula of $C_{35}H_{60}O_{13}$ and filipin an empirical formula of $C_{30}H_{50}O_{10}$. The melting points are different, lagosin having an M.P. of 230–240° C., fungichromin and M.P. of 205–210° C. and filipin an M.P. of 195–205° C. In the U.V. the ratios of the

$$E_{1\,cm.}^{1\%}\ \text{maxima}$$

at 357mμ and 339mμ of lagosin and fungichromin are different; for lagosin the ratio is 1:1 whereas for fungichromin 1.1:1. Filipin is converted to a colourless degradation product by methanol at 4° C.; no such change occurs with lagosin.

Lagosin, both as a solid and in solution is sensitive to light. The solid becomes a deeper yellow and finally a pale buff colour. Solutions (50 μg./ml. in ethanol) showed no loss when stored in the dark at room temperature for five weeks.

The microbiological spectrum of lagosin was determined by reference to the minimal concentration required completely to inhibit the growth of certain phytopathogenic fungi. Partly purified material assaying at 1760 u./mgm. dissolved in methanol and diluted with water to give a methanol concentration of 0.06–0.25%, was used. The results were as follows:

Species	Type of Inoculum: M = Mycelial, S = Spores	Minimal Inhibitory Concentration in Units/ml.
Alternaria solani	S	70
Botrytis allii	S	17.5
Botrytis fabae	S	17.5
Cladosporium fulvum	S	70
Clastrosporium carpophilum	S	70
Corticium solani	M	17.5
Diplodia natalensis	M	70
Elsinoe ampelina	S	35
Fusarium coeruleum	S	70
Fusarium culmorum	S	17.5
Fusarium nivale	S	35
Glomerella cingulata	M	70
Do	S	35
Sclerotinia camellia	M	70
Stereum purpureum	M	70
Verticillium albo-atrum	M	17.5
Do	S	17.5
Verticillium cinerescens	M	70
Do	S	70

3

Lagosin is active against a range of fungi and yeasts at low concentrations as is shown in the following table:

Species	Minimum Inhibitory Conc., μg./ml.
Saccharomyces cerevisiae	1
Riesling wine yeast NCYC 463	0.3
Champagne Moussec strain NCYC 482	0.3
Californian wine yeast NCYC 177	0.3
Hungarian wine yeast NCYC 104	0.3
Flor yeast Jerez 2, NCYC 429	0.2
Solacz wine yeast	0.6
Rabka wine yeast	0.3
Monpost wine yeast	0.3
Sauterne wine yeast	0.6
Tokay wine yeast	0.6
Torulopsis utilis	1
Rhodotorula gracilis	1
Candida albicans	0.8–2
Trichophyton mentagrophytes	5
Trichophyton interdigitale	12.5
Aspergillus niger	2
Fusarium culmorum	6
Fusarium nivale	12
Glomerella cingulata	14
Mucor racemosus	6
Penicillium notatum	0.6
Penicillin patulum	1.75
Scopulariopsis brevicaule	0.6
Trichomonas vaginalis	1

The toxicity of lagosin to mammals on oral administration is low, the LD_{50} being 2100 mg./kg. body weight for mice and 1750 mg./kg. for rats. Lagosin shows a substantially complete absence of phytotoxicity, whether applied to roots or foliage of, for example, the rose, tomato, dwarf bean and antirrhinum.

The antibiotic lagosin has a wide field of application as it is generally useful in inhibiting or controlling the growth of pathogenic and undesirable yeasts and fungi.

THE CHARACTERISTICS OF *STREPTOMYCES ROSEO-LUTEUS*

When first isolated from soil, *Streptomyces roseo-luteus* was grown on malt agar plates and sections of the colonies transferred to plates seeded with various fungi. Zones of inhibition were observed in *Candida albicans*, *Saccharomyces cerevisiae*, *Aspergillus niger* and *Trichophyton mentagrophytes*.

Streptomyces roseo-luteus grows in the form of a much-branched mycleium with characteristic aerial mycelium and conidiospores formed in chains. It is aerobic and mesophilic. Its growth characteristics vary somewhat depending on the medium on which it is grown. The growth characteristics on the media mentioned below are given by way of example only:

Asparagine dextrose agar.—Good growth; vegetative mycelium creamy white; profuse aerial mycelium white becoming light vinaceou s fawn; the reverse of the colony empire yellow deepening to yellow chrome with age; a bright yellow pigment diffused through the agar.

Yeast extract agar.—Vegetative mycelium orange becoming rufous or apricot orange with age; aerial mycelium white and at first scant; a soluble golden pigment diffused through the agar.

Bennett's agar.—Aerial mycelium abundant, white becoming pinkish grey; reverse colony light cadmium; a yellow pigment diffused through the agar.

Casein agar.—Aerial mycelium abundant, white becoming pinkish grey, then yellow and finally at 24 days a greenish grey; the reverse of the colony was bright orange-chrome and a golden pigment diffused from the colony; the casein around the colony was cleared.

Calcium malate agar.—Very poor growth; colonies smooth and cream coloured; some yellow pigment diffused through the agar.

Tyrosine agar.—Vegetative mycelium primuline yellow in colour; aerial mycelium sparse and white; no decomposition of tyrosine at 24 days.

Cellulose agar.—No appreciable growth at 24 days.

4

Starch agar.—Sparse cottony growth even at 24 days; aerial mycelium white becoming vinaceous buff.

Czapek Dox agar.—Growth sparse; initially cottony and white, becoming vinaceous fawn.

Synthetic agar with dextrose.—Good growth; aerial mycelium brownish pink; a bright yellow pigment diffused through the agar.

Litmus milk.—Peptonised with an acid reaction; heavy growth at surface covering all but centre of tube.

Potato plug.—Vegetative mycelium ochraceous orange becoming cinnamon brown; aerial mycelium maize to baryta yellow; a soluble yellow pigment diffused through the plug.

Gelatin stab.—Discrete spherical colonies grew in the stab; liquefaction only after 5 weeks incubation.

Nitrate broth.—No nitrite formed; nitrate still present after 24 days.

Glucose nutrient broth.—Thin ring of white growth at the surface and floccular growth at the bottom of the tube.

All colour descriptions referred to above conform to Ridgeway, Colour standards and Nomenclature, Washington, 1912.

The morphology of *Streptomyces roseo-luteus* was studied by growing it on cellophane discs on Bennett's agar and on asparagine-dextrose agar, the organism being examined after 10 days incubation. On Bennett's agar the spores were elliptical and borne in long closely spiralled chains, whilst on asparagine-dextrose agar the spores were oval to elliptical and borne in long chains loosely spiralled. The average spore size ranges from about 1.3–1.7μ with an average size of about 1.5μ.

The ability of *Streptomyces roseo-luteus* to utilise various carbon compounds was tested under the conditions described by Pridham, T. G. and Gottlieb D. (J. Bact., 1948, 56 (1), 113).

The following compounds were readily utilised:
Arabinose, salicin, raffinose, mannitol, sorbitol, xylose, trehalose, lactose, maltose, melibiose and dextrose.

The following compounds were not utilised and supported very sparse growth:
Erythritol, adonitol, aesculin, rhamnose, inulin, sucrose, sodium citrate, sodium acetate, fructose, dextran, sorbose and melezitose.

Streptomyces roseo-luteus is morphologically distinguished from other Streptomyces of which we are at present aware, inter alia, by the following characteristics, namely, the vinaceous fawn colour of the aerial mycelium and the production of a bright yellow soluble pigment on both organic and synthetic media, the peptonisation of milk and the very slow liquefaction of gelatine.

Following Bergey's Manual of Determinative Bacteriology *Streptomyces roseo-luteus* appears to fall in Group IA5a[2] or IA5a[3] of that manual. By comparison *Streptomyces penticus* appears to be characterised by the production of a soluble brown pigment in organic media and thus falls in the broad group Ib of the Bergey Classification; *Streptomyces penticus* is also said to be very similar to *Streptomyces rubireticuli*, which also falls into group Ib of Bergey and from which *Streptomyces roseo-luteus* is markedly different.

THE CULTIVATION OF *STREPTOMYCES ROSEO-LUTEUS* TO YIELD CRUDE LAGOSIN

Lagosin is produced by the aerobic culture of *Streptomyces roseo-luteus* in or on a medium capable of supporting the growth thereof. Suitable media are those generally used for the culture of moulds of the genus Streptomyces, and should basically contain one or more assimilable sources of nitrogen and an assimilable source of carbon and energy, and nutrient salts. The culture is preferably conducted under submerged aerobic conditions.

It will be understood by those skilled in the art that the organism *Streptomyces roseo-luteus* is capable of

5

mutation to mutant strains also capable of yielding lagosin. It is thus the practice in the antibiotic industry to produce mutant strains of antibiotic-producing organisms for the purpose of obtaining improved yields and/or more economic production. The present invention thus includes within its scope the use of lagosin-producing mutants of *Streptomyces roseo-luteus* for the production of the antibiotic.

The source of nitrogen is preferably in the form of complex organic material such as oatmeal, peptone, soya meal, maize meal, corn steep liquor, meat extract or a casein digest. Frequently such complex sources of nitrogen will be found to contain also the nutrient salts required by the organism. The source of carbon and energy may for example be carbohydrate assimilable by the mould, for example, glucose, lactose, starch, or assimilable oils or fats e.g. palm oil, maize oil or lard oil; glycerol and palmitic acid are also suitable. Such compounds may be already present in the nitrogen source or may be added to the culture media separately.

It should be noted that the presence of palm oil, maize oil or lard oil or palmitic acid to the culture media results in considerable increase in the yield of lagosin, the yield being some two to four times greater than that achieved using the same medium without one of these constituents. The palm oil, maize oil, lard oil or palmitic acid is preferably added in an amount of from 2.5-7.5%, advantageously approximately 5%. Examples of suitable media for use in the process of this invention are the following:

Oatmeal medium		Soya medium	
	G.		*G.*
Oatmeal	25	Soya flour	30
Chalk	20	Distiller's solubles	7.5
Dextrose	5	Sodium chloride	2.5
Dist. water to 1 l. pH 6.8±0.1.		Dist. water to 1 l. pH 7.6±0.1.	

Potato-meat medium		Glycerol-meat medium	
Tryptone, g	5	Glycerol, cc	20.0
Soluble starch, g	10	Peptone, g	10
Difco beef extract, g	3	Sodium chloride, g	10
Dextrose, g	2	Lab Lemco, g	5
K₂HPO₄, g	1.2	K₂HPO₄, g	5
KH₂PO₄, g	0.8		
Ferrous sulphate (0.1% aqueous solution), ml	1.0	Distilled water to 1 l.	
Potato extract to 1 l.		pH 6.9±0.1.	
pH 6.8±0.1.			

The following two media have been found to be particularly satisfactory for large-scale production.

Medium 1:   Percent
    Oatflour ---------------------------- 3
    Whey powder---------------------- 3
    Chalk ---------------------------------- 1
    Glucose ---------------------------- 0.75

(pH adjusted to 6.9–7.0 with sodium hydroxide; sterilized 45 min. at 120° C.)

Medium 2:   Percent
    Oatflour ---------------------------- 3
    Whey powder---------------------- 3
    Palm oil----------------------------- 5
    Chalk ---------------------------------- 1
    Glucose ---------------------------- 0.75

(pH adjusted to 6.9–7.0 with sodium hydroxide; sterilized 45 min. at 120° C.)

In these media oatflour may be replaced by maize meal, soya meal or corn steep liquor but we have found that higher lagosin titres are obtained if oatflour is used. Palm oil, maize oil, lard oil or palmitic acid may also be added to these media to increase the titre of lagosin, as mentioned above.

6

It will be clear to those skilled in the art that media other than those mentioned above can be used, and whether any medium will support the growth of *Streptomyces roseo-luteus* for the production of lagosin can readily be determined by trial fermentation.

In order to produce lagosin on a large scale, spores of *Streptomyces roseso-luteus* (which can be preserved by lyophilisation in dextran or soil) can, for example be transferred to a suitable glycerol-meat medium of the type detailed below (40 ml. per 250 ml. flask or 500 ml. per 2 l. flask) and incubated for 48 hours on a rotary shaker at 29° C. In this way a heavy mycelial growth is developed.

This vegetative inoculum is then used to inoculate shake flasks or stirred vessels containing a development medium, for example:

          Percent
Glycerol ------------------------------------- 5
Meat extract---------------------------------- 1
Casein digest--------------------------------- 1
Sodium chloride------------------------------- 0.5
(pH 6.8–7.0; sterilized 30 min. at 120° C.)

          Percent
Glucose -------------------------------------- 1
Meat extract---------------------------------- 0.3
Casein digest--------------------------------- 1
(pH 6.8–7.0; sterilized 30 min. at 120° C.)

In turn this is used to inoculate shake flasks or stirred vessels containing the production medium, for example medium 1 or 2 set out above.

The fermentation may be conducted at any convenient temperature which does not inhibit the growth of *Streptomyces roseo-luteus* for example between 20° C. and 36° C. preferably between 28° and 32° C. In order to ensure maximum titre good aeration is necessary; maximum titres are generally achieved after seven or eight days fermentation.

THE ISOLATION AND PURIFICATION OF LAGOSIN

Lagosin is contained in both the mycelium and in the culture broth, a far larger proportion of the total lagosin present being in the mycelium. It can be extracted from either the culture broth or the mycelium by means of a suitable organic solvent, for example butanol, amyl alcohol, ethyl acetate and butyl acetate, of which butanol is preferred. On the addition of ether to the butanolic extract, after it has been evaporated to a small volume, crude lagosin precipitates, and can be filtered off. After washing in ether it can be dried in vacuo, to give an orange-yellow solid which, in general, assays between 1,000 and 2,000 u./mgm.

Further purification of the product can be effected in any convenient manner. Thus, the crude material may be subjected to a further washing with ether, and then washed with petroleum ether and dissolved in warm methanol. Evaporation to about one-third volume and chilling gives a pale yellow precipitate assaying at about 3,000 u./mgm.

In an alternative method the crude material may be washed repeatedly with water until no further colour is removed. After drying, the product is dissolved in warm methanol, concentrated to about three-quarters volume and then allowed to stand overnight. Pale yellow solid having a potency of about 3500 u./mgm. is deposited.

In a preferred method of operation the broth is filtered on a kieselguhr pre-coated filter and the mycelial solid extracted twice with n-butanol. The combined butanol extracts are then evaporated in vacuo to a small volume and then, by the addition of water and continued evaporation, the butanol entirely replaced by water. The crude solid is collected by centrifugation, washed with ether and dried. This material is extracted in a soxhlet with methanol, the purified lagosin separating from the

7

extract on standing as a pale yellow semi-crystalline mass assaying about 4000 u./mgm. On recrystallisation from methanol the pure compound is obtained in cushions of soft, very pale yellow needles, assaying about 4950 u./mgm.

For the better understanding of the invention the following examples are given by way of illustration only:

Example 1

A culture of *Streptomyces roseo-luteus* was grown on a Bennett's agar blake bottle. After incubation at 28° C. for 7 days a scrape was taken from a well grown blake bottle and transferred into a conical flask containing 40 ml. of glycerol meat medium and shaken at 28° C. for 2 days. 10 ml. of this was used to inoculate 400 ml. glycerol-meat medium contained in a round-bottomed flask and shaken for 48 hours by which time the growth was prolific.

The contents of two such flasks were used to inoculate 100–150 litres of sterile development medium:

	Percent
Glycerol	5.0
Meat extract	1.0
Casein digest	1.0
Sodium chloride	0.5

pH adjusted to 5.8–7.0. (Sterilised for 30 minutes at 120° C.)

This was stirred at 350 revolutions per minute (r.p.m.) aerated at 8 cubic feet per minute (c.f.m.) and maintained at a temperature of 28° C. for 24 hours, at the end of which time there was prolific growth.

45 litres of this well grown culture were transferred to 450 litres of sterile "production" medium:

	Percent
Oatflour	3.0
Light precipitated chalk	1.0
Whey powder	3.0
Glucose	0.75

pH adjusted to 6.9–7.0 with sodium hydroxide. (Sterilized for 30 minutes at 120° C.)

This was stirred at 350 r.p.m., aerated at 20 c.f.m. and maintained at a temperature of 28° C. for 112 hours. At this time the broth assayed at 4275 u./ml. 2% (w./v.) of kieselguhr was added to 425 litres of the broth containing an estimated 1930 m.u. of lagosin. The mixture was filtered on a rotary filter using a kieselguhr precoat giving 58 kg. of cuttings and 350 litres of filtrate containing an estimated 105 m.u. of lagosin (by assay).

The cuttings were eluted with butanol, first with 100 litres from which 70 litres were recovered by decantation, secondly with 70 litres from which 60 litres were recovered, thirdly with 50 litres from which 40 litres were recovered and finally with 50 litres from which all the solvent was recovered. The total quantity of lagosin in the combined butanol eluates was 1040 m.u. (i.e. 53.8% of the original total by assay).

The combined eluates were concentrated under vacuum to approximately 6 litres and then water added so as to replace the evaporating butanol. The aqueous suspension was mixed with ether to remove the red oil and filtered. The solid was then re-washed with ether completely to remove a red oil which was present. The solid was then extracted in a soxhlet with methanol, the lagosin which separated being removed from the flask at periodic intervals to give a total of 247 g. of lagosin approximately 75% pure.

To remove impurities, 140 g. of this material, approximately 75% pure was extracted in a soxhlet for 2 hours with chloroform, air dried, then extracted for 2 hours with petroleum ether, air dried, and then for 2 hours with ethyl ether. The solid was finally air dried.

This solid was re-extracted in a soxhlet with methanol

8

for 8 hours. On cooling the methanol overnight 5.75 g. of pure lagosin were obtained. By refluxing the solid remaining in the soxhlet thimble for 1 hour with the mother liquor from above, filtering and allowing to stand overnight, a further 25 g. were obtained.

Example 2

The beneficial effect on the production of lagosin by the addition of palm oil, lard oil or palmitic acid was shown by the following experiment:

Twelve fermenters each containing three litres of production medium as described in Example 1 were set up. To three was added 5% palm oil, to another three 5% lard oil and to another three 5% palmitic acid. The remaining three had no addition and served as "controls." The following results were obtained, each figure being the average titre, by microbiological assay, of the three fermenters:

Hours	"Controls" (no addition) u./ml.	Plus 5% Palm oil, u./ml.	Plus 5% Lard oil, u./ml.	Plus 5% Palmitic acid, u./ml.
138	1,995	6,225	5,680	3,355
162	2,755	9,875	6,905	4,530
186	2,675	10,225	8,648	10,225

Example 3

In another experiment maize oil and oleic acid were compared with palm oil and palmitic acid. The following results were obtained which show that maize oil is of value in obtaining good yields of lagosin but oleic acid is of less value.

Oil added	Maximum titre, u./ml.
5% Palm Oil	31,700
5% Maize Oil	21,300
5% Palmitic Acid	21,860
5% Oleic Acid	865

Example 4

Lagosin may also be extracted without the prior filtration of the mycelium from the broth.

A medium consisting of 4% oatmeal and 5% maize oil was fermented as described in Example 1. Without filtration, 120 litres of the whole broth, containing 373 g. of lagosin, were mixed with a half-volume of n-butanol and the mixture separated centrifugally on two Laval separators in series. The butanolic extracts were evaporated under reduced pressure below 45° C. to about one-fifth and then two volumes of methanol were added with stirring. Unfermented maize oil separated at this stage and was removed by centrifugation. The methanol-butanol solution was clarified by filtration through kieselguhr and then evaporated until the methanol was removed leaving a supersaturated butanolic solution of lagosin. The solution was cooled rapidly with vigorous stirring and allowed to stand at room temperature for an hour. The lagosin was filtered, washed with methanol and then with ether (removing a red oil) and the material dried under vacuum, yielding 190 g. of product.

This application is a continuation-in-part of application Serial No. 815,849 filed May 26, 1959, by Christine Joy Bessell et al., now abandoned.

We claim:

1. A process for the production of lagosin which comprises cultivating an organism selected from the group consisting of *Streptomyces roseo-luteus* (NRRL 2776, NCIB 8984) and a lagosin-producing mutant thereof in a nutrient medium therefor and recovering the lagosin from the medium.

2. A process as claimed in claim 1 in which the culture is conducted under submerged aerobic conditions.

3. A process as claimed in claim 2 in which the medium

3,013,947

9

contains, as a source of assimilable nitrogen, at least one material selected from the group consisting of oatmeal, peptone, soya meal, maize meal, meat extract and casein digest.

4. A process as claimed in claim 2 in which the medium contains, as a source of carbon and energy, at least one material selected from the group consisting of glucose, lactose, starch, palm oil, maize oil, lard oil, glycerol and palmitic acid.

5. A process as claimed in claim 4 in which the medium contains palm oil in an amount of from 2.5–7.5%.

6. A process as claimed in claim 4 in which the medium contains maize oil in an amount of from 2.5–7.5%.

7. A process as claimed in claim 4 in which the medium contains lard oil in an amount of from 2.5–7.5%.

8. A process as claimed in claim 4 in which the medium contains palmitic acid in an amount of from 2.5–7.5%.

9. A process as claimed in claim 2 in which the lagosin is recovered by extracting the lagosin-containing material with an organic solvent for lagosin and recovering the lagosin from the organic solvent.

10

10. A process as claimed in claim 9 in which the organic solvent is selected from the group consisting of butanol, amyl alcohol, ethyl acetate and butyl acetate.

11. A process as claimed in claim 9 in which the lagosin is recovered from the organic solvent extract by evaporation in vacuo with simultaneous replacement of the solvent water.

12. A process as claimed in claim 9 in which the lagosin is recovered from the organic solvent solution by addition of ether thereto, the precipitated lagosin being redissolved in methanol and allowed to crystallize.

References Cited in the file of this patent

UNITED STATES PATENTS

| 2,538,721 | Colingsworth | Jan. 16, 1951 |
| 2,779,705 | Peterson et al. | Jan. 29, 1957 |

FOREIGN PATENTS

| 762,702 | Great Britain | Dec. 5, 1956 |

OTHER REFERENCES

Journal of Antibiotics, Series A, 1958, pages 26 to 29.

purification' (of lagosin). Four detailed experimental examples are included. All the claims are directed to the process of using the new strain, e.g.

'A process for the production of lagosin which comprises cultivating an organism selected from the group consisting of *Streptomyces roseo-luteus* (NRRL 2776, NCIB 8984) and a lagosin-producing mutant thereof in a nutrient medium therefor and recovering the lagosin from the medium'.

THE NATURE OF PATENT CLAIMS

Patent claims have been referred to so far as defining the scope of protection given by the patent. This concept applies especially to countries which follow legal systems of the Anglo-American type and accordingly when considering the extent of cover given by a British or United States patent, for example, the literal meaning of the words used in the claims is of the greatest importance. This is not to say that the courts in these countries will be totally rigid on this question; they can hold that the infringement of a claim can take place not only by operating within the strict wording (textual infringement) but also by the use of something equivalent to what is claimed, e.g. a mechanical equivalent or a chemical equivalent of one of the component elements in the claim. However, the doctrine of equivalent is an uncertain one and will not succeed in all circumstances and therefore the applicant must pay strict attention to the precise wording of the claims. More detailed discussion of this topic in relation to patent infringement will be given and exemplified in Chapter 10.

In contrast the German patent law as developed in the German courts regards the claim more as indicative of the inventive idea rather than definitive of the legal effect of the claim. Consequently a German patent usually extends beyond the literal wording of the claims into a penumbra which depends on how far the court is impressed by the degree of originality of the invention. It can be very liberally construed by the court in suitable circumstances, such as the absence of close prior art.

These two ways of conceiving the function of the claim, i.e. as defining the scope of protection or as defining the underlying inventive idea, do not exhaust possibilities and in some countries the form of claim imposed by patent offices is more in the nature of a generalized description of how the invention is carried out in practice, e.g. specifying the conditions of a process such as pH range, temperature range and the reactants used, even where these are not the essential features of novelty of the process. This latter type of claim seems to be preferred in some Eastern European and some Latin American countries.

Under the European patent law which is a regional patent system rather than a national system we can see how a compromise has been reached between different national traditions in the intentions of the legislator as regards patent claim interpretation. The European concept is that the literal wording of the claims represents one extreme and the indicative guideline conception of the claims represents the other extreme whereas the true interpretation is that of a position between these extremes which combines a fair protection for the patentee with a reasonable degree of certainty for third parties.

When the two parts of the specification, description and claims, are put together by the draftsman from the data provided by the inventor they should correspond well to each other in terms of content. Where the teaching is highly novel and inventive and the ground has been well studied and covered with examples the claims can be commensurably broad. The degree of breadth is of course a matter for personal judgment. It is the general custom to start at least with claims of such broad scope that no-one could possibly conceivably work outside them while at the same time obtaining even a fraction of the benefit which the invention is supposed to provide, knowing always that these can be reduced in scope should they be fairly criticized by the patent office examiner or by some third party. It is much easier to start broadly and then to narrow rather than to begin with narrow claims and to attempt later on to broaden the scope of these when wisdom dawns. There is many a draftsman of patent claims who regrets taking too narrow a view of what could be protected especially when this is discovered too late in the whole procedure to fill the loopholes. The normal course of patent prosecution results in a whittling down of the scope of the claims to an area which the applicant and the examiner accept as a fair result in the circumstances. Often the applicant will be less than satisfied with the scope of claim offered and he then has the option of making the best of it or of appealing to a higher authority at increased cost to himself.

At this stage it is the practice in many countries then to amend the description so that it is in line with the scope of the claims. This often requires eliminating parts of the disclosure which fall outside the scope of the claim and are therefore no longer relevant to the invention as now defined. In the prosecution of United States patent applications it is, however, rather rare to amend the description in this way and there is therefore often a very large measure of disconformity between the area covered by the claims and what is stated in the body of the specification as the invention or inventive step.

Inventors should bear in mind the fact that when patent specifications are cited as prior documents against the patentability of their own inventions it is necessary to look at the specification as a whole and not to pay much attention to what is actually claimed in the prior patent. Although the cited document happens to be a patent it is cited essentially as a piece of prior published literature and because the examiner considers that some part of it anticipates at least one of the claims being presented to him for examination in the case in question. Prior United States patent specifications are often cited because in the disclosure section there will be found something, even a throw-away line, which is damaging to the novelty of the subsequent invention for which protection is being sought.

With this brief exposition of the way in which specifications are composed we can now proceed to examine the kinds of invention that can be covered by patents.

Chapter 3

The Categories of Patentable Invention

The answer to the frequently asked question 'What sort of thing can be patented?' falls naturally into two parts. The first part, which is the concern of this chapter, consists in setting out the main categories or types of invention which the patent law recognizes as coming within its domain. This may be considered as a purely qualitative test of the subject matter of the 'invention' which must be applied in the first place without reference to the level of ingenuity involved. The presence of ingenuity is a necessary but not a sufficient criterion of patentability. This latter aspect, that of inventive level, is one element in the second part of the answer to the over-all question. It is best treated separately and is therefore left over until the next chapter.

It is often asked whether one can patent an idea or principle. The questioner usually has in mind some theory which has been devised or principle which has been discovered or even, for example, some chemical or biological procedure which involves an original chemical or biological change. What is being asked is whether one can protect every conceivable application of the underlying idea or principle. A qualified negative answer must be given in the sense that it is not possible to obtain protection in the totally abstract form envisaged in the question. The patent is firmly based in the economic rather than the intellectual world and therefore protection lies in the application of the idea in a physical entity or process such as a chemical compound or a microbiological method or a piece of apparatus all of which must serve some useful purpose. The patent claims define the extent to which the principle is covered in the product, process, or apparatus and the permissible scope of claim must depend on the circumstances. It is sometimes possible to draft claims so broadly that they come close to covering all important ways of putting an idea or principle into practice and this is a matter of professional skill; persuading patent offices to allow such claims calls for further and greater exercise of such skill.

STATUTORY DEFINITIONS

The patent law of any state will normally contain some attempt to define the categories of invention which can be patented or those which are excluded from patentability and it will commonly contain both positive and negative indications. For example Section 101 of the US Patent Act states:

'. . . whoever invents or discovers any new and useful process, machine, manufacture or composition of matter or any new and useful improvement thereof may obtain a patent therefor subject to the conditions and requirements of this title . . .'

and in this extract the term 'process' means 'process art or method and includes a new use of a known process, machine, manufacture, composition of matter or material'. There are no categories of invention which are specifically excluded by US statute law but according to case law certain types of invention have been held to be outside the statutory definition, such as those where the essential novelty is a 'mental step'.

In Europe, Article 52 of the European Patent Convention defines patentable inventions as those:

'. . . which are susceptible of industrial application which are new and which involve an inventive step . . .'

but the article also includes a list of topics which are not regarded as patentable inventions such as scientific theories, mathematical methods, schemes and computer programs. The article also excludes:

'. . . methods for treatment of the human or animal body by surgery or therapy and diagnostic methods practised on a human or animal body . . .'

because these are not to be regarded as susceptible of industrial application. Article 53 of the convention also excludes plant or animal varieties and 'essentially biological processes' for the production of plants or animals. Microbiological processes are not excluded. The full text of these articles is given in Appendix 1.

In the national patent laws of some countries there is a specific exclusion of some or all of the following:

1. Substances produced by chemical methods.
2. Medicines.
3. Foods.
4. Mere mixtures of foods or medicines.

Usually, however, processes for preparing chemical substances, medicines, or foods are patentable and the process claim gives protection for the product when made by the defined process.

MAIN CATEGORIES OF INVENTION IN THE BIOLOGICAL SCIENCES

Patents in this field tend to fall into four main categories: products, compositions, processes and methods of use. These are not mutually exclusive headings but are convenient to indicate the central character-type of the various inventions which arise. It is usual to include combinations of these claim-types in a single patent where appropriate.

The categories noted apply especially to inventions in biological chemistry and microbiology and will be discussed first in this context. Plant breeding and the grant of rights for new plant varieties are matters distinct from the main theme of this book and are the subject of specialist expertise rather different from that practised in relation to chemical and microbiological inventions. Nevertheless this type of right deserves discussion because of its relationship to that of the plant patent as such, and it will be briefly dealt with later.

Products

A product patent is one having a claim which directly reads on to the marketed product. It is generally regarded as the most effective form of protection because proof that the claim is being infringed by a competitor is usually readily apparent from an inspection or analysis of the competitor's product without enquiry into the competitor's method of manufacture. Under this heading the term 'product' is reserved for single substances and therefore has a restricted meaning compared to the sense in which it is used commercially to cover mixtures or combinations as well as single substances.

There are two types of product claim, the 'product-*per se*' claim and the 'product-by-process' claim. Product-*per se* claims give absolute protection for new substances. This type of claim is one which extends to the substance *per se* and covers the defined substance no matter by what method it is made even when this is quite different from that described by the inventor. Product-by-process claims are those directed to a product when made by a defined process and they are correspondingly limited in scope.

The attempt is always made to present claims to these substances in product-*per se* form provided it is possible to devise an accurate and acceptable method of identifying and characterizing the substance in itself which is not limited to the process by which the substance is made.

Another kind of product claim has been devised for the purposes of the European patent law and is applicable where the novelty lies not in the substance itself but in the proposed use. This claim is written in terms of the 'substance for use in . . .' and a particular medical use is specified in the claim (see below under 'Composition claims').

This broad category can be divided into sub-groups of product of varied origin and biological utility. The more important of these will now be discussed and exemplified.

Synthetic chemical compounds

The normal pattern of claim for a group of active synthetic new compounds is based on their generalized chemical structural formula. The essential nucleus or backbone of the structure is presented and the essential or optional radicals or substituent groups attached to it are defined in general chemical terms or by listing specific possibilities. Two examples from the penicillin field are ampicillin and the penicillin nucleus.

Ampicillin UK Patent No. 873,049

This covers a group of semi-synthetic penicillins including ampicillin and its near relations all of which are embraced by the broad main claim in the following terms:

'Penicillin derivatives of the general formula:

where X is an amino-substituted acyl group containing up to 20 carbon atoms and having the formula $R(CH_2)_nCH(NH_2)CO-$ where R is hydrogen or an amino, carboxyl, or substituted or unsubstituted alkyl, aryl, aralkyl, or heterocyclic group and n is zero or an integer and non-toxic salts thereof.'

This is an example of the standard form of claim used for new penicillins where novelty resides in the acylamino side-chain and as the compounds in this case are totally new, the claim is in *per se* form. It is followed by a graded sequence of additional claims including a specific claim covering ampicillin itself (claim 5) reading 'α-aminobenzylpenicillin'.

Penicillin nucleus US Patent No. 3,164,604

This patent contains the single product claim:

'Solid non-hygroscopic 6-aminopenicillanic and having the structural formula

and melting at about 209–210 °C.'

Although formally a *per se* claim because it is not restricted by any specific process of manufacture, it includes certain limitations as to physical properties. This is the sole claim allowed to the applicants at the conclusion of an appeal filed by them against the examiner's decision to refuse all the claims originally submitted. The examiner had cited a number of speculative references in the prior published literature to the possible 6-APA structure and these are listed as 'References cited by the examiner' at the end of the specification. In order to overcome this prior art, and distinguish their invention from it, the applicants had restricted themselves in this claim to the solid form of the substance of a definite melting point. This limitation satisfied the court. The case is a most instructive example of the problems which can arise from scattered prior references in the literature of mainly academic interest even where there is no doubt in the mind of an objective observer that a valuable invention has been made. The corresponding British patent UK Patent No. 870,396 claims 6-APA as a product having the recited structural formula and being 'capable of reacting with phenylacetyl chloride to produce benzylpenicillin, and which gives a negative Bratten–Marshall test and a negative ninhydrin test'.

Fermentation products and products of nature

It is difficult to draw a sharp distinction between the types of substance covered in this heading. One possibility is to classify fermentation products as those where the preparative method is a man-made cultivation process which may more or less resemble the process which occurs in nature whereas the true product of nature is one where the preparative method is essentially one of extraction (without multiplication) from a natural source material. Patent law so far has not quite made this formal distinction and one of the leading US cases on 'products of nature' involves a fermentation product in the above sense. The 'product of nature' problem will be discussed after some examples of fermentation product patent have first been given.

Because substances produced by biosynthesis tend to have complex structures many of which are not elucidated in the short term it is often necessary to define them in a product claim by means of physicochemical and other data, e.g. melting point, infra-red spectrum and optical rotation. The specification must disclose the organisms and fermentation conditions used, giving detailed examples, and these features can be covered by process claims in the same application. But the main commercial value of the patent lies in the product *per se* claims.

Among the early examples of product patent in this field is US Patent No. 2,449,866 which has a single-word claim to 'streptomycin' and this method of claiming has been used in later patents including the tetracycline US Patent No. 2,699,054. Penicillin V was covered in US Patent No. 2,562,410 in terms of structural formula, having arisen as a novel compound from the use of the substituted acetic acid precursor technique covered in earlier patents in process terms.

The form of product claim used nowadays for antibiotics is typified by the following claim to cephalosporin C.

Cephalosporin C US Patent No. 3,093,638

'A product of manufacture, the antibiotic substance, cephalosporin C substantially free from cephalosporin N; said cephalosporin C containing carbon, hydrogen, oxygen, nitrogen and sulphur only and being a monoaminodicarboxylic acid effective against both gram positive and gram negative bacteria; soluble in water and almost insoluble in ethanol and ether; the sodium salt having an ultra-violet absorption maximum at 270 mμ and an infra-red spectrum showing bands at $2.94\,\mu$, $3.06\,\mu$, $5.61\,\mu$, $5.77\,\mu$, $6.05\,\mu$, $6.29\,\mu$, $6.57\,\mu$, $7.17\,\mu$ and $7.36\,\mu$; stable in aqueous solution at a pH of 2.5; and having a specific rotation $[\alpha]_D^{20}$ of $+103\,°$ in the form of its sodium salt.'

Cephalosporin C is an example of a relatively simple structure synthesized by a micro-organism and one where the chemistry was determined within a few years from its discovery. Patent practitioners prefer to draft product claims in terms of chemical structures because these are felt to be more fundamental and more definitive than the combination of physicochemical data of the kind used in the cephalosporin C case and there will therefore sometimes be a question of whether to wait until the structure has been worked out before taking patent action. This requires careful judgment between the desire for the best form of claim and the need for the earliest filing date for the patent application in a highly competitive field of research. The structural formula cannot in general be added to the patent disclosure once the latter has reached a certain stage in the patenting process and, as happened in the US patent application for cephalosporin C, the attempt to introduce it will be rejected as incorporating 'new matter'. Further discussion of problems of this kind will be dealt with in the next chapter.

Where the physicochemical characterization of a product is possible it is always desirable to include this data in the specification as well as the chemical structure. This can provide a fall-back definition if there is some doubt as to the structure. Where the latter is still uncertain there seems no reason why one cannot include alternative structures with a view to selecting the correct one before the patent is granted. This tactic clearly must be used within reason and may depend on the examiner's goodwill. It has been used, for example, where the choice was between two isomeric forms.

Gibberellic acid UK Patent No. 783,611

This provides another example of a fermentation product patent, describing the production of gibberellic acid by cultivation of an 'active' strain of *Gibberella fujikuroi*. Active strains, i.e. those which produce the acid, are said to be indistinguishable morphologically from those which are inactive in this respect and therefore can only be identified by actually testing the culture in each case. The main claim is worded simply as 'gibberellic acid'. Such claims in which the compound is defined by the name given to it by its discoverers are often used in the biological field as a convenient form of shorthand for a fuller definition in terms of the physical constants and characteristic properties which are usually to be found in the specification itself. One has to read the claim with the words 'as herein defined' as understood. In this instance melting point, optical rotation, infrared absorption curve, X-ray diffraction and other data are given in the body of the specification. Separate product claims to salts and alkyl esters of the acid are also presented.

The next examples to be given are the celebrated vitamin B_{12} patents in the USA which illustrate the merging together in a single legal problem of the two sub-categories of invention dealt with in the heading under discussion. This must, however, first be put in context by a brief summary of the legal issues.

The natural product problem

The patentability of products of nature is a vexed question and has attracted a good deal of case law especially in the USA. It immediately involves this paradox—if something must be new in order to be patentable how can a substance or thing of this type be patentable when nature already produces it? The simplest way out of the difficulty is to deny patents for natural products as such and this negative approach has sometimes swayed courts of patent law in particular cases. But the discovery of a natural principle followed by the practical utilization of that discovery for the public benefit is so akin to the kind of research activity normally regarded as inventive and deserving of recognition by the patent law that courts have often applied equitable principles against the legalistic objection that a naturally occurring substance cannot be new. Precisely what the term 'new' means to the patent lawyer will be discussed more fully in the next chapter but it must be said now that in discussing the patentability of products of nature much confusion has arisen from the way in which the concept of novelty has commonly been argued between applicants for patents and Patent Office examiners. There are definite distinctions between the use of the correlative terms 'new and old', 'known and unknown' and 'published and unpublished' and it is important to apply the proper criteria to this question, in order to reach the correct legal answer.

The first difficulty to be overcome arises from the distinction some laws make between invention and discovery. Unfortunately the law usually does not define the distinction between these two terms and so gives rise to uncertainty in particular cases. Perhaps 'invention' implies devising or making something that did not previously exist hence the important historical connection of the term 'manufacture' with various notions of what can be patented. 'Discovery' on the other hand suggests finding out about something that already occurs or exists. The unpatentability of natural phenomena is justifiable on the ground that no matter how meritorious the discovery may be to the enrichment of our knowledge of nature's way no-one should expect to derive any monopoly from a purely natural event as such. The argument is straight-forward as applied to schemes which amount to no more than the reproduction of a natural process and to this extent the legislative exclusion of 'mere discovery' from patentability commands general acceptance among the inventing community.

However, to reject patents for natural products on the basis of 'mere discovery' is an oversimplification in many cases and the old assumption that one cannot or should not patent a vitamin, hormone or enzyme has been strenuously resisted by patent practitioners with a fair measure of success. It is a negative attitude which has cropped up many times whether in discussion of the patentability of inanimate substances of natural origin or of living matter itself.

Prior to the vitamin B_{12} case there had been some decisions in the USA mainly concerned with the extraction of natural products from plants and other natural sources and giving negative answers to the question under consideration. For example a claim to a product isolated from a raw plant source without substantial change except as to purity and stability was held unpatentable because the substance existed as such in the plant and was produced by nature. An alcoholic extract containing the natural product or even a pure material not differing in composition from the material as it exists in nature was also held devoid of invention. A further insight was provided in another case which held that one who first isolates the active component from a substance in which the component exists as such is not entitled to a patent on the isolated component where it has the same utility as the substance from which it was isolated, differing therefrom in degree of activity. The decision further held that increased stability of the isolated component did not make the component patentable nor did its identification by its apparent chemical formula render it patentable. The distinction of relative utility between crude and isolated forms of a natural substance proved to be an important step towards the more equitable solution adopted in later cases.

Vitamin B$_{12}$ Patents Nos. 2,563,794 and 2,703,302

These two patents derived from a complex pattern of inter-related applications the first issuing in 1951 and the other nearly four years later. The two product claims are as follows:

> US Patent No. 2,563,794: 'The compound vitamin B$_{12}$, an organic substance containing cobalt, together with carbon, nitrogen, hydrogen, oxygen, and phosphorus, said compound being a red crystalline substance soluble in water, methyl and ethyl alcohol and phenol, and insoluble in acetone, ether and chloroform, and exhibiting strong absorption maxima at about 2780 Å, 3610 Å, and an LLD activity of about 11,000,000 LLD units per milligram'.
> US Patent No. 2,703,302: 'A vitamin B$_{12}$ active composition comprising recovered elaboration products of the fermentation of a vitamin B$_{12}$-activity producing strain of fungi selected from the class consisting of *Schizomycetes*, *Torula* and *Eremothecium*, the LLD activity of said composition being at least 440 LLD units per milligram and less than 11 million LLD units per milligram'.

The production method described in US Patent No. 2,563,794 is by fermentation of suitable strains of *Streptomyces griseus* but it will be realized that the product is defined in the claim in absolute terms so that the claim is in *per se* form to a substance which occurs in nature. This is the only claim present in the patent.

The claim to vitamin B$_{12}$ of fermentation origin in US Patent No. 2,703,302 is in product-by-process form. This claim does not cover pure crystalline B$_{12}$ or B$_{12}$ from liver but it excludes compositions of such low activity as to be of no commercial or therapeutic value.

In an infringement suit on this patent the defendants attacked the patent on the ground that it claimed a product of nature which was merely a purified form of natural fermentates. The Court of Appeals, Fourth Circuit, threw out this argument and found for the patentee. In its 1958 decision the court reviewed previous case law and relied especially on cases where the isolation of the natural product effectively contributed a new utility to the art (the adrenalin and aspirin cases and others) and stated the principle thus:

'The step from complete uselessness to great and perfected utility is a long one. That step is no mere advance in the degree of purity of a known product. From the natural fermentates which for this purpose were wholly useless and were not known to contain the desired activity in even the slightest degree, products of great therapeutic and commercial worth have been developed. The new products are not the same as the old but new and useful compositions entitled to the protection of the patent'.

Both patents were sued on against another defendant in 1967 and this time the *per se* claim of the 2,563,794 patent was attacked on the ground that the patentees had not invented B_{12} but merely recovered it from an existing material in more nearly pure condition than it had been in before. It was not a newly created compound but only a purified form of the anti-pernicious anaemia factor known to be present in liver. Prior published work on the purification of this factor by others was also relied on. These arguments were dismissed by the District Court of New Jersey in a judgment which confirmed the philosophy expounded in the previous court case. One quotation is sufficient to convey the liberal view of this court:

'Before Rickes and Wood made it available to the world, pure crystalline vitamin B_{12} as described and claimed in the '794 patent did not exist. No-one had produced even a comparable product. The new product had such advantages over the earlier liver extracts that it not only replaced them but became, and remains to this day, the universal treatment for pernicious anaemia.'

The UK and British Commonwealth attitude to natural product patents

The previous patent law of the UK contained the following passage (1949 Act, Section 4.7):

'Where a complete specification claims a new substance the claim shall be construed as not extending to that substance when found in nature'.

A corresponding provision was found in the law of New Zealand and some other Commonwealth countries, that in the South African law being a vestige of the former membership of that country in the British Commonwealth.

The British Patent Office interpreted the section as referring to substances in their natural state and allowed claims to substances isolated for the first time from natural sources, especially if defined as pure substances. The pure form of the substance isolated from its natural state was regarded as no longer 'when found in nature'. It followed that it was more difficult to patent a natural product where partial isolation had been previously described in the literature; some element of novelty could be put into the claim in terms of the higher level of purity achieved but there would be doubt about basing patentability solely on the ground of purity. Where a previous publication showed the isolation of the pure substance it was subsequently impossible to patent it solely on the basis of assigning a chemical structure to the compound.

The South African interpretation of the 'when found in nature' subsection of their previous Patent Act arose for the first time in a decision of the commissioner in 1962. The case involved a misplaced attack on a patent for chlortetracycline and the meaning of the disputed clause was not central to the case and therefore the observations made on it had no binding legal force even in that country. But the commissioner did set up a distinction between 'found in nature' and 'manufactured' and concluded that a claim to a product of this kind is effectively limited by the words of the statute to manufactured forms of the substance. The patentee could not 'complain of any dealing with that substance when the other party has merely found it in nature and has taken it from where he found it'. This is clearly not a comprehensive view of the problem and the quoted passage itself is not free from difficulties of interpretation and application to the more usual natural product situation. However, a similar and highly unsatisfactory view of the effect of the 'when found in nature' clause was taken more recently in the High Court of Eire in relation to a claim to a newly isolated strain of micro-organism. This subject will be dealt with more fully in Chapter 7 but for the purpose of the present discussion the clause was virtually held to be a built-in statutory exclusion of claims to all entities of this kind.

The UK and South African patent laws now in force no longer contain the ambiguous sub-section and novelty is judged on a different basis as will be appreciated from the more detailed consideration of this topic given in the next chapter. British and European patent law should be indistinguishable on this subject.

The German law (Federal Republic)

Absolute product claims were not allowed in Germany until 1968. Following their introduction, product-*per se* claims were considered by the German Patent Office as broadly unallowable for natural products and this attitude was undoubtedly based on the traditional distinction between discovery and invention explicitly stated in the German statute.

However, in the recently decided case of the cyclic peptide antamanide the Federal Patents Court has swept this view aside. Accepting the inventor's testimony that it was uncertain whether the claimed decapeptide existed as such in the fungal source *Amanita phalloides*, the court went further and observed that such a demonstration would in any case not be an obstacle to the grant of a patent. The inventor had not only pointed to the existence of the substance, which would have been mere discovery, but had provided in addition a technical process leading to the isolation and characterization of a new product. The product defined was novel because there had been no previous awareness of its existence and no-one had been in a position to make use of such a substance. It was therefore not necessary to limit the claim to 'synthetically prepared' decapeptide.

The European Patent Office (EPO) view

The German court in the antamanide case referred to and approved the explicit guideline of the EPO which is:

'If a man finds out a new property of a known material or article, that is mere discovery and unpatentable. If, however, a man puts that property to practical use he has made an invention which may be patentable. For example, the discovery that a particular known material is able to withstand mechanical shock would not be patentable, but a railway sleeper made from that material could well be patentable. To find a substance in nature is also mere discovery and therefore unpatentable. However, if a substance found in nature and a process for obtaining it is developed, that process is patentable as is the substance itself when produced by that process. Moreover, if the product can be properly characterized without reference to the process by which it is obtained, and it is 'new' in the absolute sense of having no previously recognized existence, then the product-*per se* may be patentable. An example of such a case is that of a new substance which is first discovered as being produced by a micro-organism. Plant or animal varieties, except products of microbiological processes, are excluded in any event by Article 53, sub-paragraph (b)'.

The European law on this and related topics will apply the test of novelty over the state of the art as laid down in the European Patent Convention. It is likely to be substantially the same as the law decided in the Antamanide case.

The Japanese law and practice

This has been made clear-cut by the explicit guidelines issued by the Japanese Patent Office on the general subject of microbiological inventions. The position is broadly similar to that in Europe although there are more detailed requirements for the characterization of natural products if a product claim is to be allowed.

Summary

The various decisions in different countries now seem to converge to a more encouraging prospect for natural product patents in the field of non-living materials. Living matter will be dealt with in a subsequent chapter. Although individual inventions vary greatly in factual complexity and borderline cases occur the following summary of some commonly recurring situations can be attempted.

Situation I

The presence of a biologically active substance in a particular source has not been disclosed hitherto. The inventor is the first to discover the activity and to isolate and characterize the product chemically or otherwise. All of this happens before any publication. This is the ideal situation, rarely met with in practice, and patent prospects are very good.

Situation II

1. The presence of activity in a natural source is known from the literature. Some attempts to isolate the active factor have been

published but the crude extracts so obtained are not of practical value. The inventor is the first to isolate and adequately characterize the product and puts its practical application within the bounds of possibility for the first time. Again, prospects are good although it is not certain that absolute product-*per se* claims can always be obtained. Some purity limitation may be necessary especially in USA.

2. If a chemical structure and a synthetic method of preparation are also worked out before any publication, it should be possible to claim the synthetic substance and possibly also the natural substance in chemical terms.

(N.B. Synthetic analogues of the natural product cannot be patented on the basis of mere prediction and paper chemistry.)

Situation III

The presence of the biological activity is well known. Isolation of the active substance has been previously published and the substance effectively characterized in some way, e.g. spectrum or melting point. The inventor is first to establish the chemical structure and suggest a synthetic route. There is no simple answer here. It is open to an opponent to take the position that this is classical scientific research but not inventive activity. Insofar as structure determination is mere analysis according to standard procedures and synthesis follows well known chemical paths it is arguable that this amounts to a combination of two obvious steps lacking the element of inventiveness necessary to support a patent. In practice it will sometimes be possible to adduce good counterarguments against too cavalier a dismissal of this kind of research.

To conclude this section on natural products the following two examples illustrate inventions involving the concentration and extraction of the substance from a natural source without any cultivation stage resulting in multiplication of the quantity in which it is present in nature.

Reserpine US Patent No. 2,752,351

This claims:

'. . . a crystalline product of manufacture consisting of a member selected from the group consisting of reserpine and the therapeutically active acid addition salts thereof . . .'

The name reserpine is given to a pure compound having sedative-hypnotic and hypotensive action and obtained from plants of the Rauwolfia species. It is described as an alkaloid melting at about 263 °C and of approximate optical rotation $[\alpha]_D^{23} - 118$ ° and empirical formula $C_{33}H_{40}O_9N_2$. Other data are given in the description. Detailed working examples of its extraction and isolation from root material of *Rauwolfia serpentina Benth*, *Rauwolfia vomitoria Afz* and *Rauwolfia inebriens* are described. In addition to the product claims there are also separate claims to pharmaceutical preparations for use by injection, orally and parenterally, in the usual 'active compound plus appropriate carrier' form.

Arvin US Patent No. 3,657,416

This example is that of a patent for an enzyme which was eventually given the generic name 'ancrod'. It is obtained by chromatographic fractionation of the venom of the Malayan pit viper and is claimed as follows:

'A thrombin-like defibrinating enzyme substantially free from haemorrhagic components, amino acid oxydase and constituents which cause tissue and vascular necrosis, derived from the venom *Ancistrodon rhodostoma*, having the following properties:

(a) it is proteinaceous and substantially colourless when pure
(b) it contains at least 20% carbohydrate
(c) it has a light powdery texture when in the freeze-dried state
(d) it is adsorbable on weakly basic anion exchange materials
(e) it is soluble in physiological saline
(f) it has an electrophoretic mobility of 3.9×10^{-5} volts/cm/sec in 0.1 M phosphate buffer pH 7.0
(g) it has a diffusion coefficient D_{20} of 4.8×10^{-7} sq. cm/sec at a concentration of 4.86 mg/ml
(h) in polydisperse form the observed molecular weight is of the order of 40,000 as determined in the ultra-centrifuge, the inferred monomeric molecular weight being of the order of 30,000

(i)   it has a sedimentation coefficient $S_{20}W = 3.4$ svedbergs at a concentration of 4.86 mg/ml

(j)   it has a partial specific volume of approximately 0.7 at a concentration of 4.86 mg/ml

(k)   it is not significantly inhibited by 1×10^{-3} molar di-isopropyl fluoro phosphate within 5 minutes, and

(l)   it has activity which converts fibrinogen to fibrin and which, upon *in vivo* administration, renders blood incoagulable'.

Microbial enzymes

Since most enzymes of industrial interest are obtained by cultivating microorganisms it is appropriate to refer at this point to patents in the enzyme field. There is an extensive patent literature on processes of producing enzymes, special products containing enzymes, and the uses of enzymes in industrial processes. In the present context interest centres on the form of product claim used for enzymes and enzyme preparations. The following two examples are typical of the traditional types of patent for enzymes and enzymic compositions.

US Patent No. 4,245,050: 'Choline oxidase produced by a microorganism belonging to the species *Brevibacterium album*, *Brevibacterium cerinum* or *Corynebacterium murisepticum* characterized by (a) catalysing oxidation of choline to betaine aldehyde and that of betaine aldehyde to betaine; (b) a stable pH range of 7.0 to 8.3; (c) an optimum pH range for reaction of 7.5 to 9.0; (d) an optimum temperature range for reaction of 20 °C to 45 °C; (f) a substrate specificity to choline or a salt thereof, a slight specificity to 2-dimethylaminoethanol, and no specificity to acetylcholine chloride, sarcosine, betaine, glycine, 2-methylaminoethanol and ethanol-amine hydrochloride; (g) being stabilized by EDTA; (h) being inhibited by sodium azide; (i) a molecular weight of about 97,000; and (j) an isoelectric point of pH 4.05'.

UK Patent No. 1,243,784: 'An enzyme preparation containing at least one proteolytic enzyme of the serine type produced by cultivation of species of the genus *Bacillus*, the said enzyme showing optimal proteolytic activity against haemoglobin in the presence of urea at a pH-value above 9'.

In these examples the enzyme is defined by reference to the microorganism source so that the claim is essentially of the product-by-process type. The source may be defined in terms of the genus, species or specific strains of a species identified by culture collection number. The following *per se* claim to an enzyme has recently been published.

German Patent No. 21 67 034

'Lösliche Creatinin-amidohydrolase, dadurch gekennzeichnet, dass sie die Reaktion

$$Creatinin + H_2O \rightleftharpoons Creatinin$$

mit der Gleichgewichtskonstante

$$\frac{[Creatin]}{[Creatinin]} : K + 1{,}27$$

bei pH 8,0 und 37 °C katalysiert und für Creatinin als Substrat bei diesen Bedingungen die $K_M 3{,}3 \times 10^{-2}$ M aufweist.'

This claim is an attempt to define the enzyme by means of its characteristics but it is doubtful whether the data used are fully distinctive in this respect.

Microorganisms, viruses and cell lines

The next category of product claim to be considered is that of microorganisms and cell lines, a topic which has given rise in recent years to questions of unusual interest for inventors and patent practitioners alike. We start with examples taken from British patents granted under the former Patents Act of 1949.

Fusarium graminearum UK Patent No. 1,346,061

This patent covers a number of novel isolates of the strain *Fusarium graminearum* Schwabe useful as edible protein. The main claim is:

'*Fusarium graminearum* Schwabe deposited with the Commonwealth Mycological Institute and assigned the number IMI 145425 and variants and mutants thereof'.

This is followed by five specific claims to some of these variants identified by individual IMI accession numbers. Detailed examples of the isolation of the parent strain and of these variants are given but no mutants are described, these being stated to be producible by methods well within the knowledge of those skilled in the art.

It is clear that the microorganisms specifically described are naturally occurring and isolated by selection. Nevertheless they were novel strains isolated and made available for the first time by the inventors and on the principles of the vitamin B_{12} case, which in their intrinsic correctness can be adopted without difficulty in UK patent law as well as in US law, they were new products deserving of a product-*per se* claim.

Unfortunately, when the counterpart applications in Eire and Australia came under official criticism the product claims to the strains were rejected. The Irish High Court judgment can be questioned on a number of counts but it is sufficient here to say that the stress on the implications of the word 'manufacture' in the Irish Patent Act ruled out the allowability of a claim to a naturally occurring strain. The Australian Commissioner of Patents stated his objection somewhat differently having come to the conclusion that merely discovering a naturally occurring microorganism 'makes no useful contribution to the art'. Arguments over patentability in patent office or court proceedings always involve the question of technical merit as well as purely legal considerations and this applies both to the specific judgment on the inventive quality involved in the particular case and to the more general question of whether or not patents should be granted at all for the kind of invention under examination. The merit present in the Fusarium case ought to derive from the special nutritional properties and acceptability of the defined microorganisms as edible foodstuff when compared with known strains of the same organism but on the advantages of the defined strains in this respect the specification is silent.

Marek's disease virus UK Patent No. 1,292,803

This specification is primarily concerned with the preparation of a vaccine effective against the particular disease of poultry and based on a live attenuated strain of Marek's disease virus. The identification of the causative agent of this disease as a virus of the herpes group had been published a year or so previously and in cell culture experiments aimed at another purpose altogether the virus was found unexpectedly to attenuate, the change commencing between the twentieth and thirtieth passage. This change was accompanied by loss of the A antigen of the pathogenic virus. Most of the patent claims are concerned with the attenuation process and the process for producing the vaccine but the interest of the patent under our present heading is in its product claim to:

'A strain of Marek's disease virus substantially free of the A antigen'.

This definition was based on the assumption that attenuation and the loss of the A antigen were at least interconnected even if not related as cause and effect. Freedom from the particular antigen provided a convenient label for defining an attenuated strain and a characteristic which could be easily tested for. It served also to render the claim less open to the criticism that might have been levelled at one which merely recited 'attenuated MD virus'.

The main practical problem with the attenuated strain was the difficulty of removing it from cells without loss of stability and when cross-immunity was later discovered as a property of the Turkey herpes virus, which could be produced in the cell-free state, the Marek's disease vaccine was superseded by a vaccine based on Turkey herpes virus.

BHK cell line UK Patent No. 1,015,262

The hamster kidney cell line of Stoker and Macpherson designated BHK21 was one of the earliest cell lines to be patented. The application was filed in 1962 at which time professional opinion was generally hesitant about *per se* claims to living organisms and this uncertainty is reflected by the absence of a claim in naked form to the cell line itself. The relevant claim reads:

'A cell culture system comprising cells derived from the baby golden hamster kidney fibroblast cell line designated BHK21 in a nutrient culture medium therefor'.

BHK21 cells were not artificially produced by their discoverers but were in effect selected out of a vastly complex mixture of cells by highly skilled experimentation. Whether one regards inventions of this kind as in the 'lucky find' category or not there can be no detraction from their meritorious and patent-worthy nature and in the writer's opinion it would be pedantry to class them as mere discoveries rather than inventions.

It was evident that not all viruses would grow in BHK21 cells and this made it difficult to present a broad process claim in which the viruses were not specified. The following so-called 'functional claim' was used:

'A virus cultivation process which comprises maintaining a viable culture of cells derived from the baby golden hamster kidney fibroblast cell line designated BHK21 in a nutrient culture medium, inoculating the culture with a virus to which the cells are susceptible and cultivating the virus in the culture'.

Liver cell line UK Patent No. 1,300,391

After the BHK21 cell line, patents for other cell lines have issued in UK under the former law and apparently without serious difficulty. The claim drafted in this case is to the cell line as such:

'A hyman embryo liver cell line having the characteristics of cells deposited with the American Type Culture Collection under number CL99'.

It shows a small but possibly significant difference in phraseology and scope compared with the *Fusarium graminearum* patent referred to above.

The Chakrabarty pseudomonad US Patent No. 4,259,444—(corresponding UK Patent No. 1,436,573)

Any discussion of micro-organism patents would be incomplete without reference to the recent *cause célèbre* in the United States in which, by the barest margin, the Supreme Court finally ruled favourably on the allowability under the statute of the following claim:

'A bacterium from the genus *Pseudomonas* containing therein at least two stable energy-generating plasmids, each of said plasmids providing a separate hydrocarbon degradative pathway.'

It is unnecessary here to describe the chequered history of this claim in its passage through the US Patent Office and courts because it attracted the interest of the general public and was reported on frequently throughout its eight year odyssey. Unless and until a new patent statute is enacted in the USA this decision will remain a landmark especially for research workers in genetic manipulation. The debate over the fundamental philosophy of patenting 'life-forms' has totally overshadowed many other facets of this particular case, not the least of which is the substantial breadth of the patent claim in issue. The gene splicing method was not involved in the Chakrabarty patent but it will presumably be the foundation of most of the first generation of patents in this field. Some of those patent applications of which the public has had notice that they are in the pipeline contain rather broad formulations of patent claim and it is possible that these will be allowed. Eventually, however, once the first flush is over, one would expect much narrower claim drafting to become the norm. Genetic engineering patent situations will be discussed more fully in a later chapter.

Compositions

Where a substance is not new but has been newly discovered to possess a valuable property it can often be protected in the form of a composition claim covering the substance in admixture with other substances in a form in which it will be utilized to take advantage of the new property. For example typical claims to 'pharmaceutical compositions' and 'insecticidal compositions' define the composition as consisting of an active ingredient and a suitable carrier or diluent. Although the active ingredient and the carrier or diluent may themselves be separately known the combination may be new. Furthermore the claim is justified on the ground that until the unexpected activity of the substance was discovered it would not have entered into one's head to formulate the substance into a composition of this type.

Chemical compositions

The discovery of the insecticidal properties of the compound that came to be known as DDT is a classical example.

DDT UK Patent No. 547,874

This may not have been the very first patent in which the need arose to establish a type of claim for use where a known compound is discovered to have valuable and hitherto unexpected properties. However, it is an early example and can be regarded as a precursor of what came to be the more usual form. It is cast in manufacturing process form as follows:

> Manufacture of solid insecticidal compositions consisting in admixing a compound of the general formula $R_1R_2CHCX_3$ wherein X means chlorine, R_1 means a phenyl radical containing as a substituent in the *para* position a chlorine atom or a methyl group and otherwise unsubstituted, and R_2 is identical with R_1, with a solid finely divided or porous inert diluent or carrier.

Generally the kind of claim which has become standard is directed to a composition comprising the active ingredient and a diluent or carrier, the latter usually being qualified as 'acceptable' for the particular use concerned. Where the carrier can simply be distilled water, an organic solvent, or some other well-known laboratory chemical one is liable to run into difficulties caused by the 'accidental anticipation' of such a combination in the prior literature on the chemistry of the substance itself; this would be novelty-destroying in spite of the absence of any disclosure of the valuable property in the prior document.

Other types of composition claim are those in which, whether the active ingredient is new or not, some special method of formulation has been discovered which is particularly advantageous. A particular species of this type of claim is the claim to mixtures of substances which show a synergistic effect.

Antifungal product US Patent No. 2,968,590

This is an example of the type of claim described above, which states:

> 'An anti-fungal product comprising, in synergistic combination, boric acid and an organic compound, in an amount of from about 0.2 to about 5.0 mols per mol of boric acid, selected from the group consisting of lactic acid, salicyclic acid and propylene glycol; combined with water and sufficient base to provide a pH of between about 9 and 11.'

Also under this heading are the so-called 'unit dosage patents' mainly found in USA and directed towards products which are sold in the form of units of specified dose, the active compound usually being a known substance either of no previous known use or previously proposed for a use unrelated to the new pharmaceutical use.

Isoniazid US Patent No. 2,596,069

This contains both composition claims and unit dosage claims such as the following:

'A composition for combating tuberculosis comprising not less than 0.10 per cent of a member selected from the group consisting of isonicotinic acid hydrazide and acid addition salts thereof and a sterile parenteral water diluent at a pH of about 6.0.

'A composition in dosage unit form for combating tuberculosis comprising about 10 to about 50 mg of isonicotinic acid hydrazide per dosage unit and a solid pharmaceutical carrier'.

'Substance for use' claims

This type of claim was mentioned above as having come into use with the European patent law. It is applicable to situations in which a known substance is found to have a pharmaceutical use. Although formally a product claim it is included here because of its affinity to the older form of 'pharmaceutical composition' claim which it can now replace in modern practice. It has the advantage over the composition claim that it will not be affected by the 'accidental anticipation' complication referred to above. Unfortunately it is applicable only to the first discovery of a pharmaceutical use for a known compound and not to so-called second indications. As well as being used for European patents it is permitted under some of the newer national laws which have conformed to the European pattern. These claims take the form: 'substance or composition X for use in . . .' the use being specified as a therapeutic, surgical or diagnostic method carried out on the human or animal body.

Kit claims

Attempts to patent kits-of-parts and chemical reagent combinations which have become respectively very popular in the do-it-yourself and diagnostic fields have met with stiff opposition from patent examining authorities. Those following British precedents have rejected some of such applications on the ground of an old decision that the mere placing side by side of old integers is not a patentable combination in the absence of some working inter-relation producing a new or improved result. Putting separate chemical reagents into a multi-compartment container so that they do not mix until dispensed has been held to be mere collocation. A container including a known substance with written instructions as to a specific low dosage for use against a specific disease has also recently failed to pass the test of functional inter-relationship. But two-component or multi-component packs may be patentable if the mixture of components is novel or a new reaction is involved. Two examples are dental cement and cholesterol assay.

Dental cement UK Patent No. 1,139,430

The invention here was to substitute polyacrylic acid for phosphoric acid in the preparation of a dental cement by reaction of the acid with zinc oxide. The polyacrylic acid component was not a new substance and therefore could not itself be protected. The zinc oxide/polyacrylate cement was a new substance but a product claim to this would be of doubtful value in relation to the reagents as marketed because the cement does not come into being until it is made by the dentist at the time of performing the dental operation. Hence the necessity to claim the invention in the following terms:

'A surgical cement pack comprising a surgically acceptable grade of zinc oxide powder and an aqueous solution containing at least 40% by weight of a polyacrylic acid having a viscosity determined average molecular weight of 15,000–150,000, the powder and the solution upon mixing together in a ratio between 0.5 : 1 to 4 : 1 by weight forming a plastic mass which rapidly hardens as a surgical cement but which remains plastic long enough to be formed into a desired shape.'

Cholesterol assay UK Patent No. 1,385,320

An enzymatic method for the determination of cholesterol based on the discovery of a cholesterol oxidase which would catalyse the reaction:

$$\text{Cholesterol} + O_2 \rightarrow \Delta^4\text{-cholestenone} + H_2O_2$$

was covered by a claim to a method of assay based on estimating the amount of peroxide formed. The corresponding reagent kit claim was as follows:

> 'A kit for use in assaying the amount of cholesterol in a liquid comprising in association,
> (i) an enzyme preparation capable of oxidising cholesterol to Δ^4-cholestenone and hydrogran peroxide; and
> (ii) at least one reagent which is capable of being used in the determination of the amount in which hydrogen peroxide or Δ^4-cholestenone is formed.

Biological compositions

The final example of a composition claim is mixed culture inoculant, a US patent that figured prominently in the Chakrabarty case mentioned earlier (claim to living organism).

Mixed culture inoculant US Patent No. 2,200,532

This patent was taken out in 1940 and was litigated upon at a time when US courts were not favourably disposed towards attempts to patent 'nature's secrets'. In 1948 the Supreme Court held it to be invalid. The disclosure in the patent and the judgment of the court are given in the light of the then prevailing knowledge of nitrogen fixation in leguminous plants. The species specificity of *Rhizobium* for *Leguminosae* and the six recognized species effective for specific groups of plants had constituted a prior art background in which inoculants were used containing only one species of root nodule bacteria. Previous attempts to use mixed cultures proved unsatisfactory because different *Rhizobia* species produced an inhibitory effect on each other when mixed in a common base. Against the previous assumption that different species were mutually inhibitive the inventor had discovered some strains of each species which did not produce this inhibition and he claimed:

> 'An inoculant for leguminous plants comprising a plurality of selected cultures of difference species of bacteria of the genus *Rhizobium*, one of said cultures being *Rhizobium trifolii* alpha, said cultures being substantially unaffected by each other in respect to their ability to fix nitrogen in the leguminous plant for which they are specific'.

The case is often remembered for its ruling that the qualities in the strains were the handiwork of nature and that the mere aggregation of these produced nothing over and above the sum of their individual properties. In such circumstances there was no true 'combination' and no new effect which qualified as an invention. This reason may now seem somewhat dated but the real criticism of the claim which would apply as forcefully today came from the judge who saw that the claim was not specific enough in regard to strains which would be effective. The claim amounted to pre-empting the principle of compatibility without teaching how compatible strains could be recognized and obtained. The contemporary English judges would have described this as a 'covetous claim'. Others might describe it as a classical 'problem claim' in that it covers in effect every solution of the problem to which it is addressed.

The next category, that of process claims, covers a very high proportion of all patents granted for inventions in bioscience, extending as it does both to new processes and to new variations on known processes.

Processes

In recent years more countries have adopted the product claim as an appropriate form of protection for new substances so that this practice is no longer that of a small minority among the national systems of patent law. Before this trend, however, it was in most of the world necessary even in the case of a new product to claim the invention in process terms, i.e. a claim to a process of preparation. Not only was this a highly artificial approach to the protection of a new product but it also required the devising of alternative methods of preparation and the use of multiple process claims to cover every practical possible pathway to the product. There are still many territories outside Western Europe, USA and Japan where this unsatisfactory practice persists especially in Eastern Europe and Latin America.

The type of process claim used in the situation described above is termed an 'analogy process' claim to reflect the fact that the process is not inherently a new method but may be a standard chemical or other kind of procedure, its novelty in the case claimed lying solely in its application to a specific reactant or substrate or combination of them. The patent literature abounds with chemical process claims which cover traditional acylation and esterification reactions applied to the synthesis of new compounds. Similarly many microbiological patents exist where

58

the general conditions of fermentation recited in the claim are entirely conventional and the only novel element is the particular species or strain of microorganism used.

The genuine process invention is one where a truly novel route or method has been devised or where new conditions have been found for operating a process of generally known type in order to achieve an improved result.

For a chemical process to be new in the patent sense it is not essential for it to be some entirely new chemical reaction as such. Indeed reactions which would be considered in academic circles as truly original, perhaps justifying to be named after their originator, are found rather infrequently in patent specifications. Since the process is in general intended to produce some new useful product or class of compounds the structure of which may already be known, the newness will almost always lie in the special choice or adaptation to the particular purpose of chemical synthetic methodology which is in a broad sense within the fund of knowledge of the experienced synthetic chemist. This point must be made carefully because it is often not easy to draw a dividing line between obvious chemistry, where the structure pre-determines the required method to a large extent, and the imaginative, elegant and effective synthetic route which, once it has been disclosed, makes others ask why they did not think of it before.

Any of the parameters of a known chemical or microbiological reaction can be the subject of a process patent where a departure from standard conditions or the use of a new or special reactant or substrate gives rise to a non-obvious advantage of some kind. It is common to find patents based on a selected temperature or pH range, particular solvents for the reaction, the use of additives as precursors or for other purposes in a fermentation medium, special solvent extraction media or procedures, and so on. Microbiological processes where the essential feature of novelty lies in the use of a specially selected strain, especially a newly developed strain, give rise to a very common type of process claim.

Synthetic pyrethroid UK Patent No. 1,168,797

This is an example of an analogy process claim:

'A process for the preparation of substituted furans of the general formula:

$$Z-CH-CH-COOCH_2 \quad \underset{O}{\overset{R_1 \quad R_2}{\text{furan}}} \quad CH_2Y$$

with substituents CH_3 and CH_3 on the central C.

In which Z represents an aryl, alkenyl or carboalkoxyalkenyl group, R_1 and R_2, which may be the same or different, represent a hydrogen atom or an alkyl, alkenyl or alkadienyl group and Y represents a hydrogen atom or an alkyl, alkenyl or alkadienyl group or an aryl or furyl group which may be substituted in the ring by alkyl, alkenyl, alkadienyl or alkoxy groups or halogen atoms, which comprises reacting a substituted cyclopropane carboxylic acid or acid derivative thereof of the general formula:

$$Z-CH-CH-CO.P$$

with central C bearing CH_3 and CH_3.

with a substituted furan of the general formula:

$$QCH_2-\underset{O}{\overset{R_1 \quad R_2}{\text{furan}}}-CH_2Y$$

where –CO.P and Q represent functional groups which react together to form an ester linkage.'

Since the final products were novel compounds they were covered by a product-*per se* claim in the same British patent. The above process claim was used in the territories where the law allowed only process protection.

The legal rationale for allowing claims of this kind, where the chemical reaction involved is not new as such, was that the valuable and non-obvious level of biological activity in the final products conferred inventive merit on the process viewed as a whole. This consideration was not deemed to apply to a process in which the final product was devoid of activity and therefore in Germany and other 'process countries' which entertained the idea of the analogy process in their older laws it was not possible, for example, to obtain an analogy process claim where the product was an inactive intermediate however valuable it was for this purpose.

In the preparation of the insecticides quoted in this example the furan alcohol intermediates were novel compounds and were covered by a separate patent having product claims and also process claims to a particular chemical route for their synthesis. This provides the following example of claiming a process of this type.

Furan alcohol UK Patent No. 1,168,798

The claims cover a group of compounds but the illustration will be restricted to the preparation of the most important of these, 5-benzyl-3-furylmethyl alcohol. The process starts with the conversion of benzyl cyanide by a Claisen condensation reaction with a succinic ester to produce a condensate of formula $Ph\text{-}CH(CN)COCH_2CH_2COOR$. Hydrolysis of the cyano group and, at the same time, of the COOR group produces a β-keto acid which decarboxylates *in situ* to give the compound $Ph\text{-}CH_2COCH_2CH_2COOH$. After re-esterification and protection of the keto group as the ethylenedioxy derivative, the resulting protected ester:

$$Ph\,CH_2-\underset{\underset{\displaystyle CH_2-CH_2}{|\qquad\quad|}}{\underset{O\qquad\;\; O}{\overset{/\quad\backslash}{C}}}-CH_2CH_2COOR$$

is acylated with a formate ester to give an intermediate which can be stabilized in the enol form as the alkali metal salt

$$Ph\,CH_2-\underset{\underset{\displaystyle CH_2-CH_2}{|\qquad\;\;|}}{\underset{O\quad\;\; O}{\overset{/\quad\backslash}{C}}}-CH_2-\underset{\underset{\displaystyle O.M}{|}}{\overset{\overset{\displaystyle CH}{\|}}{C}}-COOR$$

This enol salt is then cyclized under acid conditions to give the furoic ester:

$$\text{PhCH}_2 - \underset{\underset{\displaystyle O}{\diagdown\diagup}}{\overset{\displaystyle CH \overline{\qquad} C - COOR}{\underset{\displaystyle C}{\parallel}\qquad\underset{\displaystyle CH}{\parallel}}}$$

which in the final stage of the synthesis is reduced to convert –COOR to –CH₂OH.

When faced with a multi-step process such as the one described the patent draftsman has to consider whether the invention resides in the total combination of steps or in one or more of the individual steps considered as the key to the success of the route as a whole. If one of the steps can be avoided by clever choice of an alternative route to its immediate product there will be a loophole in the claim if it is tied to the whole combination. This is a good example of a situation in which the inventor and patent agent, working together, will supply complementary constructive thinking to arrive at a formulation of the process claim which cannot be easily circumvented. One technique is to draft the main claim in terms of only the last step of the synthesis. In the example under discussion this will look rather artificial to the chemist because it will simply call for the reduction of –COOR to –CH₂OH in a particular context and he may wonder whether such wording really encapsulates the inventive content of the process. Succeeding claims will then specify the previous stages, one by one in claim by claim, until we arrive at the start, i.e. benzyl cyanide.

This last step, penultimate step, etc. type of approach is not acceptable practice under every patent system and in some countries one simply has to trust in the judgment of the patent agent/inventor team to distil out the essential idea, taking account of course of the relevant prior knowledge of which they both should be fully aware. For example the process claim used for the above process in some of the Scandinavian countries was of the following form:

'Process for the preparation of a compound of the formula specified which comprises acylating a protected keto ester of formula . . . with an acylating agent of formula HCOOR and cyclizing the resulting enolic compound of formula . . . and reducing the resulting compound to the corresponding alcohol'.

(This is a simplified form of the actual claim obtained.)

Examples of some microbiological process patents will now be given.

Use of new strain US Patent No. 3,875,010

'Process for the production of daunorubicin which comprises aerobically cultivating *Streptomyces bifurcus*, strain DS 23,219 (NRRL 3539), or a daunorubicin-producing mutant thereof, using an aqueous nutrient medium containing assimilable sources of carbon, nitrogen and inorganic substances, and separating dauno-rubicin formed during the culture.'

This patent was an important precedent in US patent practice in establishing, against objection from the patent office, that the use of a new strain in an otherwise conventional process may be patentable.

Use of new species US Patent No. 3,003,925

'A method for producing 1-glutamate selected from the group con-sisting of 1-glutamic acid and a salt thereof which comprises aerobically culturing *Micrococcus glutamicus* in a culturing medium containing carbohydrate, nitrogen source and inorganic material, controlling the pH value of the culturing medium within the range of from about 6 to about 9 by the addition of neutralizing agent, whereby a substantial amount of 1-glutamate is accumulated in the culturing medium, and recovering said 1-glutamate.'

The *Micrococcus glutamicus* patent is an intriguing example of a defini-tion for patent purposes of a new species in terms of a special property, in this case the ability to produce a particular type of product.

Use of particular fermentation medium US Patent No. 3,082,155

'A process for the production of cephalosporin C by the culture of a cephalosporin C-producing mould of the species of which *Cephalosporium* I.M.I. 49137 is a member in a medium containing suitable nutrient materials therefor, including a source of organic nitrogen, in the presence of molecular oxygen and the separation of cephalosporin C thereby produced wherein the organic nitrogen source includes corn steep liquor present in a quantity sufficient to provide a proportion of the organic nitrogen less than 20% of the total.'

Tetracycline production process UK Patent No. 952,820

'The process of producing tetracycline which comprises cultivating a strain of *Streptomyces aureofaciens* which produces tetracyline to the substantial exclusion of chlortetracycline under submerged aerobic conditions in an aqueous nutrient medium containing assimilable sources of carbohydrate, nitrogen, and inorganic salts until substantial quantities of tetracycline are produced, said tetracycline-producing strain of *Streptomyces aureofaciens* being also characterized by its ability to impart to the whole harvest mash a color characterized by a reflectance curve, when plotted linearly, wherein the vertical distance between the reflectance curve and a straight line drawn through the reflectance curve intercepts at 400 mµ and 550 mµ is greater at 420 mµ than at 430 mµ.'

The cited main claim of the tetracycline process patent was held invalid in an infringement action in the English High Court, in a case which is of especial interest in involving a conflict of scientific expert-opinion over the derivation of the strain used in the defendant's process.

Cultivation of common cold virus UK Patent No. 930,720

This was based on the fortuitous discovery that somewhat lower than usual temperature and pH ranges were necessary for successful replication of the common cold virus *in vitro*. The main claim reads:

'A process for the culture of the human common cold virus by incubation in a tissue culture system comprising a culture medium containing cells of human or monkey origin capable of supporting the growth of the strain or strains of virus selected, wherein the culture medium is maintained at a temperature of from 30 °C to 36 °C and a pH of between 6.4 and 7.4.'

Miscellaneous Methods

Under this heading are grouped various methods of treatment and methods of testing.

Methods of treatment

These include the processing or treatment of some kind of substrate such as an industrial raw material or an agricultural product e.g. plants or animals. The first example is based on the discovery of selective herbicidal properties in a known compound.

Herbicidal treatment US Patent No. 3,816,092

'A method for selectively inhibiting growth of undesirable plants in an area containing an established crop which comprises applying to said area 3,4-dichloropropionanilide at a rate of application which inhibits growth of said undesirable plants and which does not adversely affect the growth of said established crop.'

This patent recently reached the US Supreme Court in an important decision on the law of patent infringement which will be discussed in a later chapter.

Meat tenderizing UK Patent No. 913,202

As an improvement over the prior art method of tenderizing by the relatively inefficient procedure of infusion of enzymes into the meat carcass the new process can be readily understood from the following claim which gave rise to an important judicial decision on patentability:

'A method for distributing enzymes in meat comprising introducing a proteolytic enzyme in a liquid medium into the vascular system of a living animal from which the meat is to be obtained, and then slaughtering the animal after a period of time sufficient to permit substantially uniform distribution of the enzyme throughout the animal's body but before the presence or effectiveness of the enzyme has been eliminated by the animal's body processes'.

The advantage derives from the pumping action of the animal's heart which ensures proper distribution of the enzyme prior to slaughter.

The UK Patent Office and former Patent Tribunal, following a long tradition of interpretation of the term 'manufacture' in relation to patent law, had held this method to be outside the ambit of patent protection because of its 'agricultural' rather than 'manufacturing' character. This decision was reversed on appeal. The higher court was influenced by previous decisions in Australia and New Zealand on a claim to a method

of eradicating weeds (using a known substance) which had initi
rejected on the same ground of lack of industrial character. Tl
longer any doubt as to the patentability of inventions of this kinu.

Treatment of humans or animals

Under the European patent law methods of direct treatment of human
or animal subjects are patentable provided they are divorced from
primarily medical purpose. For example methods of waving hair in
humans or of increasing weight gain in animals by applying a particular
treatment or administering a certain substance are patentable.
Therapeutic and surgical methods, and diagnostic methods in which a
patient is treated directly, are unpatentable under the European law and
also under the laws of most of the rest of the world. One significant
exception is the USA where patents for methods of treatment of humans
are relatively common; they are often the only form of protection allowable especially where the therapeutic agent is a known substance. Such
method patents might appear to be of dubious commercial value but
under certain circumstances US patent law regards the sale of the
therapeutic material, or other compound used in the method, as an
illegal inducement to infringe the method claim. Typical examples of
such patents are given below.

US Patent No. 4,259,334

    '1. A process for the treatment of cardiac rhythm disorders which
comprises administering to a human in need thereof a
therapeutic composition containing an anti-arrhythmic effective amount of 1-[2-(2,6-dimethyl-phenoxy)-ethyl]-4-(benzi-
midoyl)-piperazine or a pharmaceutically acceptable acid
addition salt thereof.'

US Patent No. 4,259,075

    '1. A method for filling a tooth cavity, comprising:
       (i) Applying to the walls of the tooth cavity a lining composi-
tion comprising a phosphoric or phosphonic acid ester
compound containing at least one radical polymerizable
vinyl group and at least one

$$
\begin{array}{ccc}
\overset{\displaystyle O}{\underset{\displaystyle |}{\|}} & & \overset{\displaystyle O}{\underset{\displaystyle |}{\|}} \\
C\text{--}O\text{--}P\text{--}O\text{--}C & \text{or} & C\text{--}O\text{--}P\text{--}C \\
| & & | \\
OH & & OH
\end{array}
$$

group, wherein said lining composition contains said phosphoric or phosphonic acid ester compound in a proportion of not less than 0.1 weight percent, as phosphorus, and then

(ii) Filling the remainder of the cavity with a dental filling material which comprises a polymerizable monomer, a filler and a curing agent.

Methods of testing

Methods of testing are patentable where they are capable of industrial application and this requirement is clearly met where the test method is one of quality control or one which is connected generally with the improvement or control of manufacture especially as regards either the process or product of manufacture. There seems nowadays a willingness also to allow test method claims where the broad context is medical or diagnostic provided it is not carried out directly on the patient although in USA even this is allowed.

US Patent No. 3,925,164

In this example the main claim is:

'Method of determining total cholesterol or bound cholesterol in a sample, which method comprises treating said sample with cholesterol esterase obtained from a micro-organism, thereby releasing the bound cholesterol, and then determining the resulting cholesterol content of said sample using a standard determination'.

LEGAL RIGHTS FOR PLANTS AND METHODS OF PLANT PRODUCTION

This chapter has been chiefly concerned so far with categories of invention found in the field of chemistry as applied to the production of biologically active products and in the areas of biochemistry and microbiology. These are related from the viewpoint of patent law and fundamental legal principles apply throughout. The technology of plant breeding and the handling of innovation in this field through the special systems of legal rights which exist for the benefit of the plant breeder call for separate treatment. No more than a brief overview will be attempted here in order to relate various kinds of innovation to the legal systems under which they properly fall.

The most common form of legislation for plants is that of the plant variety right, a system which is separate from the patent law and distinguishable from it in legal protective effect. In addition there is a plant patent law in a small minority of countries of which the USA is the most notable example. These two forms of legal protection are the natural choice for the development of new varieties by traditional breeding methods. Processes for the production of plants by some methods, however, e.g. tissue culture are more appropriately regarded as microbiological inventions and can be protected by ordinary patents of the kinds discussed in previous sections. The application of recombinant DNA methods to plant genes presents aspects relevant to all three systems of legal protection and it may be a matter of choice in particular cases as to which system or combination of systems offers the best method of protecting the development. The United States provides for protection under all these systems and its laws are a good starting point for discussion of the distinctions between them.

Plant Protection in USA

The US Supreme Court, in its decision to allow the *per se* claim for the Chakrabarty pseudomonad mentioned earlier, has repeated the accepted explanation of the relatively recent origin of plant patent and variety protection law in that country. Before 1930 the belief was that plants, even though artificially bred, were products of nature for purposes of the patent law and as such were not subject to patent protection. In addition, differentiation of new plants from old was considered as not amenable to the written description requirement of the patent law. In enacting the Plant Patent Act of 1930 the intention of Congress was to extend to the plant breeder the benefits widely believed in the USA to have stemmed to industry from the existence of a patent law. The Act excluded sexually produced plants because it was then asserted (though apparently not by plant breeders) that new varieties could not be reproduced true-to-type through seedlings. However, this anomaly was removed in 1970 by the passing of the Plant Variety Protection Act.

US plant patents

The plant patent law of the USA was a separate statute in 1930 but is now incorporated in the general patent law as Chapter 15 of US Code Title 35 Patents, as Sections 161–164. Section 161 reads:

'Whoever invents or discovers and asexually reproduces any distinct and new variety of plant, including cultivated sports, mutants, hybrids, and newly found seedlings, other than a tuber propagated plant or a plant found in an uncultivated state, may obtain a patent therefor . . .'.

Some 5,000 plant patents have been granted (about 0.2% of all US patents) and the largest single group of these is for roses. The demand for patent protection came in the first instance from the rose breeders and fruit tree breeders in the USA which may account for the limitation of the statute to asexual propagation. The contrary opinion came from those who cultivate plants by seeding and so Congress evidently divided the field to satisfy conflicting interests.

There is considerable room for debate as to the scope of the term 'plant' in this statute but a US court specifically decided in 1940 that bacteria cannot be covered by means of plant patents. Although bacteria may be broadly classified within the plant kingdom and reproduce asexually the court held that the term must be given its ordinary meaning in the common language of the people. Nevertheless fungi are included. New plants found growing in nature can be patented provided they have been found in a cultivated area.

The prosecution of plant patent applications in the US Patent and Trade Mark Office is similar to that of all other patent applications except that only a single claim is allowed. Specimen plants are not routinely required and a drawing, coloured if necessary, will suffice. The claim must contain the novel and distinguishing characteristics of the new plant and these are usually stated in more relative and less precise quantitative terms than in patent claims for articles of other kinds. This will be apparent from the examples shown here.

These include the plant patent for the *Fusarium graminearum* strain quoted previously as an example of a patent (British) for a

4,612
ROSE PLANT
Samuel D. McGredy, P.O. Box 14-100, Auckland, New Zealand
Filed Jun. 12, 1979, Ser. No. 47,939
Int. Cl.³ A01H 5/00
U.S. Cl. Plt.—3   1 Claim
1. A new and distinct variety of rose plant of the miniature class, substantially as shown and described, characterized particularly by petite pointed buds opening into pure white maintaining their color well upon aging and a loose growing, spreading plant that is very resistant to blackspot, mildew and rust.

4,613
ROSE PLANT NAMED PAUL'S PINK
Paul F. DeVor, late of Pleasanton, Calif. (by Thelma G. DeVor, executrix), assignor to DeVor Nurseries, Inc., Pleasanton, Calif.
Filed Jul. 2, 1979, Ser. No. 53,933
Int. Cl.³ A01H 5/00
U.S. Cl. Plt.—18   1 Claim
1. A new and distinct variety of rose plant substantially as herein shown and described, characterized by its beautifully opening high centered blooms which have a very soft pink coloration and strong fragrance, its vigorous and free branching growth habit, and its profuse year-around production of long lasting flowers.

4,614
DISTINCT VARIETY OF BLACK WALNUT TREE
Walter F. Beineke, West Lafayette, Ind., assignor to Purdue Research Foundation, West Lafayette, Ind.
Filed Sep. 5, 1978, Ser. No. 939,833
Int. Cl.² A01H 5/00
U.S. Cl. Plt.—32   1 Claim
1. A new and distinct variety of black walnut tree substantially as illustrated and described, which has excellent timber quality, is fast growing, has strong central stem tendency, little

sweep, few crooks; late in time of leafing, pistillate flowers very late, pollen sheds late, and a nut crop is seldom produced.

4,615
APPLE TREE
Irving H. Wrigley, 2550 Wrigley Rd., Eureka, Calif. 95501
Filed May 7, 1979, Ser. No. 36,787
Int. Cl.³ A01H 5/03
U.S. Cl. Plt.—34   1 Claim
1. A new and distinct variety of apple tree, substantially as described in this application, and in particular, characterized by the solid red colored fruit which it bears.

4,616
PEAR TREE
Kenneth L. Turnbull, Depew, Okla., and Daniel K. Hybskmann, Shenandoah, Iowa, assignors to Henry Field Seed and Nursery Company, Shenandoah, Iowa
Filed Apr. 20, 1979, Ser. No. 31,985
Int. Cl.² A01H 5/00
U.S. Cl. Plt.—36   1 Claim
1. A new and distinct variety of pear tree, substantially as shown and described herein, distinguished by the physical characteristics of the fruit including its size, shape and taste.

4,617
PEACH TREE
Aram Kevorkian, P.O. Box 409, Reedley, Calif. 93654
Filed Jul. 5, 1979, Ser. No. 55,026
Int. Cl.³ A01H 5/00
U.S. Cl. Plt.—43   1 Claim
1. A new and distinct variety of peach tree substantially as illustrated and described, characterized by its bearing of freestone fruit having yellow flesh striated with red and by its general resemblance to the Redtop Peach Tree (unpatented), but which is distinguished therefrom by its fruit ripening from seven to ten days earlier and by having more highly colored skin.

5

4,347
NON-TOXIC STRAIN OF *FUSARIUM GRAMINEARUM*
Gerald L. Solomons, High Wycombe, and Gerald W. Scammell, Chinnor, both of England, assignors to Ranks Hovis McDougall Limited, London, England
Continuation of Ser. No. 417,190, Jan. 7, 1974, abandoned, which is a continuation of Ser. No. 140,303, May 4, 1971, abandoned. This application Dec. 19, 1975, Ser. No. 642,610
Claims priority, application United Kingdom, May 14, 1970, 23452/70; Jun. 24, 1970, 30584/70
Int. Cl.² A01H 15/00
U.S. Cl. Plt.—89   1 Claim
1. A novel non-toxic fungi *Fusarium graminearum* as shown and described in the foregoing specification and drawings which has been deposited with the Commonwealth Mycological Institute and identified as *Fusarium graminearum* Schwabe I.M.I. 145425.

microorganism. The claim to the strain was evidently not allowed in an ordinary US patent and so the applicants resorted to protection in the form of a plant patent.

The plant patent law has the same novelty and inventiveness requirements of the general patent law and in particular also has the concept of 'enabling disclosure' according to which a mere published description of a plant or other article which would not have enabled the public to reproduce the plant or article in question would not be destructive of novelty. The general law on patentable novelty and inventiveness are discussed in the next chapter.

As to the nature of the plant patent right it must be emphasized that the patent is directed to the plant itself, rather than to its flowers, fruit, seed or other products. Section 163 defines the plant patent right as the right to exclude others from asexually reproducing the plant or selling or using the plant so reproduced.

US plant variety rights

These are covered by the Plant Variety Protection Act 1970 which applies only to plants propagated by seed and provides that:

'The breeder of any novel variety of sexually reproduced plant (other than fungi, bacteria, or first generation hybrids) who has so reproduced the variety, or his successor in interest, shall be entitled to plant variety protection therefor . . .'.

Although the reasons for excluding fungi and bacteria are not known hybrids were said to have been excluded because these have their own built-in protection for their developer since he can control the in-bred or parental stocks and the hybrid cannot be reproduced from hybrid seeds.

Applications for protection under this legislation are handled rather differently from plant patent applications. The authority for the granting of certificates of protection is the Department of Agriculture rather than the United States Patent and Trade Mark Office. The rights attaching to the certificate include the ordinary patent right of protection against unauthorized marketing or importing or inducing others to perform these acts. In addition unauthorized propagation from marketed seed is forbidden where the object is to market seed for growing purposes. However, the seed of a protected variety may be used by a grower whose primary occupation is the growing of crops for food or feed and not primarily for seeding purposes.

Plant Protection Outside USA

In the law of most countries other than USA the plant patent is over-shadowed by the plant variety right as the dominant type of protection.

Plant patents

In a small number of other countries patents are granted for asexually reproduced plants along the lines of the US law. Germany and some other European territories have allowed patents for plants as for other types of invention and have not hitherto made any special legal distinctions in their respect. In Japan new plant varieties could be protected *per se* under the patent law from 1970 but in 1978 a new 'Seeds and Seedlings' law was enacted. Parallel protection under both Japanese systems may be possible.

In Western Europe the more usual modern approach is to exclude plant varieties from protection under the patent law. The prototype of this policy is Article 53(b) of the European Patent Convention which specifically denies patent protection for:

'Plant or animal varieties or essentially biological processes for the production of plants or animals; this provision does not apply to microbiological processes or the products thereof'.

It is not evident that this article textually excludes all claims to plants as such and however produced; the intention was to exclude the processes and products involved in traditional plant breeding techniques the protection of which is provided for under other legislation, i.e. plant variety rights.

Plant variety rights (general)

This type of national legislation is widespread throughout the world. There is also an international agreement known as the International Convention For The Protection Of New Varieties Of Plants (in force since 1968 and text revised in 1978) which is a sort of skeleton law designed to achieve a high degree of uniformity of national legislation but flexible enough to accommodate differences required for local reasons in one state or another. This international union comprises Belgium, Denmark, Eire, France, West Germany, Israel, Italy, Netherlands, New Zealand, South Africa, Spain, Sweden, Switzerland, UK and USA.

Whereas with plant patents of the US type the protection is for the whole plant it is a general characteristic of plant variety protection that it is directed to the reproductive material of the plant. The convention provides, as a minimum requirement, the exclusive right to:

1. The production for purposes of commercial marketing.
2. The offering for sale.
3. The marketing of the reproductive or vegetative propagating material, as such, of the variety.

The corresponding provision of the UK law (Plant Varieties and Seeds Act 1964) gives the exclusive right:

'. . . to sell reproductive material of the variety for which the grant has been made (the protected variety);
'to produce reproductive material of the protected variety in the United Kingdom for the purpose of selling it, and
'to exercise such further rights, if any, as are specified in the plant breeders' right scheme for the species to which the variety belongs;
'or to authorize, i.e. licence, others to carry on these activities'.

The rights attaching to this form of protection are more limited in scope than those of ordinary patents because they cannot be exercised against a third party who reproduces the variety for the purpose of selling consumption material, e.g. grain for milling, potatoes for human consumption, or the better quality fruit of a new variety of fruit tree. The typical owner of a plant variety right, or the body that licenses it on his behalf, is not normally in the business of selling the ultimate consumable product to the public. For example the owner of the right may sell basic seed to a seed merchant and license him to sow it to produce a first multiplication (C1) which he then sells to the grower who will sow it to produce consumption material (C2). It has been recognized in plant variety right legislation that protection that extends only to the right of sale of initial reproductive material, e.g. basic seed is insufficient to achieve an adequate return on the investment of the plant breeder. Hence the multiplication of the reproductive material as far as the first generation is also an express component of the right but the C1 to C2 stage is outside it.

Ordinary patents for methods of plant production

The propagation of plants by special methods which are classified as general methods of manufacture as distinct from techniques directed to producing an individual new variety is open to protection under the ordinary law of process patents. One example is US Patent No. 3,514,900 directed to a method of asexual multiplication of an individual

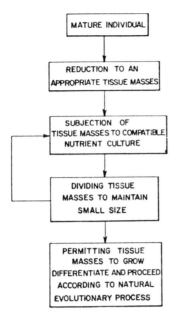

Figure 1. Method for rapidly reproducing orchids, US Patent No. 3,514,900, June 2, 1970

plant selected from the orchid family by a series of steps which are apparent from Figure 1.

In general, other plant cell culture methods which are operated for the purpose of producing secondary metabolites such as perfumes and flavours rather than the plants themselves involve the same patentability consideration as process inventions of the usual kind. The same also can be said in relation to genetic manipulation of plants for this and related purposes, a strategy which falls clearly under the heading of microbiological process invention. The types of claim obtainable and useful to inventors in this connection will be touched upon when some of the special difficulties of patenting this kind of technology are discussed in a later chapter. There are no test cases so far under the new European ideas of patentability to indicate how *per se* claims to genetically altered plants will be considered.

An example of a plant culture method patent which would presumably be classified as one for a microbiological process, and therefore patentable under modern European patent law principles, is UK Patent No. 1,310,119 covering a technique for protoplast fusion defined in the main method claim as:

'A method for effecting the fusion of isolated protoplasts derived from plants of the class *Angiospermae* which comprises treating the isolated protoplasts with an aqueous solution containing sodium ions in the absence of magnesium and calcium or other cations or anions which are physiologically unacceptable to the protoplasts or inhibitory to their fusion, and allowing or constraining protoplasts to move towards each other and to fuse together'.

Chapter 4

Conditions for Patentability

Chapter 3 has dealt with typical examples of invention which arise in biological chemistry and other disciplines in biological science, and has shown how these fit into categories which the patent law has come to recognize over more than a century of practical experience of dealing with patent applications and with patent litigation. The examples given attempt to provide a short catalogue of possibilities some of which may bear relation to the reader's own area of research. The necessity for guidelines of this kind arises from the fact that the first recognition of a patentable invention or, at the least, the awareness that the research done (or about to be started) may present patent possibilities must originate with the inventor. Industrial inventors with associated patent departments which scrutinize research reports for patentability are in a more fortunate position in this respect than those without a screen of any kind, but even here the proposition remains true that unless the inventive source is tuned into the subject to some extent there is a chance of something being missed.

From the identification of categories we now proceed to examine the principles upon which the merits of any particular case are evaluated. Given that the invention falls into a clear-cut process, product or method category, the prospects of obtaining patent protection for it and the scope of claim that is likely to issue have to be assessed according to certain fundamental conditions of patentability stipulated in the patent law.

The merits of the case are conveniently dealt with under three headings, (1) novelty, (2) inventiveness and (3) utility or industrial applicability, and this trinity is broadly common to the patent systems of all countries having a well-developed law on this subject. However, the application of these three main criteria by patent office examiners and courts in different countries varies considerably. In the past, inventors would often be advised that some particular process or product might not be considered sufficiently new or inventive in the 'difficult' territories, e.g. USA, Germany and Holland, but would be patentable without difficulty in others, e.g. UK and France. In future this distinction may become blurred in Europe as national laws become harmonized. It is doubtful whether it will disappear altogether because the interpretation of law is affected by differing national attitudes towards invention and the extent to which it should be recognized by monopoly rights.

NOVELTY

Novelty is the most basic of all the conditions for the grant of patent rights. The invention must be seen to teach those skilled in the art something which they do not already know from prior publications or experience. It is difficult to discuss novelty in total isolation from the topic of inventiveness for there is often only a fine line between the two. Nevertheless a true legal approach must involve maintaining the distinction between novelty, where the question is whether what is claimed is already fully disclosed in the prior art, and inventiveness, where there are differences, however slight, between what is claimed and what is previously in the public domain of knowledge.

In dealing with the law of novelty it is necessary to consider the kinds of public disclosure which, if made prior to the filing of the application for protection, can be detrimental to patentability. The law on this subject is strict but fair, although it may at first sight present problems to inventors who want to discuss their work freely and openly with others before deciding whether patenting is worthwhile. The patent law makes allowance for disclosures which are clearly made in confidence and it will in appropriate circumstances protect the inventor against the effect of such disclosures and, to some extent, against unauthorized leakage of information flowing from them. Before discussing the topic of confidential disclosure the general rule of novelty must be outlined.

The patent systems of most countries now apply the test of absolute novelty, as opposed to mere local novelty, at least as regards documentary publications. Thus a publication anywhere in the world is a bar to novelty. Under modern conditions of rapid communication this may seem an obvious provision but until recent times many important countries insisted on the document being available in their territories before it could constitute a novelty bar. The laws of some continental European countries specify that there should have been no previous publication anywhere whereby the invention is sufficiently publicly known to be put into practice by an expert; it should not have been pre-viously patented anywhere nor put to prior public use in the specific territory (this part of the requirement does carry a local restriction); and it should not have fallen within the public domain in any other way.

In all patent laws the test for novelty is applied to what is commonly referred to as 'the state of the art' and this includes everything on public record or in public use. The state of the art is defined, for example, in Article 54 of the European Patent Convention (Appendix 1) as:

'Everything made available to the public by means of a written or oral description, by use, or in any other way, before the date of filing of the European patent application.'

This definition is the most modern and comprehensive requirement that inventors and patent practitioners have to work under and it has increasingly been adopted in a corresponding form by those states that have harmonized their national law with the regional law of the European patent. The 'prior use' section of this particular law has no territorial limitation and the term 'public' is similarly broadly intended.

Prior Publication and Use

The requirement for novelty is construed strictly with reference to prior literature and all other knowledge already in the possession of the public before the inventor's patent application has been filed. It is applied to the inventor's own publications as well as to publications of other research groups and therefore any relevant publication by an inventor before the application is filed can be suicidal. There are some exceptions to the generality of this rule and some countries have special provisions for certain types of publication but it is dangerous to overestimate these concessions and best to seek protection before any publication occurs. All prior published documents are citable by the examiner irrespective of whether they are scientifically well founded or mere paper proposals or even mere science fiction. Examiners will also try to combine bits from separate documents and make up a mosaic in order to show that the invention has been anticipated, but this attack is strictly speaking more relevant to the question of inventive step than to novelty.

At the very beginning of any patentability study it is necessary therefore to ask whether the invention has already been disclosed in a public manner to any extent whatever, either fully or partially, or even by mere mention of it. The industrial inventor will usually be aware of the importance of strict confidentiality over research results until the time is ripe commercially for disclosure and this may often mean keeping the more publicity-minded staff of the company away from the laboratory at certain times. But for all inventors, those in industry, the researcher in a university or similar environment, and even for the lone inventor funding his own research, some sort of check list is a useful self-discipline. For example, one would ask whether there has been any prior disclosure:

1. In the open literature.
2. By inclusion in a thesis or other document deposited in any library (including 'private' collections associated with and indexed in the library).
3. By oral disclosure at scientific meetings or in any circulated abstract or pre-print of a paper to be read at such a meeting.
4. In any talk or demonstration at an open day, colloquium, lecture, or the like.
5. To any visitors to the laboratory, in a non-confidential manner.
6. By being put to use for any length of time (other than solely for experiment).
7. By advertisement, sale, or any other form of commercial activity which is public.

A prior use of an invention which puts the invention or sufficient information about it into public knowledge is just as damaging as the literary form of publication.

Experimental Use

It is important to be clear about the effect of experimental use e.g. clinical trials and, following on from this, the extent to which an invention may be put into use after the trial period without jeopardizing the patent position. Reasonable trial and experimental testing of a drug or device do not in themselves constitute a prior use which would prejudice a later-filed patent application, but the problem is that it is often difficult to arrange such trials without a certain amount of leakage of information or active publicity, with the result that the invention is effectively pre-disclosed before anyone has thought about the question of patent protection; and by then it is often too late. Some inventors are unaware of this and have been known to launch their eventual patenting attempt on the basis that the product or technique has been successfully used openly by doctors and nurses for a considerable period of time. In some cases, of course, practical trials have to take place in a public manner, and the old British law catered for that by allowing a period of one year for public working of this sort of invention before the patent application was filed. The new British law is not explicit on this topic and, until the interpretation of these matters is clarified it will be advisable to exercise caution.

Under the old UK law any use of an invention, after the trial period, would invalidate a patent based on a later-filed application because it would be either a prior public use or a prior secret use and both these were grounds of invalidation and hence of revocation of the patent. Consequently, it was necessary to make up one's mind about the question of patents before the substance or method was put into routine use, and it probably made little real difference whether the intended use was commercial or not and whether it could be carried out without the knowledge of it coming into the possession of the public. The new UK law is possibly less clear on this point because, for the purpose of refusing a patent application or of invalidating a patent, the anticipatory use must be a matter which has been made available to the public. Thus, if the invention is used in a laboratory to which the public do not normally have access, for example, a hospital laboratory, one has to ask whether it is available; possibly it can be said to be available to the public in the sense that the use has been carried out for the benefit of patients, even though they did not know precisely what method or device was in fact used.

One example of the difficulty involved in deciding whether a use is public or not arose in the case of a patent application claiming, as a new product, ampicillin trihydrate. This was opposed successfully (in UK) by a competitor who produced evidence of having previously made a few batches of what must have been the trihydrate but who had blended it with other material before sale, it being accepted that the presence of the trihydrate in the blended product could not have been detected by analysis. A great variety of opinions on whether this was secret use or public use were expressed in the course of the case, leading to a close final result (three judges to two) in the House of Lords in favour of it being public use.

Special provisions in USA and Canada

The foregoing remarks apply in substance to the great majority of patent laws whether national or regional. However, there are exceptions to the general rule as regards the inventor's own publications and the patent laws of the United States and Canada are the most important examples of a different approach to the question. The novelty conditions of US law and the principles of originality or priority of invention are set out in Section 102 of the current statute (Appendix 2). They are rather involved and it is difficult to state their combined effect in a few words. In combination, they embody the 'first-to-invent' philosophy in US patent law which contrasts with the 'first-to-file' principle of most other patent systems. The application of the test of 'first-to-invent' in determining the question of originality or priority as between rival inventors (the so-called 'interference' procedure) has provided an enormous growth of case law and is now a specialist topic. For our present purposes it is sufficient to note only the first two of the seven subsections:

'A person shall be entitled to a patent unless:

(a) the invention was known or used by others in this country, or patented or described in a printed publication in this or a foreign country, before the invention thereof by the applicant for patent, or

(b) the invention was patented or described in a printed publication in this or a foreign country or in public use or on sale in this country, more than one year prior to the date of the application for the patent in the United States, or . . .'.

The important message for the inventor is that if he has already published, perhaps having not thought about patenting, all is not lost in these two countries provided action is taken to file a US patent application within one year of the publication (and in Canada within two years). The wording of the US statute on this point refers not simply to 'publication' but uses the term 'printed publication' and there is much case law on the meaning of this term. It is generally held not to cover mere oral disclosures but the more cautious practitioner will play for safety and calculate the one year as running from the date of any public disclosure assuming that the grace period has not already run out by the time he is called upon to act.

For all inventors, the printed publication occurring more than one year before actual filing of the US application is a 'statutory bar' under Section 102(b) and this sub-section also includes public use or sale of the invention in USA as denying patentability if it occurred more than a year prior to filing. Sub-section (a) of 102 also deals *inter alia* with prior public knowledge or use by others in USA, and prior printed publication anywhere, before the applicants *invention* date (as opposed to filing date). Unlike 102(b) this last sub-section does not apply in the same way to *all* inventors because a distinction is made between inventions made in USA and those made abroad. An invention date for inventions made in USA can be established by appealing to laboratory notebooks and other records and this is known as 'swearing back'. Inventions made outside USA, apart from those made by US inventors serving abroad on behalf of their country, cannot benefit from the 'swearing back' privilege and thus cannot be accorded a date any earlier than the corresponding home-filing date of the inventor in his own country of residence. One consequence of this distinction is that the US inventor at home may be able to 'swear back of' a publication occurring *within* one year prior to his US filing date whereas the 'foreign' inventor usually cannot obtain the benefit of any date earlier than his filing date in his home territory. The preference that the US system gives to the US inventor over the foreign inventor in this respect is admitted by professional opinion to be an anomaly, but it remains the law. Canada also has the 'first-to-invent' concept, but unlike USA, will allow evidence of activity outside its territory in determining invention date.

Duty to disclose prior art

Before leaving special provisions of US patent law attention must be given to the vital requirement of candour by inventors themselves, and anyone else connected with the prosecution of a US patent application, in relation to prior art known to them. It is not sufficient to leave it to the US patent examiner to search for prior art in his investigation of the application and its patentability. Inventors and patent advisers have the duty to disclose to the patent office any pertinent prior art of which they are aware at the time of filing or subsequently so that there can be no question of the patent being granted without taking a comprehensive view of the issues in the light of what is already known. Reticence or carelessness in this matter is highly dangerous and can give rise later to the question of 'fraud on the patent office'. A finding of fraud not only renders the patent unenforcible but can in some circumstances result in more serious penalties to the patent owner. Recent developments in law and practice in USA have laid further stress on the applicant to shoulder the burden of exposing all prior art known to him which could conceivably be relevant to questions of both novelty and inventive step.

Other documents within the 'state of the art'

Attention has so far been confined to documents or activities of an open and public nature. A further category of prior knowledge exists that does not have the same fully public character as the open disclosure and this must also be considered. This body of knowledge consists of the contents of prior pending patent applications.

The older patent laws of many countries dealt with the problem of conflicting claims in concurrent applications under the heading of 'prior claim' rather than 'prior publication' for the good reason that the earlier-filed application, being still pending, was retained as a secret document in the patent office until it was accepted and eventually published in printed form according to official procedure. Because this period of gestation could be rather lengthy some patent offices began a practice of early publication of applications (before complete examination and acceptance) but even so there was a definite period in which the application remained secret. Until official publication of the specification in any form the document was in fact not available to the public at large. Consequently it could not be treated as a prior publication in the normal sense. Nevertheless it could not be ignored and the practice of the patent office was to attempt to prevent two patents issuing for the same invention or to avoid as much overlap as possible between the two claims which finally issue. Therefore the existence of a prior pending application could affect the scope of claim allowable to the later applicant but would only rarely pre-empt it completely.

The current solution in the European patent law, which in this respect also is the model for many modern national patent laws, is to adopt what is known as the 'whole contents' approach. According to this, provided the prior application is eventually published, the contents of the as-yet-unpublished application are deemed to be part of the state of the art as of its application date. This is of course a legal fiction because until the contents are actually published neither the later applicant nor any other person can have knowledge of them. The effect of this highly artificial but practical expedient is mitigated, however, as far as later applications are concerned because Articles 54(3) and 56 of the European law apply it only for the investigation of novelty and not for the determination of the closely related but separate issue of inventiveness.

It is worth noting at this point that the unpublished research activities of others are not counted as in the state of the art unless they have been the subject of a patent application. It follows that inventor A cannot object to inventor B's patent simply on the ground that A researched the field first even if A discovered the precise invention first, assuming that A did nothing about it by way of protection or publication.

In this area of law the USA rule has long been different from those elsewhere in that, for the purposes of US patent prosecution, published US patents are considered to be prior art as of their application date and are therefore citable against later applications even though the cited patent has not issued, and therefore become actually published, until after the filing date of the later application. Moreover their status as prior art counts for the assessment of both novelty and inventiveness, a more rigorous application of the 'whole contents' principle than that of the European law.

Summary of Principles of Novelty

From the foregoing discussion of novelty requirements it will be clear that the novelty-destroying act is one which in intention and effect freely discloses something to the public, not necessarily the general public but at least the interested person or persons in a particular art, and in such a way that the content of what might have been claimed in a subsequent patent application is already known to another. Disclosure of anything less than the whole of what is claimed will not be sufficient to invalidate a patent on this ground alone or prevent one from being properly applied for. It was noted that one section of the US patent law specified the prior disclosure as being in the form of a printed publication thus stressing the intention of wide dissemination of the knowledge. Japanese law also has this characteristic that the novelty bar must be a document which is intended for distribution. In most countries, however, the implication of multiple readership is not necessary and any act, by oneself or another, which discloses the invention sufficiently to enable an 'expert' or, as sometimes stated, a person of 'ordinary skill' to put it into practice is citable as part of the state of the art. In practice patent office examiners will often cite documents as novelty destroying which on analysis turn out to fall short of being such. The patent agent has a primary responsibility here to see that a proper analysis of the document is made to determine what its teaching really is and whether it can carry the examiner's burden of argument that it anticipates the invention claimed.

Sometimes the patent agent will be able to make this analysis but over the complex range of disciplines operating in the biological sciences not many patent practitioners will be able to achieve this without substantial help from the inventor.

Anticipation and Infringement

The term 'anticipation' is usually reserved in patent practice as a description of a prior document or use which discloses or involves the totality of the invention which is being claimed. It is strictly speaking tied therefore to the ground of novelty and not to that of inventiveness. Infringement is a topic that will be discussed more fully later but it will already be apparent that the term 'infringement' means an unauthorized making or using of the invention defined in the patent claims. Research workers sometimes overlook the distinction between these two concepts.

If a document cited as an anticipation is a patent specification it is usually being cited because its disclosure taken as a whole or in part contains something which the later applicant is attempting to claim as new. The claims of the prior patent are in most cases irrelevant to this issue and the force of the prior document as an anticipation usually cannot be overcome by pointing to limitations in the language used by the prior patentee in framing his own particular claims. The claims of the prior patent can sometimes be pertinent to an understanding of the intended meaning of certain passages in the text (and vice versa) but the fact that the prior inventor left some loopholes in framing his protection does not mean that they can be plugged by the later inventor. The inventor's gleeful claim that 'they did not cover this, therefore we can' will meet with disappointment if in the descriptive disclosure of the prior patent there is something tucked away, even a casual or gratuitous observation or unsupported piece of speculation, which nevertheless discloses something within the claims that the later inventor is presenting as patentable over the prior art.

On the other hand the claims of the prior patent and any limitations they contain are highly significant when the question is not whether the later invention is patentable over the first but whether the later invention can be put into practice without infringement of the earlier patent. Now the earlier claims become central to the issue and the descriptive part of the prior patent is relevant only to the extent that it may affect the interpretation of the scope of these claims. If therefore the earlier description contains something which, if it had been claimed, would have affected the later applicant's 'freedom-to-use' it is of no account if in fact the earlier applicant neglected to include it within the scope of his protection.

The possession of a patent does not convey the automatic right to make or use the invention which has been patented. The invention may have been held patentable over an earlier patent but the latter may still dominate the use of the second invention in which case a licence under the first patent will be a precondition to be met by the second patentee before exploitation and commercialization of the second invention can take place.

Confidential Disclosure

Previous discussion of the law of patentable novelty has dealt with public knowledge deriving from prior documents disclosing the work of others or from the free act of premature disclosure of the inventor's own work by the inventor himself. In practice this accounts for most of the novelty problems faced in the prosecution of the majority of patent applications. As regards disclosures by the inventor however the law distinguishes those made to individuals or small numbers of other people which clearly have the character of confidence or privilege or, in other words, are not intended to put the invention into the free possession of the public. Patent law rarely writes this distinction into the statute itself and our understanding of it must be learnt from particular cases in which courts or other tribunals have considered whether or not a particular disclosure amounted to a 'publication' in the full legal sense, that is, a making available of the information to some member of the public who is free to make use of it or under no restriction against passing it on to others. Statute law touches upon publication resulting from a breach of confidence, for example in Article 55 of the European patent convention (Appendix 1) but that is usually as far as it goes.

Disclosing of the invention to some individual who is under no restriction as to the use he may make of the information or who is under no obligation of secrecy is not confidential and therefore is public disclosure. This is true where it is clear from the circumstances that the inventor did not mind what use was made of the information or even intended the recipient to put it to use but perhaps had a change of mind later. This kind of situation can often arise with inventors who have an inclination for taking a piece of commercial equipment (possibly loaned by the manufacturer) and modifying and improving it and who communicate their improvement to the firm freely and enthusiastically. A type of disclosure which is becoming a topical problem is the relatively unconditional distribution to others of biological material such as new strains or cell lines which are developed further by the recipient into something of commercial value. Another sort of free disclosure is one to groups of academic colleagues or industrial contacts involved in particular information exchange or liaison groups where it is clear that no fetter is being applied. This kind of disclosure makes it very questionable for the inventors independently to attempt to obtain patent protection subsequently. It is open to the recipient of the information, such as a commercial firm which may by then have put effort into developing it, to take the view that its freedom to proceed further should not be suddenly curtailed and it may even contest the validity of the patent. The only way to avoid this embarrassment is to make it clear in the beginning that the disclosure is privileged and that the inventor is at least taking advice on the possibility of protecting the invention or improvement.

The most obvious kind of confidential disclosure is one to an agent, adviser, or consultant and there is rarely any doubt that confidentiality is implied in any disclosure in this category. But it is often necessary or desirable to disclose to others who are independent entities and in this situation caution is advised. A disclosure in confidence is one where the freedom of the recipient is qualified either by express statement or by implication. It clearly applies where the research is at an early stage and where it would be a breach of confidence for the recipient to go ahead independently or disclose it to others. Frequently, imparting this kind of information is connected with a suggestion of collaboration in the research and the intention to create some kind of partnership in a particular project. Where, however, the research is well advanced and the proposal has the character of a commercial deal then it may be difficult to argue confidentiality in the legal sense because the parties have entered the zone of commercial exploitation which the law might consider to be prior user. This may well happen more between industrial parties, e.g. where a design or a product is shown with a view to getting an order. A confidential disclosure does not prejudice a subsequent attempt to obtain patent protection. Even where patenting is not possible, or is decided against, a confidential relationship still exists and must be respected by the parties.

The courts are very ready to support the donor of information if it has anything of the character of confidence about it. The English courts have developed the famous principle of the 'springboard'. This arose out of a case involving two industrial parties one of which received confidential design information from the other in order to manufacture a product and, after the arrangement between the parties had terminated, went on to design its own product. The judge held that the second designer 'could not have avoided starting his dive into the future from the spring-board of confidential information acquired'. Of course this is a difficult doctrine to apply and we can easily think of examples in which a person may be baulked from using his own additional contributions. It would be unrealistic to expect him to withdraw from the field or postpone activity until the original information had been published and lost its confidential character. The judge in another case said 'businessmen concentrate on their business and very sensibly do not constantly take legal advice before opening their mouths or writing a letter so that business may flow and not stagnate'.

There is a reluctance in industry to become too closely involved in confidential relationships with independent individual inventors (excluding their own selected consultants) and industrial firms have to guard against unsolicited disclosures which may set up such relationships. This puts the outside inventor in a dilemma because for his own proper protection he does not want his disclosure to the firm construed as a public disclosure but he is keen to have their comments and perhaps an expression of interest. It should be possible to steer through this difficulty by making it clear that the communication is special, is made for the purpose of assessment only, and is therefore not freely conveyed in order for it to be utilized without qualification. These provisos firmly take the disclosure away from the character of public communication and they protect the inventor's position without binding the firm to a wider commitment than is reasonable and acceptable.

INVENTIVENESS

It may sound trite to say that in order to be patentable an invention must be inventive. However, the term 'invention' is being used in this context to mean 'the subject matter of the patent claim' and this is convenient as shorthand because of the frequent need to refer to it in this discussion and in the arguments used in real cases.

There would be common agreement that the assessment of the quality of inventiveness, being highly subjective, gives rise to the greatest uncertainty in patent law and in the making of practical judgments by businessmen and their advisers over specific patents. The only help the written laws give us in this matter is the well-nigh universal statement that for something to be inventive it must not be 'obvious' over the state of the art. This may appear to do little more than substitute for the original term one which is just as difficult to apply in practice but it makes the question fractionally easier to answer and we have to make the best of it.

The lawyers say that 'obviousness' is a question of fact. They do not mean by this that it is not a matter of opinion but rather that it is not in itself a matter of law. It is a matter of fact to be established by evidence from those skilled in the art whether or not what is claimed would have been obvious to the reasonably skilled worker in that art in the light of what was already published in the literature or generally known in other ways. The courts have the privilege of making the judgment itself but they are assisted by the contestants in the case who can bring forward expert witnesses to give evidence of the state of public knowledge in the art. Courts will vary in the degree to which they are willing to delegate their prerogative to the expert witnesses and as these will often be in dispute in matters of scientific argument the judge usually has a difficult decision to make.

Because of the almost universal distribution of scientific knowledge and the widespread possession of technology it ought to be possible to arrive at common standards in the quantum of inventiveness necessary to justify the grant of a patent. In the century and more during which patenting and patent litigation have been indulged in on a significant scale, this goal has so far eluded us. The patent practitioners' guidelines in this matter are set by court decisions and enshrined in the resulting body of precedents in which judges attempt to enunciate principles which can be extended to other instances of a similar nature within their own national tradition. There are evident limitations to this kind of extrapolation but it is possible to form an opinion on the basis of case law and at the very least this enables the problems to be anticipated and the arguments prepared in advance by the joint cogitation of the inventor and patent agent. If we are to proceed, we should certainly see a good argument in support of non-obviousness before embarking at all but frequently the potential importance of obtaining protection forces the pace and the arguments tend to mature and become polished as the benefits of the invention are realized from experience.

Convincing the Patent Office of Inventiveness

The topic of inventiveness has been introduced by mentioning the approach of courts of law but in order of time the first challenge in this respect arises long before courts are invoked because it can be raised by patent office examiners in relation to the prior art revealed in their search. It is almost invariably raised in the patent offices of USA, Germany and Holland where the demand for inventive level, especially by the Dutch, has always been high and in no field more so than in chemistry and the biological sciences. This aspect of the patent system is the least satisfactory for it may well be doubted whether examiners are by background or experience equipped to make the difficult practical judgments that are called for in the evaluation of inventiveness. Challenge there must be, for the law requires it and public policy is not served by the grant of worthless patents devoid of inventive substance, but the scales are loaded in favour of the examiner because he is not always under the same obligation, as is the applicant, to produce a reasoned case for his position. It is easy to say, after the event, that this particular 'invention' was obvious in view of reference A taken with reference B in view of reference C etc. and examiners rarely give reasons for connecting the various references they combine into a mosaic in this way. It is heartening to note that European patent office examiners are officially urged not to overplay hindsight arguments of this kind in their approach to inventive step.

The foregoing points have been stressed in order to arouse support from inventors in the defence of the degree of innovation and ingenuity in what they have done. Patent professional men can also fall into the trap of totally equating patents and other documents with the real world and the tendency to apply legal principles in the abstract. Attorneys require frequent and sustained contact with inventors and the practice of technology in order to conform their professional thought more to the nature of real technological problems. This is nowhere more clear than in relation to the assessment of what is obvious or not to the man skilled in the art. There are few attorneys including the most eminent patent lawyers whose judgments are not influenced greatly by a conference with inventors and technical men who appreciate at first hand the knowledge which is common to those of ordinary skill, that which is the possession of a few specialists of extraordinary insight, and that which skilled workers have failed to see even though it may be latent or implicit in the state of the art.

In biological chemistry, microbiology and the other biological sciences we are dealing, in the majority of cases where patents are involved, with the production or isolation of some compound or other substance having valuable biological properties. This may be for example a chemical end product or intermediate or a microorganism or some other substance of intermediate complexity such as an enzyme. The inventiveness in such cases usually resides in the unexpected nature of the biological properties of the substance produced or in the level of biology activity exhibited or in the special advantages of the particular method specified for producing it. This applies clearly where the invention is protected in the form of a product claim such as one covering a new antibiotic or a therapeutically valuable synthetic chemical. It also applies where claims to the preparation of such substances are allowed only in process form, because the hidden properties of the new product carry over their merit, so to speak, into the process of making it even where the process in itself is a known synthetic method e.g. a standard acylation or esterification.

The prospects for patents of the above kind must therefore persist so long as structure/activity relationships cannot be unfailingly predicted by the skilled worker. Where known fully defined chemical structures and configurations are associated with biological activity of a particular kind one must of course allow the predictability argument to some extent to apply to other substances of close chemical relationship, especially the near homologues, and in practice the argument often centres about this issue. Hindsight is easy to apply here but there may well be situations in which the art has taken a long time to get round to looking at homologues or isomers and there is an unexpected bonus to be had from some related compound. The US Patent Office is particularly difficult to convince in these cases where they commonly argue that the compound being claimed, though it may have surprising properties, is nevertheless 'structurally obvious' over some known substance of similar composition and therefore not entitled to protection in *per se* form.

Another category which has been noted above is that of the discovery of unusually high levels of activity or sometimes of an additional biological utility in compounds having a structure which is not broadly new as such. These compounds must of course themselves be new, as individual members of a known class, in the sense of not having previously been made or specifically pointed to in prior published work. But once having passed the first hurdle of novelty of the claimed compounds the obstacle of inventive height can be jumped on the basis of unexpectedness as to the level or type of activity shown by them. These particular compounds cannot be obvious, so the argument runs, because nothing in the prior teaching leads one to make them rather than other members of the broad class which do not have these outstanding properties. A special case of this category is that known in British patent law as the 'selection patent' which represents a sub-group of compounds picked out of a previously known broad class and possessing some special advantage peculiar to the selection.

Before giving examples of the application of the principles stated above one more aspect remains to be discussed generally. It applies more frequently to biochemical and biological processes than to synthetic chemical processes and concerns the use of techniques and procedures of producing or handling biological materials. Where some methodology is known and possibly extensively used in practice in one context, say for the extraction of an enzyme from cells or for the treatment of a virus for vaccine production, it is sometimes difficult to argue inventiveness in its application to a similar context i.e. for another enzyme or virus. No-one should be put off by this statement for an inventor is entitled to expect some imagination on the part of his professional adviser in seeing distinctions between the two parallel uses of what looks to be the standard technique. Usually the inventor himself will be the first to see the distinctions and subtle differences although he may need to be con-ditioned to think on these lines by the questioning and prompting of the patent attorney. It is helpful to find some contra-indication against routine extension of the method from the one substrate to the other or some prejudice on the part of the art which had to be overcome in the new application.

The following examples are taken from reported cases illustrating the types of patentability question that arise everywhere although varying answers are given in different countries.

British case law

Homologues (mere verification)

From 1927, when it was reported, down to recent times the case of Sharpe and Dohme *v.* Boots was a leading case in this field. The patent was for a process of producing alkyl resorcinols of formula:

by a two-stage conversion involving the known sequence of a Friedel–Crafts condensation followed by a Clemmensen reduction. At this early date chemical product-*per se* claims were not allowable under UK law.

The process was already known for the preparation of lower alkyl resorcinols and the properties of these products were also known. For novelty reasons the claim was limited *inter alia* to the production of compounds in which the alkyl group R contained more than two carbon atoms. The patentees failed to sustain their patent in spite of the evidence quoted by their eminent expert witness that 'there is no prevision in chemistry'. The case is famous for the formulation by Sir Stafford Cripps, counsel for the patentee, of the obviousness question in the following terms:

'Was it for all practical purposes obvious to any skilled chemist in the state of chemical knowledge at the date of the patent (which consists of the literature available and general chemical knowledge) that he could manufacture valuable therapeutic agents by making the higher alkyl resorcinols by the condensation and reduction processes described?'

Though this became the celebrated Cripps' test its content hardly takes one very far from the simple original formulation and this for the good reason that it is not easy to define any intermediate ground between the general proposition and the specific question on the facts of the individual case.

In the Sharpe and Dohme case the courts answered the Cripps' test affirmatively because to go higher up the homologous series and establish the persistence of antibacterial properties amounted to no more than mere verification of what could have been reasonably predicted by the skilled worker. Some commentators have developed from this case a no-man's land theory that in drafting claims in such cases a gap should be left between the prior art and the start of the claimed area. There certainly was a surprising sudden peaking of activity in *n*-hexyl resorcinol, the product marketed by the defendant, and a claim limited to that compound might have been more easily defended on selection principles.

Substitution of groups

A more recent re-statement of the Cripps' test came in 1970 from the case of Olin-Mathieson *v*. Biorex where in a phenothiazine structure:

base
|
$(CH_2)_n$
|

the alleged invention lay in the choice of substituent X. Compounds in which X was chlorine were already known (chlorpromazine) and the question was whether compounds in which X was CF_3 (trifluoroperazine) were inventive.

Following a review of phenothiazine developments and some evidence on the use of the CF_3 substituent in other types of biological activity the obviousness question was put as follows:

'Would the notional research group at the relevant date, in all the circumstances which include a knowledge of all the relevant prior art and of the facts of the nature and success of chlorpromazine, be directly led as a matter of course to try the CF_3 substitution in chlorpromazine or in any other body which has the other characteristics of the formula of claim 1 in the expectation that it might well produce a useful alternative to or a better drug than chlorpromazine or a body useful for any other purpose'.

This time the negative answer was given. Experts called in to give evidence claimed that no sound prediction of the effect of varying substitution could yet be given. This statement of the obviousness test, which we must remember is in keeping with the sympathetic view of British patent courts, is a good summary of the current approach. It strikes a compromise between the 'obvious-to-try' and 'not obvious that it will succeed' positions which the protagonists will usually take.

New use of known material

The case of Johns Manville reported in 1967 is a good example of a commonly recurring question. The claim covered the use of polyacrylamides as filtration aids in the shaping of articles from asbestos cement slurries. It had to contend with prior publications showing the same materials used in the same or similar fashion for filtration of minerals and metals, industrial waste and chemical precipitates and in paper making for flocculation of clays.

The effect on the skilled worker of the prior documents was questioned in various ways. Would he be 'alerted to the possibilities that', would he 'see without difficulty that . . .', the polyacrylamides would be useful in his own situation. The British Court of Appeal held that: 'It is enough that the person versed in the art would assess the likelihood of success as sufficient to warrant actual trial'.

US case law

The US case law on obviousness is legion. The Supreme Court has laid down the principle, in a number of mechanical engineering cases, that the achievement of new and unexpected results is one predicate of patentability and this rule can be applied to new chemical compounds and other substances which are discovered to possess valuable properties. The proliferation of the case law on this subject stems from the justifiable concern of applicants to obtain product claims rather than to accept claims drawn to the use which flows from the properties discovered in the new substance. The legal issue becomes most acute when the compound or group of compounds though individually new is in structure closely related to a previously known compound. If one looks at structure alone it may be difficult to see invention in a structure that is not radically new; *per contra* it is not the structure that is being claimed but the compound.

Most of the decisions of interest to the research worker are those made by the Court of Customs and Patent Appeals (CCPA) this being the court which hears appeals from final rejections issued by the US patent examiner and supported by the three-man Board of Appeals in the patent office. The line of cases decided by the CCPA began in 1944 with a ruling (*In Re* Hass) on the patentability of homologues in organic chemistry. A claim to a particular nitro-olefin was held unpatentable over a known homologue differing by only one methylene group because the new member of the series did not possess some 'unobvious or unexpected beneficial properties not possessed by a homologous compound disclosed in the prior art'. Most would concede that where a certain biological or other type of utility has been recognized in a known structure and recorded in the literature it must be obvious that there is a likelihood of similar activity in a chemically very closely related substance. But if the activity has not been recognized in the known compound what incentive is there for the skilled worker to synthesize the homologue and test it for the particular activity? The CCPA dealt with this question in a remarkable decision in 1950 (*In Re* Henze) in which the presumption of obviousness was rebuttable only by showing the absence of the useful property in the prior art homologue. Mere lack of recognition of such a property was not enough; the comparative properties of the new and the old compound must be established by testing.

To bring under control the tendency to reject compound claims on the basis of structural obviousness alone the CCPA in the leading case of *In Re* Papesch (1963) stressed the inseparability of properties and structure. It also confirmed the practice of overcoming the presumption of obviousness over an inactive prior art compound by a demonstration of an unknown and unobvious pharmacologically advantageous property.

Another facet of this complex subject is exhibited by cases in which there is a discovery of a new utility additional to one which is common to the new compound and its known structural relatives in the prior art. In the 1969 case of *In Re* Mod the claim for the compound was sought on the basis of its unexpected antimicrobial properties. However, it was closely similar in structure to a known insecticide and itself possessed insecticidal activity. The court reasoned that it would therefore have been obvious to produce the compound as an insecticide and the discovery of the additional utility was not sufficient ground for holding that the subject matter as a whole was unobvious. The justice of this decision may seem rough but it has this logic about it that if a *per se* claim to the new compound were allowed it would cover its manufacture and sale as an insecticide as well as for its antimicrobial uses. Nevertheless to the extent that the insecticide art and the art of discovering substances active against bacteria, yeasts and moulds have become differentiated it must seem harsh to workers in the one to be denied product protection for reasons extraneous to their own research problems.

Even though the unobvious properties of a 'structurally obvious' compound are a proper basis for patentability the view that the patent must be directed to the method of use rather than the compound itself has been supported by some US courts. The discovery of the herbicidal properties of 3,4-dichloropropionanilide (DCPA) provides an example of this trend. The method of use claim for this invention was given in Chapter 3 in the section on methods of treatment. The owner of the method patent had previously successfully invalidated a patent for the compound held by another corporation on the ground of obviousness over the prior art homologue (DCAA). In that litigation the District Court had held DCPA to be structurally obvious, to have the same properties as the prior homologue, and to differ from it in this respect only in degree. The court also stated more generally the proposition that 'the purposes of patent law will be adequately served if patents on compounds which are structurally obvious from the prior art are limited to method patents directed to the new and useful characteristic or property which is the essence of the discovery or invention' (Monsanto Co. *v.* Rohm and Haas Co., 1970).

The cases cited under this section are leading cases but represent only a selection of the plethora of available precedents covering chemical compounds and the question of adjacent or remote homologues, isomers, stereoisomers and analogues. There are few corresponding cases on product patents in microbiology for reasons which will be clear from the product-of-nature problem outlined in Chapter 3. Similar arguments have been used against process patents for the use of new strains of microorganism in analogous manner to that of known organisms. Thus in the daunorubicin process claim cited as an example in Chapter 3 of this category of claim the patent office had applied the obviousness objection that the organism *Streptomyces bifurcus* was used in the manner conventional for other strains of *Streptomyces* and without unexpected result. This was reversed by the CCPA on the ground that the new strain was hitherto unknown to the skilled worker so that its use was not therefore a simple matter of choice of a different strain from a range of available organisms.

In the British case law outlined in the previous section the number of leading cases on obviousness in the field of chemical compounds is relatively small. Moreover these are invariably decided in High Court actions for infringement and revocation of the patent in which competitors confront each other and leave no important issue untouched. They therefore constitute a central tradition of precedent which must be carefully considered in any subsequent case coming before the court. By contrast the CCPA are in the main called upon to decide between the arguments of the applicants and the patent office officials in the very numerous appeals which the formidable adversary standpoint of the US Patent Office inevitably creates. The sheer numbers involved, the shades of difference between one case and another, and the ability of the patent office to find reasons for not accepting arguments based on precedents cited by the applicant in prosecuting his case generate a corpus of case law not without its vacillations and inconsistencies. It is to the skill of the US patent attorney that inventors and the patent professionals of other countries must turn to be piloted through these strange waters.

Inventive step in European patent law

The 'Guidelines for Examination in the European Patent Office' published by the European Patent Office (EPO) discuss the inventive level requirement for the benefit of applicants and examiners and in terms familiar to practitioners from previous practice under national laws. The following attempt is made to give meaning to the term 'obvious':

'The term 'obvious' means that which does not go beyond the normal progress of technology but merely follows plainly or logically from the prior art, i.e. something which does not involve the exercise of any skill or ability beyond that to be expected of the person skilled in the art'.

Invention, it is said, can be based on the appreciation of the problem to be solved, the devising of the solution of a known problem, or the insight into the cause of an observed phenomenon, and combinations of these factors. The examiner must assume that the ordinary skilled worker is familiar with all that is in the 'start of the art' and he is allowed to combine different documents, or parts of them, to support his argument provided that a skilled worker would have also aggregated bits of knowledge in this way and no incompatibility would result.

The guidelines list a number of stock situations which are assumed to involve no inventive step. One consists of the choosing from a number of equally likely alternatives, e.g. ways of heating a reaction mixture, selecting dimensions and other parameters, extrapolating quantities, and selecting particular examples from a broad field without any special advantages. Examples of non-obvious findings include the selection of special operating conditions or materials having unexpected advantages and the overcoming of prejudices on the part of those skilled in the art. The relevant chapter in the guidelines after exemplifying many specific situations closes with advice to the examiner of which the following extract can give nothing but hope to the hesitant applicant:

'Once a new idea has been formulated it can often be shown theoretically how it might be arrived at, starting from something known, by a series of apparently easy steps. The examiner should be wary of *ex post facto* analysis of this kind. He should always bear in mind that the documents produced in the search have, of necessity, been obtained with foreknowledge of what matter constitutes the alleged invention. In all cases he should attempt to visualize the over-all state of the art confronting the skilled man before the applicant's contribution and he should seek to make a 'real life' assessment of this and other relevant factors. He should take into account all that is known concerning the background of the invention and give fair weight to relevant arguments or evidence submitted by the applicant'.

The case law of the European patent system is in its infancy. Decisions of the Technical Boards of Appeal are now beginning to be given on questions of obviousness. One of the earliest decisions supporting the applicant shows how the provision of impressive test data establishing the superiority of selected compounds for use in a known process can overcome the presumption that they are an obvious choice from among the available range of materials.

Searching the Prior Art

The scientist is in no doubt of the advantages of a literature search before taking a research programme very far experimentally. Therefore by the time the research results have to be evaluated for patentability the inventor will be able to bring considerable prior art knowledge to the attention of his patent advisers for investigation in the light of the novelty and obviousness criteria discussed above. However, because of the differing attitudes between the scientist and the patent law as to what constitutes significant prior art it is frequently the case that the inventor's knowledge must be supplemented by a wider search if a full appraisal is to be made. The patent literature is an obvious place to begin, first because this is where the patent office examination will itself concentrate and secondly because inventors do not normally concern themselves with this peculiar literature apart perhaps from noting those patents which get into the abstracting journals.

It is often a misconception on the part of an inventor or indeed some company representatives in consulting professional advisers that the latter, in accepting instructions to seek protection, will automatically include a search in the service they perform. The point must always explicitly be made, and it is the responsibility of the patent agents to make it, that individual agents or professional firms rarely know the art in anything like the depth that the inventor knows it and that they will act on their client's indication of what is relevant prior knowledge unless a fresh search is made. The main purpose of the search is to see whether any attempt to seek protection is worthwhile and to avoid fruitless expenditure. More usually the search results will suggest how best to deploy patenting effort to forestall any prior art likely to be cited against the application. In this connection the way the specification is written and supported in order to highlight the differences from prior proposals and the relative merits of the invention can be of crucial importance to the outcome; the supporting disclosure necessary to achieve this must be there from the start and cannot be added later. The searching under discussion here is of course the preliminary investigation carried out before any patent action is taken or at the latest before the patenting process has reached a stage at which the specification can no longer be rewritten with complete freedom. This is usually well before the results of the official patent office search have been communicated to the applicant although there are ways to procure an official search early enough in the timetable to take it into account in drafting the definitive text of the specification.

The message will now be clear that the best professional work is done when no effort and expense has been spared to determine in advance the obstacles that lie ahead. Expense is certainly a key factor and if this kind of preliminary investigation is to be made thoroughly in every case the applicant must either set up a comprehensive searching facility in his organization or commission a firm of professional searchers to do this job. The larger research-based industrial firms will usually choose the first alternative and since their technical field is specialized and well delineated they will be able to turn up relevant art very effectively. For those less well placed a balance will have to be struck between the expense of searching and that of abortive patent activity and it will in many situations be necessary to play the hunch as to the likelihood of a knock-out anticipation in the prior literature. Because the principle of absolute novelty dictates that a publication anywhere in the world can be a bar to patentability on the ground of lack of novelty or inventiveness it follows that searching cannot always be totally foolproof. For example a Ph.D. thesis in the more obscure of academic establishments, provided it can fairly be said to be available in its country of origin, is citable as a publication but may well be missed in the official search and in the routine search by the applicant himself. Indeed it may not come to light without extensive excavation of the kind that is called for by the prospect of an infringement action. The great advances that have been made in information technology in recent years offer the prospects of minimizing the risks entailed in searching. It is perhaps not too fanciful to suggest that a time may come when the law might consider the argument that documents which cannot be revealed by these most sophisticated systems of information retrieval are not 'available' to the skilled worker in the true and practical sense of the term.

INDUSTRIAL APPLICATION, UTILITY AND MERE DISCOVERY

The economic context in which the patent system is rooted demands some form of practical utility in the invention if it is to qualify as patentable. This is the foundation of the exclusion from patentability of theories and schemes and purely mental steps as such. Of course there is often a theoretical basis to an invention but it is to the physical processes and products which result from the theory that patents are directed. For example an inventor may be able to correlate empirical observations of insecticidal activity with the stereochemistry of the compounds tested and the relationship of this to receptor sites in the insect or its constituent enzymes but this knowledge alone will not allow him to protect all applications of the theory. Patent examiners are down to earth on this point and will require exemplification of the theory by test data for a fair number of compounds before allowing a claim of any great breadth. Since the scope of claim depends critically on the number and distribution of practical examples covered in the specification it is probably unhelpful and even unwise to bring the theory in at all.

The need for industrial character or industrial applicability of an invention is with one major exception an almost universal feature of patent laws and is the basis for the unpatentability of many methods and procedures which have the nature of diagnosis or therapy especially those directly involving the patient, human or animal. The significant exception is the US patent law, in which utility is required but does not have to be of an intrinsic industrial character.

Mere Discovery

A category of 'invention' which patent laws everywhere agree to exclude, including US law, is the mere discovery of natural phenomena. The reasons here are more primarily derived from considerations of novelty and the basic philosophy that the laws and handiwork of nature must be free and open to all to utilize, but the absence of a utilitarian context in the act of invention itself is also involved in the negation. The US Supreme Court in its judgment on the patentability of living matter (Chakrabarty case) has reminded us that Einstein could not have patented $E = mc^2$ and Newton would not have been able to patent the law of gravity. Such exceptional examples are rather far fetched and do no more than illustrate the principle involved for one cannot begin to judge the question of patentability until one has formulated the patent claim, which would be rather difficult to do for the theories of relativity and gravitation.

The European Patent Office Guidelines explain the EPO view of discoveries and inventions considered to be susceptible or unsusceptible to industrial application. The mere discovery of a new property of a known material is said to be unpatentable although we are told in the European Patent Convention (EPC) and elsewhere in the guidelines how the first medical use of a known substance can be patented. The discovery of products of nature has been dealt with in Chapter 3.

Industrial Application

For the European law, according to EPC Article 57, to be susceptible of industrial application means that the invention can be made or used in any kind of industry including agriculture. The term 'industry' is given a broad interpretation as covering the useful or practical arts as distinct from the aesthetic. It is, however, to be of the nature of physical activity of a technical character and the invention itself must have similar character as contrasted with schemes or plans, e.g. for running a farm or other business. It is difficult to deal with this topic without mentioning another exclusion, namely that of plant or animal varieties and essentially biological processes for their production although this is the subject of a different article of the convention, Article 53(b) (Appendix 1).

In excluding patents for methods of therapeutic, surgical or diagnostic treatment of the human or animal body Article 52(4) of EPC defines such methods as not susceptible of industrial application. This standpoint is unwelcome to some commentators but is consistent with the widespread prejudice on the part of law makers the world over against bringing the procedural steps of the physician and surgeon within the control of patent protection. However, US patent law allows claims to such methods and a New Zealand Court has approved a claim to a method of treating leukaemia in humans by administration of a known compound. A few other territories are said also to allow the grant of such patents but on the whole the answer is negative. The value of such patents is debatable unless the local law has a doctrine of contributory infringement according to which the supplier of the drug or other substance or device (itself unpatentable) who knowingly supplies it for the intended use is also held to be an infringer of the method claim. The EPO guidelines stress that this exclusion applies only to the methods as such and not to new products and devices for use in such methods. Moreover, other methods of treatment are patentable where the purpose and effect is purely economic and not connected with a diseased condition in the human or animal recipient. It is also important to note that methods of treatment of body tissues or fluids are patentable provided these have been removed from the body and this opens the door to the patentability of many assay methods used in hospitals and elsewhere. It is interesting to ask whether this removal must be permanent or whether, for example, a return of treated blood to the patient would bring the method back into the forbidden area.

It is difficult to see why the treatment of animal diseases has been excluded from patent protection. Although there is a humane aspect to it the economic aspect is usually the predominant motive. There is no corresponding restriction on the treatment of plant diseases. Methods of testing are generally patentable if applicable to the improvement or control of a product or process which itself has an industrial application.

Utility

Under United States patent law the emphasis is laid on the utility of the invention to society. The application of this principle to inventions in the fields of chemistry and biology and the abundant case law on the subject require resort to textbooks of US patent law and interpretation by specialist US lawyers. Only the barest of attempts to guide inventors can be made in the present work. Further reference to this topic will be found in Chapter 7 but the basic points can be stated simply at this stage. There must be a utility, the utility must be disclosed in the specification positively and not tentatively, and there must be a disclosure of 'how to use'. So fundamental is utility that it is not conceived as an adjunct to the invention but as an integral part of it, something without which the invention is incomplete. Furthermore the prosecution of US patent applications in which biological utility is asserted almost invariably requires some proof of utility to be supplied to the examiner beyond what is declared by the inventor in the specification and other application documents.

SUFFICIENCY OF DESCRIPTION

The conditions for patentability which have been discussed above relate primarily to the nature of the invention itself and to the terms in which it has been expressed in the specification. There must now be added a fourth condition, one primarily literary in character, which has already been touched on in Chapter 2 and which is that the specification must describe the invention adequately to enable a worker of ordinary skill to put its teaching into effect.

A failure to provide adequate information in the specification can give rise to an 'insufficiency' attack on the patent or application which is fatal because the defect cannot be made good subsequently as will be explained in the next chapter. The problem has an insidious nature because it can go unrecognized by the inventor who is so immersed in the knowledge and experience of his invention that he takes too much for granted and also by the draftsman of the specification who may not know and sometimes cannot know what he is missing. This latent difficulty is exemplified in two rather old British cases on insufficiency where in one the success of a metal pipe rolling process depended critically on the undisclosed composition of the alloy used and in the other the ability of a particular chemical reaction to proceed depended on the use of an iron vessel rather than one lined with porcelain. In this sort of case neither the inventor nor the patent agent may be aware of the criticality of the precise conditions used by the inventor but not described in the specification and there is no avoiding the resulting invalidity of the patent. The responsibility for ensuring as far as possible against this situation lies in practice with the patent adviser, who must detach himself frequently in the drafting exercise to ask 'how will this read?' or 'how would the reader carry out this particular set of instructions?' and, of course, to ask the inventor for answers if he is in any doubt.

In chemical process or product inventions, for example, it is standard practice to include a description of the preparation of any compound used as an intermediate of which there is no preparation given in the prior available literature. It may be debatable whether this is vital in every case for the question always is whether the ordinary skilled worker would be able to prepare such a compound from his ordinary stock of chemical skill and knowledge or whether he would have to exercise inventiveness in order to do so. Most draftsmen play for safety on this point. In a microbiological process similar questions must be asked with regard to the availability of particular strains of microorganism necessary for the process or the possibility of critical media or other requirements to make the process work. Indeed the question of strain availability has become one of the dominant issues of patent law and regulation over the last decade in relation to microbiological inventions and is an extreme application of the sufficiency-of-description requirement which applies universally in patent law. It will be discussed in detail in a later chapter.

One may ask who is the notional skilled worker and what level of skill and knowledge he must be assumed to possess. The courts do consider this question from time to time in relation to sufficiency though not so often as they do for the question of obviousness. Generally we must not assume too much imagination on the part of this legally fictitious character and once again err on the safe side by supplying more rather than less instruction in experimental detail. If the inventor can write the method down in sufficient detail for it to be followed faithfully by an average laboratory technician new to the job with results comparable to those the inventor himself would obtain then we are on reasonably safe ground. The court will expect the addressee of the specification to interpret sensibly the directions given by the inventor and with a view to achieving success rather than failure.

The requirement of sufficiency is in principle and practice much the same in all national patent laws. It is taken somewhat further in the US law where the inventor must not only provide a sufficient description of 'how-to-use' but must also disclose the 'best mode', i.e. the best method known to him for operating the process or preparing the product claimed. A US patent would be invalid if at the time of filing the inventor knew of a better method for carrying out the invention and did not disclose it in the application. This applies even if someone else has discovered the better method. It is sometimes difficult to draw the line between this situation and one where the better method is a separate invention altogether.

The notion that a patentee can hold back essential information and yet obtain a valid patent which is exercisable against others is thus seen to be unfounded.

Chapter 5

The Mechanism of Patenting

Happily the mechanism of patenting can be left to a large extent to the patent attorney. Patenting procedures and mechanisms have become heavily loaded with formalities under modern legislation, especially in connection with international patenting activity, and the wise practitioner will do as much as possible to insulate the inventor from their impact.

The first essential message for inventors is that the success of the operation depends critically upon the amount of experimental effort put into the setting up of the patent position, primarily before filing the first application and, to a lesser extent, during the following year. This remark applies mainly to the individual patent as distinct from the building up of a multi-patent portfolio, which is usually a progressive development over a number of years. For each individual invention the same time-scale and tactics apply to the method of protecting it and these must now be outlined.

PREPARING THE GROUND

Inventors must realize that what is written into the specification filed in the patent office at a definitive point in the patenting process very largely determines the outcome. This is not to say that what is first written is indelible; it will often have to be amended in response to official objections. What cannot be done, however, is to add to the disclosure in any significant sense. By the time that the application has worked its way through the patent office machine and received its first critical report from the examiner the inventor may well know much more about his invention, as to its scope and its important parameters, but as far as this particular patent application is concerned the last word of its technical disclosure content has virtually been said. Additional knowledge can be used in argument in support or confirmation of what is already explicit or implicit in the specification but it cannot be incorporated in it. An examiner may ask for clarification of certain terms used and with his permission this can sometimes be written into the document but that is rather different from the point now being emphasized.

Order of Events

When an inventor submits his research results to patent professional opinion e.g. to his internal company patent department or to an external firm of patent agents or attorneys, it will in most cases be necessary or at least highly desirable for a discussion to take place to enable the invention to be scrutinized and analysed against the conditions for patentability described in the last chapter. Such discussion has a two-fold purpose, first to determine whether a sufficient degree of novelty, unobviousness, and utility attaches to the inventor's findings to support a patent position of any kind and, secondly, to assess the nature and scope of claims to be used to protect the invention. Consideration of this second point brings in the amount of experimental ground covered by the research to date and the expectations of any further research planned by the inventor. An inventor may sometimes be advised that in order to protect his position more effectively certain further experiments should be carried out, for example, to synthesize more compounds within the general formula contemplated for use in the main patent claim, or to try the effect of related strains of virus or species of microorganism, or the effect of a variety of other reagents suitable for use in the process. The question that will inevitably arise is 'how much data must I produce before I can confidently begin the patenting process?' To answer it we can start with the unusual position of the British inventor and then see how his counterparts elsewhere will fare.

Formerly it was possible for a UK resident inventor to initiate patent action by presenting to the British Patent Office a specification of the invention in a provisional manner. In the provisional specification it was not required to present the patent claims; it was enough to describe the invention sufficiently well to establish that the inventive concept existed and could be formulated explicitly at an early date, a fact of importance whenever it came to a dispute over priority between two or more parties claiming the same idea. Some practical demonstration of the concept was usually very desirable at this stage, but a further period of one year was allowed for presenting the complete specification which would include the claims and which would be the definitive document to be examined by the patent office. This system had certain advantages for the applicant. First, it allowed for developments arising within the year following the provisional specification to be included in the complete specification and, up to a point, it permitted some rethinking of the original presentation. This was a very convenient element of flexibility where the essentials of the invention were not clear-cut at the provisional stage, for in such cases it was possible in the provisional to foreshadow alternatives and a possible shift of emphasis as regards the crux of the invention after a preliminary study of previously published work. This facility was subject, however, to the check and balance that any claims made which were not 'fairly based' on the provisional disclosure were not entitled to the priority date of the provisional but only that of the complete specification. The provisional/complete specification system operated in the UK and still exists in some British Commonwealth countries, being generally appreciated by inventors resident in these territories. However, in continental Europe, the United States, Japan and indeed virtually everywhere else, an inventor was, in fact, obliged to file the equivalent of a British complete specification in the first instance, there being no such thing as the provisional in their own national law. Inevitably, the tendency would be for the non-British inventor to delay filing his application for patent protection until he was in the position to draft an effective specification having claims well supported by the data and the degree of disclosure required.

The new British law has done away with the provisional and complete specifications as such, although it has replaced them by something rather similar. Thus, it is possible to inter-relate for priority claiming purposes two separate patent applications if they are dated within one year of each other. Furthermore, it is possible to file what we now call an informal specification, i.e. without claims, and supply these claims within a prescribed period. Although this sounds rather like the provisional specification in another guise, there will be some important legal distinctions to make between the two.

INTERNATIONAL ARRANGEMENTS

To recapitulate then, the first step for the inventor is normally to file an application for basic protection in his home territory, what we shall term a basic national filing. The application is given a number and a filing date which establishes a priority date in relation to other applications for the same or a related invention in that territory. It also achieves something even more valuable to the inventor because this priority date can be accorded international significance. Under the International Convention for the Protection of Industrial Property (Paris Convention), first established in 1883, any contracting state to this convention agrees to treat the priority date of the basic national filing by inventor A as effective against competitive patent applications made by inventors B, C etc. in its own national patent system, provided that inventor A files a corresponding application in that state within twelve months of his basic national filing. The foreign application has been described as a 'corresponding' application because it must obviously be one for the same invention. It need not be word for word identical with the basic application and it can include additional data and developments of the original invention. However, the priority date which is accorded to the contents of the foreign application must depend on the extent to which the respective parts of it are also present in the basic national filing, which is usually referred to as the 'priority document'. Different claims can have different priority dates for the territory concerned and some may be entitled only to the actual filing date of the corresponding application in that country.

Thus all the research carried out before the zero point in the patenting time scale should be properly reflected in the basic national filing. Any further research which is concerned with the same broad inventive concept can be included at the 12-month stage in the specification for foreign filing and in any further related filing allowed in the basic national territory. The previously mentioned British practice of interlinking a first and second application for the same invention also extends to the combining together of the subject matter of any number of relevant applications (all filed within a span of one year) into an omnibus application which can supersede its precursor filings and carry over from them the subject matter of a series of claims having a gradation of priority dates. Most recent German, Dutch, Swedish and Finnish practice also allows this very convenient practice of interlinking their own national applications in this way. The US patent law has an even more generous policy of interlinking a series of so-called 'continuation' or 'continuation-in-part' applications without any timespan restriction on their respective filing dates except that the precursor filing (of which the new one is a continuation) must still be pending before grant. But these territories are still rather exceptional to the general rule that the basic national filing is the definitive event in the laying of the foundation for protection.

The whole scheme and timescale for obtaining protection outside the home territory can be grasped more easily by reference to Figure 2 but the remaining stages of the process must be described before the Figure can be fully appreciated.

European Developments

In addition to patents obtainable through the individual national systems of patent law which continue to exist, there are two new types of European patent offered to inventors, the present European patent, which is the subject of the European Patent Convention (EPC) signed in Munich in October 1973 and the future Community patent dealt with in the Community Patent Convention (CPC) signed in Luxembourg in December 1975. One might well ask why two such systems have been created. In continental Europe the concept of a Community patent as a unitary right having the same effect throughout the Common Market and subject to no nationalistic barriers has enjoyed strong motivation. To the prime movers of the European patent concept, the European Patent Convention was only a first stage, open in principle to all states of the European continent and effective in any state which would sign and ratify the convention. The second stage (CPC) was expected to follow rapidly upon the first but so far has not done so. EPC provides for one examining and granting system leading to, effectively, a bundle of 'national' patents in designated states. It is only with the CPC that the truly single patent, having the unitary character referred to above, emerges.

The governments of some EEC and other European states moved sufficiently rapidly to enable the first Convention (EPC) to enter into force thus allowing the European Patent Office to begin receiving patent applications in June 1978. It was not necessary for all EEC states to ratify it to achieve this object. The coming into force of the Community Patent Convention, however, is still delayed because it is of the essence of the thing that all states of the Community ratify it. There are therefore certain transitional provisions which interlink the European and Community patent systems from a practical point of view.

If the European route is chosen, the applicant can file his European application in the European Patent Office in Munich or The Hague or in a National Patent Office e.g. in London which acts as a branch office of the EPO. English, French and German are the three official languages which can be used for the specification and any proceedings relating to it. One may start with a selection of any of the states which are parties to the convention; this selection must be designated at the outset and cannot be added to later. It may embrace all states of the Community. If all are included in this way the applicant must make his choice at the outset whether he wishes to obtain a European patent (i.e. a European patent bundle covering designated states which can be dropped individually and selectively at a later stage by non-payment of renewal fees), or whether he intends to obtain a unitary Community patent. In the latter case it will be understood that conversion to a Community patent can only be effected after the Community Patent Convention has come into operation.

On the question of relative cost, it is considered that if patent protection is required in three or more European territories it should be cheaper to proceed by the European route rather than the individual national routes. The European route involves the risk that in prosecuting the patent application all the eggs are in the one basket. Many inventors and, indeed, many industrial firms may well not require protection in more than about three European territories and they may prefer to use the traditional national routes if the higher costs of maintenance of the full Community patent are not warranted. The cheaper option of selecting European territories including part of the EEC (perhaps only those in which manufacture of the invention will occur) remains open but once CPC comes into effect this option will only exist for a limited period.

International Applications: The Patent Co-operation Treaty (PCT)

Unlike the EPC and CPC systems, which result in regional patents, the PCT route produces national patents which ultimately are granted in accordance with the strictly national laws of the territories selected for protection by the applicant.

PCT applications are described as international because they are initially processed by an international body, in the so-called 'international phase', before they are formally introduced into the national systems (before they 'enter the national phase'). The international phase is concerned mainly with the formal preliminaries, search and preliminary publication of the application rather than with substantive examination as such. It is conducted under the supervision of the World Intellectual Property Organization (WIPO) based in Geneva but involves the participation of many national Patent Offices (acting as receiving offices) including their searching arms (as International

Searching Authority) and their examining divisions (providing International Preliminary Examination).

The PCT system is very broad indeed, embracing USA, Japan, the Soviet Union, the European patent system and numerous other territories which can all be designated at the outset by the payment of modest designation fees in addition to the basic charges. In effect the applicant reserves the right to activate the national phase for as many of these territories as he wishes after he has received the search report. Although the basic fees of the international application are not small the system allows postponement of translation charges until the national phase is reached. The International Convention (Paris Convention) applies to PCT applications as well as to European applications so that a PCT filing can be made twelve months after the basic national filing. The International application is published at the 18-month stage and the national phase begins at 20 months. The latter can in some countries be postponed until the 25-month stage if the applicant elects to subject his application to international preliminary examination, a procedure designed to elicit a preliminary and non-binding official statement on the merits of the case, a *prima facie* view of its patentability.

The Official Response

Having collaborated with the patent attorney in the preparation of the first specification at the initial filing stage and of its developed form at the second or foreign filing stage, the inventor has to stand back and allow the mechanism to take over for a time. The patent department or firm of agents or attorneys will complete the documentary formalities and arrange for the lodging of the applications in the appropriate patent offices. Since this last mentioned step must be done before the passing of the anniversary of the basic national filing date and time must be allowed for the transmission of documents abroad and for any translation of the specification into a foreign language, it is clear that the drafting and other preparatory parts of the process must be started some months earlier. In practice therefore the effective period between the first and second stages shortens from twelve months to perhaps nine or ten months and all who have been through this exercise will know how rapidly this time runs out! In an ideal world the inventor will have made contact with his professional advisers at times even during this period so that any important developments which have arisen in the interim and which justify further filing will have been protected specifically with the earliest possible priority date.

The mechanism which then takes over operates silently in official channels where the requisite novelty searches are carried out. Under the European model, the search report which is sent to the applicant's professional representative will identify prior patents and literature citations regarded by the official searcher as relevant to what is claimed in the application. The normal pattern under the European patent system and many national systems in Europe is for automatic publication of the application and search report to occur at 18 months after the claimed priority date. At the same time the applicant can propose amendments to his claims in the light of the cited prior art if it is clearly apparent that he cannot in the circumstances hope to sustain their original breadth.

The real in-depth examination of the application must then be initiated by a request of the applicant for 'substantive examination' and most countries have a specific period within which this must be done if the application is not to lapse. Depending on how difficult may be the objections raised by the examiner the inventor may be recalled to activity by the patent agent to support him in devising counter arguments and an effective response. The separation of the official search stage from the substantive examination stage is now a general feature of national practice in European countries and under the European Patent Convention. In USA, Canada and elsewhere the search and critical examination are carried out by one and the same examiner who then reports his various objections. Under all systems this report is known as an 'official action' or 'office action' and it requires a written response within a set period. It is a virtually universal rule in patent procedure that all the various actions which have to be taken, including the filing of responses and amendments of the claims, to overcome official objections must take place within legally prescribed time limits which if exceeded can result in the sudden death of the application. The inventor or other member of staff of the applicant company who anxiously awaits news or activity from his patent adviser should bear in mind that the agent works to a calendar that is heavily dotted with deadline dates of this kind which relate to and constitute the summation of work entrusted to him from all his clients. All deadlines are equal from the professional point of view and there is no question of some being more equal than others when the interests of different clients are involved.

Sometimes it is not possible to deal adequately with the examiner's objection by letter and an interview may be necessary. The examiner may call for an interview with the agent but more often it is the agent who sees the need for face-to-face discussion to remove misunderstandings or to advance a point of view more forcefully. Occasionally the agent will ask for the inventor to be present to resolve difficult technical matters. The correct tone of such an interview has been set poetically by the US Patent Office in the following terms:

'An interview between an applicant and examiner is not an adversary proceeding. It is a joint and co-operative voyage of discovery to reveal and define the proper boundary between the applicant's invention and the public right'.

Regrettably, principle and practice rarely meet in the ideal portrayed by this statement.

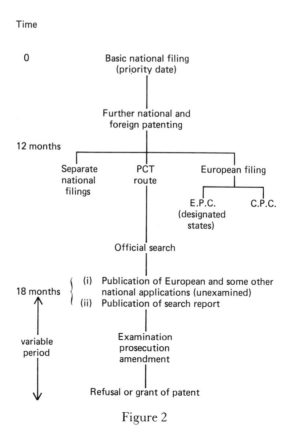

Figure 2

In most cases this period of negotiation with the examiner which is known technically as 'prosecution of the application' results in agreement being reached as to what scope of claim is reasonable in view of the prior art. Where this cannot be achieved by compromise the applicant and the examiner must continue the argument up to the highest tribunal the law provides unless one side gives way en route. The term for which a patent lasts when granted varies around the world. The 20-year term running from the application date is now becoming the standard pattern in European countries. USA and Canada are among the most important countries where the term runs from grant of the patent (in their case 17 years). Lesser periods apply in many other countries. Maintenance is usually conditional upon payment of renewal fees.

Figure 2 can now be given to summarize the procedure outlined so far. The section between official search and examination refers mainly to the European type of procedure. In USA, Canada and many other countries no official publication of the application is made until the patent has been granted.

Opposition and Revocation

It has been the practice of many countries to allow a further period, after acceptance of the application by the examiner, within which an opponent can file a formal opposition to the grant of a patent on the application. A period of two or three months for the filing of opposition was the norm and if one was filed in time it would have the effect of postponing grant until the arguments between the parties were resolved. In an opposition the patent office now changed its role of direct protagonist for one in which it held the ring between the contestants and then decided the winner. The older British law provided specific grounds of opposition which went beyond the powers of objection given to the examiner during normal prosecution and in most other European countries there was even more freedom for the opponent to argue that a patent should not be granted. In practice the opponent was a kind of new examiner 'writ large' who could argue even more strongly on the prior art cited in prosecution and who could usually dredge up more documentary art than the examiner's search had revealed and sometimes a prior public use which the examiner could not have known of. He could also bring forward technical expert evidence in support. The opposition could often drag on for years and could go to appeal at the instigation of the loser in the first round. Usually an applicant in these circumstances could not exert his rights against any infringing use of his invention until it was finally determined that he was entitled to such rights and what their scope was to be.

Following the European patent model it is now widespread practice also under national systems in Europe to grant the patent at the conclusion of prosecution and to allow a subsequent period for any challenge to be made by a competitor. It is still called opposition according to EPC but the term used in UK national law is 'revocation'. The period now common for the lodging of this challenge is nine months from grant. Any unauthorized interim use of the invention after the very first publication of the patent application can be the subject of a claim for compensation by the finally successful patentee.

Japanese law also provides for opposition and allows a claim for compensation in respect of 'infringing' use to be made in court in parallel to the conduct of opposition proceedings. The United States system has never favoured a full-blooded opposition system of the European or Japanese type. It has allowed 'protestors' to participate in any attempt by the patentee to amend his patent after grant in so-called re-issue proceedings and the resulting protest could be a formidable burden for the patentee in re-opening many issues. The most recent addition to the US patent law allows any party, including the patentee, the Commissioner of Patents, or a third party, to call for a re-examination by the patent office of any patent it has granted. This allows one to call into question even those patents which have been established for many years. For the process to be permitted it must be based on the citation of prior patents or printed publications only and must raise a substantially new issue of patentability. Re-examination proceedings cannot be described as opposition for it is not *inter partes* as between the patentee and the third party. It can, however, result in the cancellation of some or all of the allowed claims.

What has been said of the rules of novelty in the previous chapter can now be related to this discussion of the mechanism of patenting by way of review and reminder to the inventor as regards plans he may have for publishing or in any way disclosing details of his invention. Figure 3 sets out the important points.

In the period from invention date to basic filing date non-disclosure or at least confidentiality is essential in relation to patents that might eventually be sought in any country that has the rule of absolute novelty and provides no grace-period for the inventor's own publications. In the one-year period between basic national filing and the extension to over-

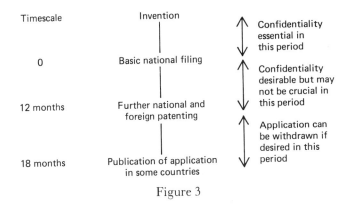

Figure 3

seas protection publication of the invention in outline or in detail will not be harmful as regards those countries that are party to the Paris Convention, assuming always that the effective foundation of protection has been laid in the basic application. The cautious inventor may still be willing to delay publication in this interim if the invention is developing so rapidly that the original description in the first application will need major re-vamping for the final specification. Few inventors are cast in such a patient mould. At the twelve-month stage comes the need to settle the final draft of specification on which subsequent prosecution will rest. Publication after this point usually cannot affect the outcome and in any case the specification will itself be published officially at the 18-month stage if an application has been filed in such an early-publishing country. There is the possibility of withdrawing the application before this time thus preventing official publication provided action is taken before the patent office procedure has gone too far. This is sometimes necessary where a particularly relevant piece of prior art has turned up in the search or in any other way and the applicant needs to re-think and substantially re-draft his presentation of the invention in order to distinguish it more clearly from prior knowledge. Abandoning the application at this stage results in loss of the original priority date because the re-presentation referred to can only be achieved by filing a new application thus starting the whole process afresh from a new priority date.

Chapter 6

Inventorship, Ownership and Contractual Relationships

Inventorship is a subject that arises at the start of any proposal to patent research results. Logically it must take second place to the preliminary discussion of patentability for the simple reason that one must first appraise the nature of the invention and the claim structure envisaged to protect it before asking who invented it. There may be a sole inventor or a small number of joint inventors and in some countries there is a concept of the team invention. A purist school of thought recommends making a review of the inventorship towards the end of prosecution of the application in the light of the final shape of the patent claims. There is logic in this view but it is practised only in a minority of cases and is probably totally justified only where a drastic re-assessment of the nature of the invention has been forced upon the patent attorney in the face of substantial and close prior art. It is hardly likely to be popular with the originally named inventors. There is no general judicial authority calling for such a review and the need for it is debatable. The essential point to be appreciated in these opening remarks is that inventorship is a legal question which can affect the validity of the patent and therefore cannot be left to the research group to decide alone.

Having identified the invention and the inventors to be named in the application documents it is a short step to decide to whom the invention belongs. However, the legal ownership of inventions takes us into other waters than those of the patent law and can involve the general law of master and servant and the law of contracts and fiduciary relationships. It is yet another instance where national laws vary from country to country and where a full survey would require a specialist work. A reading of this chapter will give the inventor an awareness of the main issues but will not equip him to form conclusions without professional advice based on the relevant guiding law applied to the detailed circumstances in which the invention has arisen. Having stated this precaution the topics of this chapter can now be discussed in turn.

INVENTORSHIP

This is a concept elaborated by the patent law which applies relatively straightforwardly where the invention or discovery is the work of one person working alone or, at most, with the assistance of technicians who perform prescribed tasks of a routine kind. Where more than one person is involved in the work to a significant degree the question is whether they are all, or some of them, to be ranked as co-inventors. This consideration cannot simply be equated with that of authorship of a scientific paper. It is difficult to give a precise statement of the criteria on which a particular worker would be judged as a co-inventor which would not apply also to the naming of co-authors and it would be strange to find a person named as a co-inventor who did not figure as a co-author of the relevant scientific paper. The converse is by no means true and it is frequently the case that more authors will appear on the paper than can be judged as having participated inventively in the work in the strict patent law sense. The US examiner will often pick up an apparent discrepancy of this kind and call for an explanation. A disclaiming declaration by the co-author concerned is the best possible answer but an explanation by the named inventor(s) of the nature of the work done by the omitted person(s) can also suffice to remove objection.

Invention may lie in the idea or in the method of putting the idea into effect or it may be in the combination of idea and execution. This principle, which is primarily related to the assessment of inventiveness, must also apply to the question of inventorship. Some may find it strange that in settling the question of inventorship more weight is given to the person responsible for the idea than to the person who performs the actual experiment. Nevertheless there are many judicial decisions in support of the practice. At one end of the scale a person who merely performs experiments devised by another is not normally judged as an inventor although if he were left to his own devices and exercised ingenuity in executing his prescribed task, the position would be different. At the other extreme, a person whose contribution is of a general supervisory character would not be properly named as a co-inventor. The problem in practice is that most cases lie between these extremes and require an objective and fair attempt to disentangle individual contributions.

There are few legal decisions on the criteria for judging whether a co-worker is a mere auxiliary or a co-inventor. The approach which is usually taken in practice is to ask not whether one could have produced the results without the other but whether the conception was complete without the co-worker's contribution in the sense that it needed nothing more than verification or confirmation. In the experimental sciences on which our study is focused it is probably rare for the pure idea to remain unmodified after some experimental work has produced results and it is then necessary to see how much independently creative thought has been given by the experimentalist in devising and performing that work. Should such a question arise in relation to postgraduate research for a higher degree it will be found that the supervisor will often clearly understand the distinctions being pointed out in discussing whether the student's work amounts to a co-inventive contribution. Sometimes the correct conclusion is that the student is the sole inventor especially where it is the student who has decided on the particular track to follow which has revealed the invention.

Occasionally the inventorship problem becomes metaphysical. Let us suppose the case where one worker synthesizes a new compound and a different worker discovers that it has an unexpected utility. This situation must be distinguished from the usual one in which the chemists prepare a group of compounds as part of a research strategy to produce a certain biological activity or level of activity and these are passed to the pharmacologists for the specific test or a routine screen. The biological tester has to concede that his work is normally to confirm or dispel a hunch on the part of the chemist who will be considered the inventor if indeed there is an invention at all. But where the synthesized compound is not particularly impressive for the original purpose and somebody has the bright idea of looking for a different type of activity which is then discovered to be present and to be significant it seems very rough justice not to consider the invention a joint one. Some years ago a US court held that even in these circumstances the invention was in the compound whereas the properties of the compound were not the invention but only the utility that made the invention patentable. The US courts are authority as to the law in that country but the law of inventorship is not in all respects the same in USA as elsewhere. A chemical compound without a recognized utility is an academic curiosity until its properties are discovered whereupon it takes on the character of an invention recognized in patent law. Different practitioners have their own view of the way to handle problems of this kind. One way is to file two patent applications, the first claiming the compound and citing the chemist as sole inventor and the second claiming the use of the compound or a pharmaceutical composition containing it and directed to the discovered utility naming as inventor (sole or joint) the person who discovered the special properties of the compound.

One should exercise some control over the number of inventors named and follow the principle that entities should not be multiplied unnecessarily. In some cases there can be up to, say, six or seven inventors named without violating this principle and we are likely to see more of this in the area of genetic engineering inventions covering a broad area of research. In traditional microbiology inventors could be quite numerous in the series of developments involved, say, in the development of a new strain of microorganism and its use for the production of a new antibiotic. The person who discovers and isolates a new strain which is later shown to have valuable properties may be an inventor. The one who notices the special type of antibiotic activity produced by the strain (not in the routine screen) has certainly made a contribution without which the strain may have simply remained as a laboratory specimen. A third person might then be brought in to determine how to cultivate the strain for the purposes of producing significant levels of the biological activity so that extraction procedures can be worked out. So the chemists now enter the field to devise extraction and purification procedures and to characterize the antibiotic. The process and product to emerge from all this work may thus incorporate contributions made along the line which are combined into the final patent specification and which must be evaluated for the determination of inventorship. The specification may include a variety of claims of the type met in the examples given in Chapter 3 and these will focus thought on the question under discussion. The US patent law again presents special considerations because in joint invention situations it is required that the invention defined in every claim be the joint invention of all the named inventors. It is therefore commonly found that the total subject matter will for US patent purposes have to be distributed among more than one application and according to inventorship criteria. This can also be done for equivalent filings in other countries but the consequential multiplication of patent cost usually dictates against this course unless it is considered necessary or desirable on other grounds. Before leaving the inventive aspects of chemical contributions something further must be said about product characterization. Although it is unwise to make sweeping statements about invention or inventive activity it would seem safe to say that performing analytical determinations on pure compounds supplied by others does not qualify. A knowledge of structure is not itself an invention although it may lead to ideas about structural modification, e.g. synthetic analogues of a natural product, which result in further inventions. The generator of such ideas would of course be the inventor, or one of them, of these further inventions.

The investigation of inventorship must to a great extent be the professional responsibility of the attorney because thorough knowledge of the legal principles is essential to a proper determination. The attorney must be given an accurate account of the facts pertaining to the generation of the ideas, experiments, results and inventive conclusions of the workers involved. It is also advisable to record the nature of the various contributions and the reasons which dictate the choice of names. To have the written agreement of the named inventors to this record may also prove useful later when memories have become rusty. If the persons named as inventors in a patent application are not truly the inventors the resulting patent could be invalid and could be attacked, particularly by others who believe they have contributed to the making of the invention.

The correct joinder of inventors is of particular importance in US patent law and as special considerations apply to this subject it is often necessary to seek specialist advice when preparing an application for filing in that country. Mistakes made in naming inventors (misjoinder) can be cured if made without fraudulent intent. Other countries will also permit corrections but it is usually necessary to act while the application is pending.

OWNERSHIP

This section is concerned with the question of ownership of inventions insofar as it falls to be determined primarily by operation of law as distinct from contract. The two topics cannot be totally divorced, however, for in most cases there may well be a contract which, in order to eliminate doubt, explicitly achieves the same result as would be decided in a court of law.

For the private inventor working without financial support from another party there is clearly no doubt that he owns his invention. The basic principle that the product of a man's ingenuity belongs in the first place to the individual is a basic right recognized anywhere except the total Marxist state. But most inventors do depend on financial support and most are employees of the body which provides it and this therefore poses the question whether or not the inventor merely holds his invention in trust for his financial backer or employer. Because of variations in national law there is no simple single global solution to the problem of deciding where complete ownership resides in these circumstances and the inventor is advised once again that it depends very much on what he is and what work he does in the establishment and what law controls the situation.

Employee Inventions in UK Law

For the British inventor, i.e. one who is resident in and makes the invention in the UK, the position was controlled by common law until dealt with by explicit statutory provisions in the Patents Act of 1977. The need for frequent application of common law principles arose from the absence of express terms relating to inventions in the hitherto typical contract of service of many employees and most of the cases in which the relevant principles have been established are of early vintage. The 1949 Patents Act made an attempt to provide for the possibility of an apportionment between employer and employee of the benefit of an invention but this was emasculated by a decision of the House of Lords that it could only operate where an agreement to share the benefit actually existed. In the absence of such an agreement the provision could not displace the ordinary rule governing the relation of master and servant. The ordinary rule could be stated fairly easily although its concrete application was sometimes difficult. It was that an invention made by an employee 'in the course of his employment' belonged to the employer. This phrase was never restricted in application to inventions made during the course of working hours and with the employer's materials and facilities for the obvious reason that the problems of the working day often follow an employee into his bath and, like those of Archimedes, are sometimes solved there. It was concerned more with the nature of the invention in relation to the employer's business and more especially with the specific work and duties attached to the employee's job. The disputed cases are those in which it was evidently not part of the normal duties of the employee to do research or to design new processes and products or improvements in the existing processes and products of the employer's manufacture. Anyone working in research or development and at a level at which creative ideas are expected to emerge from time to time can hardly have been in doubt that if any of these came into the category of patentable invention it would be the rightful property of the employer.

The new provisions of the 1977 Act are said to codify the pre-existing law and they attempt to develop the meaning of the common law precept quoted above. The test of employer ownership in Section 39(1) of the Act is whether the invention

> '. . . was made in the course of the normal duties of the employee or in the course of duties . . . specifically assigned to him, and the circumstances in either case were such that an invention might reasonably be expected to result from the carrying out of his duties . . .'

It is not possible for the employee to escape from this wording by the simplistic 'I am not paid to invent' argument. Very few are explicitly paid to invent and a substantial proportion of valuable research work is not of the type for patenting in any event. The first part of the test points rather to the circumstances in which the invention was made, so that if Fleming, for example, had been an industrial employee on whose Petri dish the stray microorganism alighted which produced penicillin we could expect his fortunate employer to claim the benefit under modern principles. It would be arguable whether the second part of the test would be met by someone who was not supposed to be studying the effect of various substances on microorganisms, and the chance discovery of this kind is somewhat rare but the 'reasonable expectation' relates to 'an invention' and not necessarily 'the invention' which transpires. The next sub-section of the quoted part of the Act omits the test of reasonable expectation in relation to employees who are under 'a special obligation to further the interests of the employer's undertaking'. This is thought to apply to high level staff whose special position overrides the fact that they are not engaged in day to day research or similar work and it is believed to codify one of the strands of case law relating to inventions made by company directors and the like.

The more controversial part of the 1977 Act on this subject deals with circumstances in which although ownership resides with the employer the employee is nevertheless entitled to some compensation, i.e. additional to his normal remuneration. The main example is where the patent is of 'outstanding benefit' to the employer; it is clear that this provision can only apply to the somewhat extraordinary type of invention.

There is a popular notion that whether an employer can lay claim to the full ownership of an employee's invention depends on whether its scope is reasonably related to the employer's business or the specific work of the employee. It does indeed happen on occasion that an inventor set to a particular task will devise a solution that has far wider application than in the specific problem tackled and may indeed be the basis of a patent that is relevant outside the direct business interests of the employer. As regards 'out-field' uses, however, British law knows nothing of the concept of shared rights or ownership either in common law or statute law. The right of ownership is uninfluenced by the scope or value of the invention although these factors would certainly be relevant to the question of compensation if the patent rights were exploited extensively outside the pre-existing commercial field of the employer either directly or by licensing.

Academic inventions

The common law principles of ownership of inventions made by employees have been developed chiefly in the context of the master and servant relationship in industrial life. The corresponding provisions in the British statute reflect a similar pre-occupation with an industrial setting. In both these departments of law it has always been difficult to classify the invention arising from research in a university or similar academic environment. Academic institutions have felt uneasy in applying these principles to their own situation in life and there have been doubts as to the correctness of equating the relationship of academic research staff and institutions totally with the traditional employer/employee relationship in industry. The question is one which has not in the past admitted of a strict legalistic answer of the kind that would be generally acceptable in all academic institutions and these have tended to favour an approach based on *ad hoc* agreement with the inventor or with his department. It is still not crystal clear from the British statute how the principle should be applied to university workers. However, the concept of shared benefit has always been strong in university thinking on this subject and if along with this there is included the idea of shared responsibility for appropriate exploitation of the invention it may not be of fundamental importance to settle the legal question of absolute ownership. In the report of a working party set up to study the whole question by the Committee of Vice-chancellors and Principals of the Universities of the United Kingdom there is the strong recommendation to universities to grasp the nettle and 'promulgate detailed procedures for all categories of staff and students to govern the patenting and commercial application of research results'. The report includes an excellent analysis of the spectrum of possibilities arising in university research and some British universities have already adopted many of its proposals including the one dealing with the desirability of contracts of employment which are clear as to the normal duties of the employee.

Employee Inventions in US Law

In the absence of express agreement between the parties the common law of the United States also determines ownership of inventions as between employer and employee. The US common law has perhaps been more ready than its British counterpart to give explicit recognition to the concept of being 'employed or hired to invent' in the sense that the employee is paid for and assigned to the task of inventing a solution for a particular problem. In such circumstances the Supreme Court in 1890 observed:

'Whatever rights as an individual he may have had in and to his inventive powers, and that which they are able to accomplish, he has sold in advance to his employer'.

This type of employment has been described as 'specific inventive' employment. It is, however, not to be restricted to the terms and understanding of the original contract of hiring and is held to obtain even where the employee is assigned to a task which may be somewhat removed from the original duties specified. This may be compared with the distinction in the British statute discussed above between normal duties and duties specifically assigned both of which give rise to employer ownership of any resulting invention.

Other types of employment have been described as 'general' in which no specific inventive end-product is contemplated although the intellectual level of those in these jobs may not be significantly lower than in the specific inventive category, and 'non-inventive' in which even the expectation that invention might arise is not apparently in the mind of the employer. Inventions actually made by employees in these types of work belong in common law to the employee. A minority opinion holds that inventions made by those in 'general' employment ought to be assigned to the employer where they are within the field of the employer's business. But in a case where, of two employees, 'never was there a word said to either of them, prior to their discoveries, concerning invention or patents or their duties or obligations respecting these matters' and 'in no proper sense could it be said that the contract of employment contemplated invention' a Supreme Court majority ruling in 1933 decided that the inventors need not assign their patent applications to their employer (the US Government). Where invention arises outside the assigned work of the employee, it is this middle ground which is so difficult, uncertain, and generally unsatisfactory to both sides that has in course of time brought about the specific contractual arrangement which is now the norm in the employment of highly skilled personnel in the USA.

Basic ideas on the ownership of inventions arising from research funded by the commercial employer are deeply rooted in the entrepreneurial spirit of the industry and people of the United States and it is recognized that those who venture are entitled to gain if the research succeeds. The *status quo* is apparently so entrenched that attempts to introduce protective legislation on behalf of the employee have so far foundered. The prevailing climate of reducing the role of government will presumably maintain the view that the parties to a contract of this sort must determine their respective rights according to the principles of the free market. Some States, however, have legislated to regulate contracts which contain excessive ownership and assignment provisions favouring the employer. The sanction against such grasping clauses is that they are unenforceable against the employee in the State concerned.

Employee Inventions in Europe

In addition to the UK other countries in Europe have special laws governing this subject. The relevant statute laws in force in Austria, Germany, Holland and Sweden pre-date the British counterpart and of these the German is the most well known and comprehensive. In Germany the Employee Inventors Act 1957 distinguishes between 'tied' inventions (service inventions), deriving from the employee's work or from the experience gained therein, which belong to the employer and 'free' inventions which are not so derived and are the property of the employee. Even for the tied invention, however, the right must be claimed by the employer within four months or it becomes free to the employee to patent at his own expense. Furthermore the tied invention can still attract compensation to the employee over and above his salary and there is no restriction to cases of outstanding benefit as in the British law. Compensation is decided by a complex system of assessment of the value of the invention. This system adds considerably to the work of the 'in-house' patent departments in industry and has produced its own specialist lawyers in both industrial and private practice.

Employee Inventions in Japan

The Japanese patent law also makes the distinction between the 'service invention', i.e. one within the employer's field of business and deriving from the employee's present or past duties, and the 'free invention' which arises in other circumstances. The law allows employment contracts to contain a clause which provides for the employer to acquire the patent or the right to apply for the patent. The employee is entitled to reasonable compensation in respect of service inventions assigned to the employer and this can be decided in court proceedings in which allowance will be made for the salary already received by the employee. Rather than entering into individual contracts with their employees most Japanese companies tend to adopt service invention regulations along the lines of the model suggested by the patent office in 1964. This sets down procedures for reporting on inventions made, the filing of the application, notification of the inventor, determining compensation and other matters. Monetary compensation is not the only reward for employee inventors in Japan, where other factors in the total employment practice provide incentives for employees to invent.

CONTRACTUAL RELATIONSHIPS

In this section there are grouped together contracts of employment, contracts of consultancy, and other kinds of relationship. The following brief discussion is aimed at identifying and distinguishing types of arrangement in outline only. Actual situations can involve so many variables that specific legal advice will be necessary for any research worker or group contemplating employment or collaboration with another organization where room for manoeuvre exists in the setting up of the initial agreement.

Employment Contracts

As research and development in the area of bioscience has become more and more the province of industrial concerns, of government and of other bodies commanding the large amounts of funding necessary to conduct it under modern conditions, so have contracts of employment tended towards standardization. The individual seeking employment with the large firm has little choice but to accept the standard package in the form of either the old-style contract, full of 'whereas' clauses, still in use in Britain or the simpler form of a letter setting out the main points more colloquially as is now popular in the United States.

In the USA patent applications must be filed in the name of the inventor(s) and no other and therefore as the employer claims ownership and insists on establishing it formally and publicly there must be an assignment for recordal in the US Patent Office. In other countries applications can be filed in the name of the employer or any other person or body that possesses ownership or, as is now possible in UK, can establish it before the patent is granted.

The older style of clauses used in British industry required the employee (1) to acknowledge the employer's right of ownership, (2) to file a patent application or join with the employer in the filing of such, and (3) to assign the beneficial ownership and execute all documents necessary to vest the legal ownership of the patent in the employer. When it became possible for an assignee to file an application in his sole name with the mere appendage of a signature of assent by the inventor, or a mere naming of the inventor, a newer style of clause came into being which was more comprehensive and effective. It provided that any invention made while in the employment and related to the employer's business would belong absolutely to the employer. This would therefore obviate the need for any further formal assignment except where dictated by the laws of the countries in which corresponding patents were applied for, such as in the USA as noted previously. Contracts of service in which the employer claimed the right to 'all' inventions made while in his employ were always considered by the better opinion to be too wide to be enforceable although such broad wording was often used because of the difficulty of being more specific as to the type of invention intended to be caught, especially in a developing and diversifying business situation.

The statutes mentioned previously also contain provisions against contracts which seek to avoid the consequences of legislation and to reduce the rights of the employee. Section 42 of the UK Act 1977 holds such a contract unenforceable 'to the extent that it diminishes his rights in an invention . . . or under a patent for such an invention or application for any such patent'. Likewise the German law holds such agreements 'invalid to the extent that they are manifestly inequitable'.

Consultancies and Other Contracts

The employee inventor and the independent consultant are in clearly distinguishable categories as regards ownership of inventions but in practice the end result may be much the same. There is a middle ground in the form of someone taken on for a regular salary on a short-term basis. One such example of a temporary 'consulting engineer' came before the British court in a disputed case in which the outcome was that the employee, though different from other employees, was not so different as to make him an independent consultant and therefore the decision upheld the employer.

The true consultant is one who is technically not an employee and whose position therefore is determined primarily by his contractual relationship with the firm or body engaging him. Old-fashioned forms of consultancy agreement sometimes omitted specific reference to inventions and patents and it would therefore be necessary to resolve the consequent difficulty by looking for an implied term in the contract such as would follow, for example, from a clear relationship of trust between the parties. There is nowadays no excuse for leaving this point unsettled in the consultancy agreement, and in the highly patent-conscious industries concerned with innovation in the chemical and biological sciences the expectations on both sides are now well established and clear-cut.

The first distinction to be made is between arrangements where the consultant is engaged to offer suggestions, ideas and guidance and those where some experimental work is involved. The former may be regarded as the norm for the individual consultant whereas the latter is more usually the province of the private firm of consultants or some other kind of consulting laboratory or service. The normal individual consultancy is often dealt with by means of a short but formal letter of agreement defining a technical field, more or less limited, and a period of time over which services are required. There will be a modest annual retainer and a more realistic daily rate of payment for time spent by the consultant as well as expenses. For our purpose the two most important features of the agreement will be those covering confidentiality and inventive rights. The consultant will be privy to important 'commercial in confidence' information over which the firm has total ownership and control and therefore the consultant will have no power of publication of anything learnt in this way or indeed of any of the suggestions he himself makes unless the consent of the firm has been given. Similarly the ownership of any inventions made by the consultant will be claimed by the firm. These may be sole inventions but more often will be joint inventions of the consultant and employees of the company who perform experimental work of the kind to justify nomination as co-inventors. The consultant will agree to joining in the patenting activity as required by the company and signing all necessary documents. The remuneration of the consultant is normally regarded as sufficient consideration for the claim to ownership without further sum but the generous firm may in the event of successful commercial application of the consultant's ideas undertake to pass on some share of the proceeds of exploitation. Thus it will usually enter into *bona fide* discussions based on the relative contribution of the ideas and inventions of the consultant gauged against its own research and marketing effort to arrive at some additional payment; this might be a rather small fractional royalty payment based on product sales. The open-ended nature of this last commitment is inevitable and not objectionable. It must be distinguished from a situation in which there is total vagueness in the whole matter of remuneration or compensation as can sometimes be met in loose collaborative arrangements between academic laboratories and certain firms.

Industrial collaboration with academic institutions

In the normal consultancy arrangement discussed in the previous section it will be very common for the consultant to be a member of the academic staff of a university or similar institution or of a publicly-funded research establishment. Such a consultant will require clearance to accept the consultancy and where the individual has not been clearly freed for this purpose the industrial firm may ask the employing institution or other body to join as a party to the transaction in order to be sure of access to full title to patent rights. The institution may wish also to benefit from the arrangement in some way especially if use is being made of its facilities in the course of the consultancy.

Another type of arrangement under this heading is not the consultancy as such but the collaborative research project between industry and the university research group or its counterpart in other bodies that are equally willing to form relationships of this kind. Closely related to this is the research project funded by governments or other public bodies in universities and the like. A variety of possible situations can exist which promote this kind of association. The industrial firm can have its own secret proprietary information or specialized knowledge or problem which nevertheless requires expertise at the level which is only to be found in a particular institution and which may require the combined skills of the resident research group. This is now common in the field of genetic manipulation and in such a new and competitive field it can bring unusual problems into academic life. The technology agreement entered into between the firm and the university, university department, or the research workers as a group will provide for funding of research, for individual fees to the persons concerned, and for the assignment or at least the exclusive licensing to the firm of any patent and other rights generated by the academic team. Alternatively the initiative can originate within the institution, either from the research workers or from administrative staff whose job is to stimulate industrial liaison and attract funds through contract research. In these circumstances it is desirable for the research group in possession of a valuable discovery or invention to establish the foundation of its patent position before disclosure to the firm and before any undertakings are given. The original basis for such a collaboration might be a type of evaluation agreement in which the firm commits itself to a speedy assessment of its interest in the invention and, contingent upon this, to acquire the interest in the invention according to financial terms specified in the agreement (lump sum or royalties or both). The company will usually undertake full costs of patenting and may be persuaded to re-assign the rights if it fails to market a product within an agreed period unless it can establish diligence and reasons beyond its control which have prevented commercialization.

Government funding of academic research usually claims ownership or at least the right to direct the manner in which exploitation of resulting inventions shall be secured in the public interest. This funding may be direct or through government agencies or research councils having allocations of funds for this purpose. Government may direct exploitation by other public bodies established for this purpose but will often contemplate some sharing of exploitation revenue with the academic source. A US statute enacted in 1980 provided for the disposition of patent rights in inventions made with Federal assistance in small businesses or non-profit organisations such as universities. This allows the recipient contractor to elect to retain title within a reasonable time after disclosure of the invention to the Federal Agency provided it files patent applications within reasonable time.

Chapter 7

Special Considerations of Chemical and Microbiological Inventions

The nature of patent practice is far from uniform over the whole of technology. The requirement of the law for inventiveness translates in practice into the need to demonstrate to patent office officials some advantage or superiority of the invention over close prior art. This is true of all cases whatever their field of technology but when it comes to satisfying examiners that protection is justified one finds that standards vary not only from country to country but also from one discipline to another.

CHEMICAL INVENTIONS

As regards proof that an invention has utility, patent practitioners in the mechanical and electrical fields are faced with the problem relatively rarely compared with their chemical counterparts. The operability and usefulness of a mechanical or electrical device described and illustrated by the drawings can usually be directly assessed by the examiner from a reading of the specification whereas the same cannot be said for the utility of a chemical substance. It is not sufficient simply to say that a new chemical compound is a good antioxidant for elastomers or has antitumour activity; these assertions must be proved in some way either by including experimental evidence in the specification itself or by supplying it as the case proceeds through the patent office. Even here, however, there is a distinct difference in burden of proof as between an antioxidant and an antitumour agent and nowhere is the difference more acute than in practice before the US Patent Office.

The problems met in the prosecution of pharmaceutical patent applications are due in part to the foregoing considerations but stem also from public policy in the granting of monopoly rights in the field of health and medicine, restricted though they are in scope and duration.

Public policy in this respect is manifest both in the specific statutory restrictions on the patenting of foods and drugs in various countries and in the attitudes of examining staff to attempts to protect inventions in nutrition and pharmacy which are squarely within the ambit of what is allowed by the written laws. It may seem once again that the US Patent Office is being singled out for comment in relation to the inventor's problems but US Patent Office officials have made no secret of their view that the granting of a US patent is seen by the public as an *imprimatur* amounting to an endorsement of the claims made by the patentee that his product will alleviate or cure disease. This justifies the official caution shown toward the applicants' assertions of biological utility and the demand for high standards of proof. This viewpoint is challenged by the spokesmen of the pharmaceutical industry who point out that it is the function of other government bodies or agencies to determine matters of medical efficacy, safety and professional acceptance of new drugs and other remedies and that these issues should be separated entirely from the assessment of innovative merit.

Some of the major difficulties in the way of obtaining satisfactory protection for inventions in the chemical and microbiological field can be set out in the order in which they arise for consideration in practice.

Public Policy

The first problem we meet derives from the policies of different countries to patents for biologically active substances and processes for their production. In some countries only medicines are excluded from patentability but in others there is an exclusion of all substances produced by chemical methods. The term 'medicine or drug' is often given wide interpretation, e.g. in India where it includes insecticides, fungicides and other such substances and even those chemical substances which are ordinarily used as intermediates for the production of the above mentioned types of compound. In Brazil and Turkey no patent protection is possible either for such products or processes of producing them.

Brief mention can be made here of patents for foodstuffs where in general it is not possible to patent mere mixtures of component foods. This is either expressly forbidden or will be refused on the ground of lack of invention. Processes for producing foods are usually patentable but Denmark still refuses protection for these.

The Type of Protection Available

The nature of the protection available depends on whether the substance is new or old. If new, we have to consider whether product claims or only process claims are available. If old, it is usually possible only to claim certain kinds of composition containing the active substance assuming such claims are allowable under public policy.

In Western Europe the tendency continues towards the granting of product patents for chemical products and new substances generally but a minority clings to the older philosophy of allowing only process protection in these fields. This is no longer quite so much the problem of territorial variation that it once was. The European Convention favours product patents and any territory joining it can only opt out of this feature for a transitional period.

The Scope of Protection

The scope of protection is one of the most acute problems in the scientific disciplines in which we are interested. A novel piece of machinery or electrical circuitry can often be patented in the generalized form using the terminology of the mechanical or electrical engineer. Devices of this kind can be claimed in terms of a combination of features each being expressed in the form of a 'means plus function'.

In chemistry and biology the existence of special languages and the classification of materials and organisms into genus and species offer the possibility of extrapolation from limited experimental data and the use of broad definitions in patent claims. The applicant will naturally desire to cover his invention broadly so as to make avoidance of the patent difficult. There is therefore a great attraction and temptation to draft claims of very broad scope but this carries with it obligations. First there must be support for the scope of the claim presented. With the public interest in mind, the patent office cannot be seen to grant extensive monopolies on the basis of limited experimental data. This points to the clear necessity for inventors to cover the experimental ground sufficiently well to demonstrate the breadth of the discoveries or concepts that underlie the invention claimed.

For the chemist it is necessary to mention the problem of substituents in general formulae used to define the group of compounds of interest. It is clear that any formula containing a benzenoid, heterocyclic, or other ring system offers the possibility of substitution that could provide a possible route to evasion of the claims and therefore the matter must always be considered. Examiners will not allow broad and speculative reference to substituents and are justifiably provoked by 'dangling valencies' in structural formulae. Unless the inventor is able and willing to explore the effect of substituents sufficiently to provide some basis for a reasonable extension of the claim in this respect a point of weakness must remain. In this and other related matters it is difficult for professional advisers to make predictions or give guarantees as to the amount of experimental information which will secure claims of the desired scope but they frequently have to give their client some estimate by way of guidance; some are lucky enough to have clients who will follow the advice given. This point arose in the phenothiazine case mentioned under 'Obviousness' in Chapter 4 wherein the scope of defini-tion of the N-substituent side-chain was also challenged (see structure on page 93). The benevolent view of the British court on this question was that the data given enabled a 'sound prediction' to be made as to the possession of biological properties across the area of chemistry covered by the definition of the side-chain.

A risk attached to the use of over broad terminology is that on a strict view the benefits and advantages of the invention must derive from everything falling within the scope of the claim and not only selected parts of it. If some possibilities falling within the wording used do not give a useful result the patent may be invalid. This risk applies more to laws which have a utility requirement than to those having a mere industrial applicability provision. To express these problems in other words, the structure/activity relationship in biologically active com-pounds and the problem of variability and unpredictability in living systems both point to the need for sufficient experimental data to enable a reasonable judgment to be made as to the scope of the claim necessary to provide effective protection.

The problem of definition

Although related to the foregoing discussion of scope of protection, this problem is not so much that of broad or narrow claims but is one of pre-cision in definition. In the traditional area of relatively simple organic chemistry structural formulae can be readily worked out by modern methods but in the field of large molecules of complex structure derived from biological systems many difficulties remain. There have so far been very few cases in which the courts have had to consider the questions of identity or close similarity in regard to such complex materials and it is clear that these can only be resolved by expert evidence in the light of scientifically established criteria for the characterization and identification of substances such as enzymes and living cells.

One example of the special difficulties involved in the characterization of large molecules is that of the snake venom enzyme arvin quoted in Chapter 3, where a combination of various physicochemical and biological data was used to define the substance. The draftsman of such a claim must carefully question the accuracy and permanence of the data provided by the inventor and should refrain from using individual numbers and other results unless the inventor is emphatically positive about their reliability. In the arvin case one of the original items in the list of properties failed to stand the test of time; the enzyme was first stated to show two precipitin bands on immunoelectrophoresis and this property was included in the main claim. It was later shown, however, that one of these bands was due to a minor impurity and was lost after running the product on a Sephadex column. This was discovered during prosecution of the patent application and the attempt was made to remove this item from the list. The wording could not be changed to specify a single band because this would be 'new matter' and inadmissible, as noted in a previous chapter. But the mere removal of something stated in the specification is not in itself to be equated with the addition of new matter and can be justified under the time-honoured practice of cancelling subject matter from the disclosure in response to the examiner's objections and for other reasons. The difficulty here was that some examiners regarded the cancellation as in effect broadening the scope of the claim and refused to permit it.

In the case of enzymes and other materials difficult to define there has been little official guidance in the past and applicants were obliged to deal with each situation *ad hoc*, arguing that certain data and combinations of properties would be accepted in the art as sufficient for the demarcation of the particular substance being claimed from known enzymes or the corresponding known materials. The Japanese Patent Office has been the first to supply guidance of a systematic kind by issuing its 'Examination Standard for Inventions of Applied Microbiology' in which the information required to be present in the specification as filed is thoroughly prescribed. For example, for an enzyme which is claimed to be new a list of eleven items is given including activity, substrate specificity and optimum pH range and stable pH range, which should be complied with where the case permits or substituted by other data of a more suitable kind. Similar and very detailed requirements are also explained for inventions involving new strains and other microbiological process parameters.

Another example of the definition problem arose in UK litigation of an antibiotic patent in which the derivation of the strain of microorganism used by the defendant was in issue; this case is pertinent to the even more special difficulties involved in patents for certain microbiological inventions which will be discussed in the next section.

The foregoing complications apply especially in the prosecution stages of patent applications in our field of study but they do not end there because they are relevant also to questions of enforcement of patent rights. Indeed it is no exaggeration to say that all patent prosecution is undertaken with the possibility of this ultimate sanction in mind.

MICROBIOLOGICAL INVENTIONS

If biotechnology is defined as the application of biological processes and organisms to industrial ends and the apparently great potential of this activity is to be exploited even more vigorously in the future it is clear that the patent laws must relate to microbiological inventions more effectively than in the past. Although inventions in microbiology are no strangers to the world of patents and a number of them have come before the courts in the first half of this century, a sense of unease with and even hostility towards patents for the 'handiworks of nature' can be detected in the early decisions. Inventions in the inanimate areas of the natural sciences such as physics and chemistry have been readily absorbed along with those of mechanics and electricity into the sphere of patent law with its emphasis on the effectiveness of the written description and the principle of operability and reproducibility of written instructions. But in recent years the difficulty of fitting biological systems neatly into the same conceptual package has given rise first to tension and uncertainty and then to the insertion of more explicit provisions in the law in order to deal with the peculiarities of living matter.

Microbiological processes and products of classical methods of fermentation of bacteria and fungi and the cultivation of viruses to produce clinically useful and other valuable materials have in the past been accommodated to the patent law straightforwardly following the practice established for chemical processes and products. The development of new strains of microorganism by selection, mutation or genetic manipulation has proved more controversial and practice has varied nationally from the most liberal policy of the former UK patent law to the more exacting 'unpatentable product of nature' viewpoint in older US patent jurisdiction.

In discussing the claim to a specific strain of *Fusarium graminearum* in Chapter 3 the difference of approach was noted in the UK, Australian and Irish patent systems and to some extent these divergent views may persist. However, following the narrow but firm majority decision of the US Supreme Court in the Chakrabarty case mentioned in Chapter 3 the US Patent Office has now included in its 'Manual of Patent Examining Procedure' a new section pertaining to practice in this field from which it is clear that a genuine conversion of mind has taken place. It is encouraging to note that a liberal attitude will now be shown to the patenting of microorganisms where the hand of man has been involved in their procurement although the substantive issues of novelty and inventive step of course remain in full effect. In parallel with this development the British and European Patent Offices have also declared informally that a similar policy will apply in their own jurisdictions. It may be convenient at this point therefore to recapitulate the principal types of patent claim open to us in this field which are:

1. Process of producing a new microorganism.
2. The new microorganism as produced by the defined process.
3. The new microorganism *per se*.
4. Process of cultivating or otherwise using the defined microorganism to produce an end product which may be:
   (a) A form of the multiplied microorganism itself e.g. vaccine or edible biomass.
   (b) A by-product of microbial growth e.g. an antibiotic, enzyme, toxin, or an otherwise useful industrial product (even if inactive biologically).
   (c) Some other product or substrate which is produced or improved by the culturing process e.g. a purified industrial product or effluent.
5. The products of any of the processes defined in (4)—defined by a *per se* claim or product-by-process claim as appropriate.
6. Particular formulations of new strains or cultures thereof, including combinations with other substances, designed to utilize and exploit their special properties, e.g. in human or animal foods or for industrial uses.

At present, the interest of many scientific workers concentrates mainly on the scope of item (3) in this list and various aspects of it must be mentioned. The first is that it is not limited to 'artificial' micro-organisms produced by some direct manipulation of the genetic components of the cell as in the case of recombinant strains obtained by DNA splicing techniques. It must also include non-naturally occurring organisms produced by mutagenic means such as have been used in the past for strain improvement. It is true that for these improvements a policy of industrial secrecy has generally been preferred to that of patenting and has been largely successful among reputable organizations which are enthusiastic for patents on other kinds of commercial development. When 'found' organisms are considered there seems no good reason to distinguish these from non-naturally occurring organisms where their isolation from nature makes available some valuable material or property which can in no real sense be said to be within the state of the art prior to the inventor's efforts. The merits of the contribution to the art can be independent of whether it is achieved by selection and isolation or semi-synthetic and manipulative processes.

Microorganism Claim Terminology

Another aspect of claiming new microorganisms *per se* is that of claim terminology. Since the function of a patent claim in most countries is one of definition a proper method of defining such entities must be found. The accepted procedure for describing or referring to new strains in such a manner that the addressee of the specification can obtain or reproduce them for himself will be considered shortly but at this point the discussion is concerned only with the content and language of the claim. Microbiologists will no doubt approach this question along lines traditional to their science and point immediately to generally accepted schemes of classification and taxonomy such as Bergey's Manual. Thus for defining purposes we can already use the name, morphology and biochemical characteristics of the new strain as the essential body structure of the claim. Although these may be alone sufficient to distinguish the strain from previously known and recorded strains it has been customary also to rely on the accession number of the deposit of the strain in a culture collection and indeed many practitioners have been content to rely almost entirely on culture collection number alone as seen in some of the examples in Chapter 3. While this may continue to be sufficient for the purposes of the claim, modern legislation and the practices developing in patent office circles on this topic strongly point to the need to include in the specification maximum data on the characterization of a new microorganism and the inventor cannot escape this burden if he wishes to secure his position with a product claim of this kind. The most comprehensive attempt so far to systematize these requirements has come from the Japanese Patent Office and a study of the 'Examination Standard for Inventions of Applied Microbiology' would be a good starting point for the inventor who wishes to co-operate fully with his patent advisers in this respect. The US Patent Office are now granting patents for 'biologically pure cultures' of organisms defined by culture collection number and a fairly brief recitation of properties usually in terms of the ability to produce specific antibiotics or other products.

With regard to claims based solely on culture collection number it should be noted that relatively little judicial consideration has yet been given to the limits to which such claims must be construed. One question for example might be whether claims drafted in terms of the deposited strain cover only the strain actually deposited and its direct descendants obtained by sub-culture of a sample of the deposited strain or whether they should be construed as also extending to independently prepared isolates which are indistinguishable in essential respects from the deposited strain.

A third possibility for the definition of a microorganism is in terms of what it will produce or how it will perform, a so-called functional definition. This is one which many inventors will find congenial because it offers a neat solution to the problem of embracing everything that achieves the same result as the strains actually obtained by the inventor. Unfortunately such an easy solution is rarely possible. In Chapter 3 US Patent No. 3,003,925 was given as an example of a claim to the use of a new species for the production of glutamate and this was a case where the functional definition succeeded. The inventors declared that they had found strains of a species of *Micrococcus* which could not be identified with species listed in Bergey's Manual and they listed a series of morphological and physiological characteristics justifying the recognition of a new species designated *Micrococcus glutamicus*. It is difficult to resist the conclusion that the significant characteristic of the new strains was their ability to produce high yields of L-glutamic acid and that therefore the claim to their use for this purpose was based in effect on this particular function or property.

This last mentioned technique of claim drafting is presumably valid where a number of strains have been isolated with a common property which gives a new result. It will not succeed, however, where the property or result to be obtained is an obvious desideratum for those skilled in the art. An illustration of the failure of the functional definition is the case involving UK Patent No. 952,820 which was decided in the British High Court and reported in 1973. The patent claim, which is set out in Chapter 3, specifies use of:

'... a strain of *Streptomyces aureofaciens* which produces tetracycline to the substantial exclusion of chlortetracycline ...'

and these strains were characterized later in the claim by reference to a harvest mash reflectance curve and a numerically defined parameter which became known as ΔR. Much of the argument in court dealt with the question whether or not such strains had to be descendants of the type strain A-377 but apart from this difficulty of interpretation the court also found that the other parameters used to define the strain were lacking in real substance or relevance. Applying again the modern version of the Cripps' test (as re-stated in the phenothiazine case, see Chapter 4), the court found that to search for a high tetracycline-yielding strain derived from A-377 was simply to follow in the path of previous workers and amounted to an obvious desideratum. The patentee's method of framing his definition in this way went unjustifiably beyond the novel strains actually disclosed in his specification and was lacking in fair basis.

In both the *Micrococcus glutamicus* case and *Streptomyces aureofaciens* case the claim was in process form but the point being made applies to the strain nomenclature used and is independent of claim form.

Finally mention must be made of another form of functional definition which is popular with draftsmen and used extensively in the 'process countries', i.e. where no product claim is obtainable. It applies especially where the product X of microbial growth is a new substance. It is based on the definition of the micro-organism as 'an X-producing strain', the strain being usually further qualified as belonging to a particular genus or species. A typical form of process claim would be:

'Process for producing X which comprises cultivating an X-producing strain of the genus (or species) Y on a nutrient medium ... and recovering X or a fraction having "X-activity" from the medium'.

This type of claim has something of the character of a circular definition and must not be so broadly worded as to constitute the mere statement of a problem. It will avoid this criticism if the content is specific enough in various respects including, for example, a precise mention of the genus or species from which the X-producing strains can be found by relatively straightforward experiment. It must of course be supported by at least one example of such a strain isolated by the inventor.

Deposition of Microorganisms in Culture Collections

It is generally admitted that where a patent relies on the use of a new strain of microorganism (not available to the public) it is difficult if not impossible to write into the patent specification a sufficiently full description of the organism and the method of obtaining it to enable the reader to reproduce the procedure and obtain the strain for himself. The practice therefore grew up under more sophisticated patent systems of depositing strains in culture collections either on a voluntary basis or as an official requirement of the patent office concerned. Practice, however, was non-uniform and on a country by country basis. Thus decisions were required for each country as to:

1. Whether deposit was necessary, where to deposit, and when to deposit.
2. Whether to make the strain publicly available and, if so, when.

Prior to the European Patent Convention (1973) no patent statute had ever dealt specifically with this problem. In the national courts there were three landmark decisions:

1. In the USA, the Argoudelis case (1970) laid down that sufficiency of disclosure could be completed by the deposit under certain specified conditions in an officially recognized culture collection prior to the date of filing the US application and on the understanding that the culture would become available to the public once the patent was granted.
2. In the UK the House of Lords, in Dann's application (1970/71) ruled that all that British law required was a written description and that the 1949 Patents Act did not superimpose the requirement of deposition as a complementary and necessary physical act. In other words the House of Lords pointed out a deficiency in existing law.
3. In Germany in the Bäckerhafe (Baker's Yeast) case (1975) the

Supreme Court held that deposition of the strain can complement the patent description but that the strain must be available upon first publication of the patent application. (This is at the early stage before there is any grant or promise of grant of the patent.)

The European Patent Convention originally included in its regulations a specific rule (Rule 28) requiring an applicant having an invention in this category to do the following:

1. Deposit the new microorganism in a culture collection not later than the European application date.
2. Add to the application identifying details of the deposit.
3. Make the deposited microorganism available from the culture collection to any person from the date of first publication of the application (18 months after the priority date).

Certain conditions and undertakings were attached to item (3) and certain timelimits applied, the most important of which was in effect that the third party could not use the strain industrially (other than experimentally) while the application was still pending prior to grant of the patent. These restrictions could not however compensate for the irrevocable loss of exclusive possession of something of vital importance at an early stage when the prospect of obtaining protection was still uncertain. Worse still, the availability of the strain remained even if no patent was granted.

Throughout the debates on this rule during the drafting of the convention many arguments were heard from participating governments and industrial and other interested circles alike against its severity. It was common ground that deposition is an integral part of providing a sufficient disclosure of the invention and must take place before or simultaneously with the filing of the application to complete the effectiveness of the written description. But availability of the strain at the time of first publication went beyond reasonable requirements and such restrictions as were imposed by the rule would be difficult to police and enforce. However, in 1973 the prevailing majority governmental view was that microbiological inventions must be treated on the same footing as all other inventions in respect of the necessity to publish the application at a specific date and therefore availability of the culture at the same date was a logical necessity. Rule 28 duly came into force for European law and provided a model for use in the updating of many national patent laws in Western Europe including the new UK Patents Act of 1977.

European industrial and professional circles could not, however, accept Rule 28 as sacrosanct and continued to seek for some amendment, first by submitting arguments to representatives of the separate national patent systems and later by expressing their views to officials of the European Patent Office after it began to function in 1978. Eventually the EPO allowed a partial concession over the controversial date of availability of the microorganism. There are two conflicting considerations which need to be reconciled here. The typical applicant for protection argues that in making the microorganism available to third parties he is supplying the physical means of performing the invention whereas all other inventors supply nothing more than information; the microbiological inventor who supplies the self-replicating cellular factory which produces the desired product is therefore a special case justifying special consideration. Moreover the point at which the full sufficiency of the disclosure is of primary significance in relation to the procedure of the patent application itself is not the date of first publication of the unexamined application but the later date on which the officially examined and accepted application is published in connection with patent granting procedure. From that time an enforceable right is obtained so that there is a *quid pro quo* for the disclosure and for making the strain available. The counter-proposition is one which looks beyond (and is strictly irrelevant to) the application itself because it is motivated by the desire in official circles to validate the early publication as a document which then becomes part of the state of the art which is citable against later applications. The latter requirement has no legal foundation in the convention but is part of patent office philosophy in some countries in Europe. By contrast in USA and Japan availability of the microorganism is not required until the enforceable right stage has been reached. The final compromise amendment accepted by the EPO applies to the period between the first and second publication stages of the European application. It allows an applicant to limit availability of the new strain in this interim to an independent expert acting on behalf of third parties but bound by certain conditions including that of not passing the strain out of his hands. It fulfils the publication status of the first publication because any independent expert on the official list instituted by the EPO is in the same position as any other skilled worker who could have obtained the strain under the original rule. The only difference in his impartiality between the applicant and the applicant's competitor. After the second publication and grant of rights has taken place, the conditions of the old rule take over in effect and the patentee must rely on his patent right to control his competitor's activities.

Subject to the officially approved experts acting in full conformity with the new rule and ensuring some measure of control over the culture while the applicant is unprotected it would seem that all parties to the debate should be satisfied. The amendment of Rule 28 is set out in full in Appendix 3.

Recognition of experts for the purposes of Rule 28 (microorganisms)

The European Patent Office has established a procedure for the recognition of experts for the purposes of new Rule 28. The formation of the initial list of recognized experts was mainly by recommendation of industrial and professional contacts and of course by the initiative of any such experts to whom this kind of work proved interesting and congenial. The experts are required to act in a personal capacity and therefore institutions as such cannot act as experts for the purpose of this rule. Experts are asked to indicate their suitability for work of this kind by reason of their independence (especially lack of conflicting interests), their technical expertise in relation to a specific area of microbiology, and their access to the necessary equipment and other experimental facilities.

The expert is expected to carry out as much as possible of the experimental work personally for reasons of security but it is recognized that the use of assistants under the control of the expert may be unvoidable for the performance of certain tasks. The use of assistants is to be minimized and in any event the expert must accept responsibility for them.

Microbiological experts need to have an indication of the kind of work entailed by their inclusion in the official list. Typical examples of topics in which the expert's advice will be required are questions of taxonomy, identification of microorganisms and reproduction of experimental details given in patent specifications for the cultivation of the new strains and the assessment of products produced by microorganisms as regards properties, chemical identity and so forth. An expert who is prepared to be entered on the list must be assumed to be willing to enter into commitments of this kind for appropriate remuneration by the party represented but unreasonable demands on the time and effort available will not be made; the expert will be free to decline involvement in specific cases if there is any incompatibility with the expert's other duties and indeed for any good reason.

The Budapest Treaty 1977

Given that deposition of a new microorganism in a culture collection is necessary in connection with a patent application and given that it must be made available to the public at a certain stage of patent procedure two questions arise—where must the culture collection be and who are the public to whom it must make cultures available? Since patent laws have historically been essentially national laws there would inevitably be a logical tendency to answer these questions on a territorial basis. Indeed the original Argoudelis ruling in the USA though not explicitly demanding that the culture collection be on US soil was stated in terms which could have been thus interpreted and accordingly there was some uncertainty as to the essential location of the collection under US practice. This uncertainty remained until a later court case gave a non-restrictive answer to the question. Japanese practice was quite positive about deposition in a Japanese culture collection although it accepted the re-deposit there from another collection during the pendency of the Japanese patent application. Since the public to which any patent is addressed is primarily the public in the territory covered by the patent it would have been reasonable though highly inconvenient for every patent examining body to require a deposit in its own territory.

Recognizing the need for general agreement over the procedure for deposition the UK Patent Office raised the matter with the official body responsible for international aspects of patent law and practice, the World Intellectual Property Organization (WIPO) and in 1973 attempts began to internationalize this procedure so that deposit in any one officially recognized culture collection would suffice for the purposes of multiple patent applications on a broad international scale. This led to the signing in 1977 of the 'Budapest Treaty on the International Recognition of the Deposit of Microorganisms for the Purposes of Patent Procedure' and its ultimate ratification by a sufficient number of signatory states to bring it into force by the end of 1980.

Under the Budapest Convention a culture collection can become recognized as an 'international depository authority' by the furnishing of assurances by a contracting state that it will comply with the specific requirements of the treaty as to acceptance and storage of microorganisms, documentation, furnishing of samples etc., indeed all the things that the leading culture collections of the world have been doing for many years as a matter of course for the scientific community. In 1981 the first culture collections to become recognized were the two

US collections ATCC and NRRL, the Japanese FRI, Dutch CBS, German DSM, and in early 1982 the British NCYC and NCIB.

The value of the Budapest Convention is in the first place the practical one that deposition in a single depository is effective for a patent application in any country that ratifies the convention. The fortunate inventor who has an international depository in his own country can make the deposit more easily than if the culture has to be sent abroad. Sending cultures to other countries may involve the obtaining of import licences, e.g. in USA, and this can cause delay and have even more serious consequences if a licence is refused. For all countries which have ratified the convention the national patent law requirement is met by deposit in a single culture collection and so there is no impediment to the grant of valid patents in these countries. If there is a legal impediment to the import into any country of the biological material necessary for the performance of an invention it must follow that the value of a patent in that country becomes questionable and may even reduce to zero except in relation to the importation of final products of the process concerned. The distinction between the validity of a patent and the value of the patent to its owner finds yet another application in this situation. The convention is also helpful in case of loss of viability of a deposited strain, the status of the deposit being unaffected if the depositor promptly redeposits the same organism.

The furnishing of samples of the deposited microorganism by an international depository authority is governed by Rule 11 of the regulations of the convention. The depositor is mainly concerned here with the part of it which deals with release to third parties (Appendix 4). One procedure is for the third party to obtain a certificate from an industrial property office which has published the patent application referring to the strain and identifying its accession number in the collection. All this procedure is handled by prescribed forms of document but the essential purpose of the certificate is to inform the culture collection that the requesting party has the right to receive the strain under applicable national law whereupon a sample can be issued by the culture collection without fear of legal complications. The necessity to proceed in this way stems from the fact that there are still differences of national law and practice regarding the stage or stages at which patent applications are published. For USA, as noted above, the patent is not published before it is actually granted and therefore instead of the certification procedure, which is inapplicable in the case of US patents, the alternative is for the patent office to notify the culture collection from time to time of the grant of US patents which refer to deposited strains, this being the signal that there is no patent law impediment to the release of the strains to others. In practice culture collections will prefer to hear directly from patentees in this connection.

The Problem of Reproducibility

It will be appropriate to refer here to the problem of reproducing experimental conditions and reported results of which practising biochemists and microbiologists are aware. Organic chemists are not immune to this problem and it sometimes takes some repetition before reported yields can be reproduced for a chemical process but with biological systems the many unknown factors which affect the behaviour of microorganisms even when all prescribed conditions have been met present a special difficulty in patent law. The German patent law has always demanded a high standard from the applicant in respect of reproducibility. It was experienced in acute form long ago by plant breeders in connection with the German plant patent law under which the German Patent Office insisted on a description of a repeatable plant breeding process which would result in the new variety. It would not accept the argument that once a new plant variety had been brought into existence the new plant would itself be the progenitor of all future individuals of that variety. Provided the new variety would breed true the legal requirement of utility was fulfilled and there would be no purpose served in describing the long and arduous process of arriving at it. The same attitude can be detected today in German decisions on claims for new microorganisms. According to these if the claim is to the strain *per se* then a reproducible method of preparing it must be given and mere deposition in a culture collection (as a source of supply) is insufficient. This strict view of the law imposes an impossible standard in the case of the isolation of many new strains from soil or other sources because there can often be a low probability of repetition of the isolation method with precisely the same results. This is not due to the shortcomings of the inventor or his descriptive powers but is inherent in nature itself. Fortunately, the US, UK and European Patent Offices do not follow the German courts on this question.

Chapter 8

Patents in Genetic Engineering

In order to make the research worker familiar with some of the key concepts of patent law and the way patents are obtained previous chapters have dealt with aspects of this subject on which a wealth of experience has been gained by patent attorneys practising on behalf of inventors in areas of classical chemistry and microbiology. With the science of genetic manipulation, however, we come to a subject which is strange ground to the patent lawyer and one where he is called upon to go in for prediction to a more than usual extent. The genetic manipulators think in abstract conceptual terms to a high degree and speak in a recondite language which is formidable to patent practitioners with the standard background in chemistry and the other natural sciences. It presents them with unusual difficulty in achieving the level of comprehension which is necessary before any effective patent work can be undertaken. The special problem of communication between research worker and attorney in this field therefore commands preliminary attention.

In the discussion between inventor and patent adviser about any new piece of research it is usual for the latter to take much of the initiative because he shares often the same technical background as the inventor. He is therefore usually well placed to cross-question the inventor over the 'metes and bounds' of his invention and sometimes to explore avenues which the inventor may not have examined. With the present subject, however, there may well have been too much specialization to enable this cross flow to occur readily and it will probably be more than ever necessary for the inventor to recognize his obligation to communicate a considerable amount of background knowledge to his advisers as well as the novel gems which he has discovered.

The inventor will want to hear from the attorney what sort of things can be patented in genetic engineering and the attorney will want to know from the inventor what he has done which is patentably distinguishable from the increasing body of literature on this subject. Those who have to meet the costs of patenting will want to consider whether

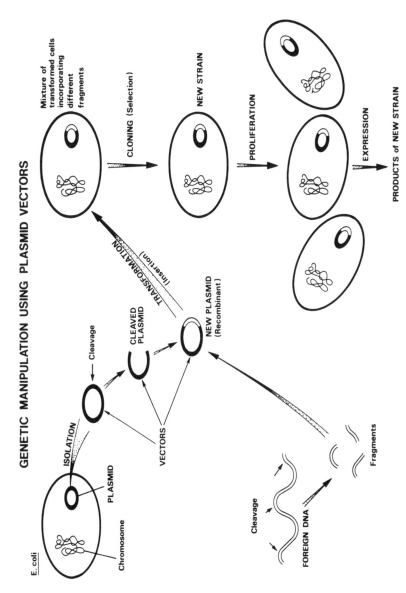

Figure 4. Genetic manipulation using plasmid vectors

what can be patented is worth patenting, i.e. whether it can result in a piece of property which can be effectively exploited, policed, exercised or licensed.

Our simplest way into this topic is to consider a basic ground plan of genetic manipulation using plasmid vectors as set out in Figure 4. This points immediately to a selection of typical items suitable for protection under the categories studied in Chapter 3 including process techniques and new products. A similar approach could be followed for the application of viral replicons as vectors but it will be better to concentrate here on plasmid methodology in order to simplify the analysis. Before identifying the items which might qualify for patent protection one might pose the general question of whether we can expect to find anything patentable in this branch of research. Bearing in mind the requirement for novelty and inventiveness are we not dealing here simply with the application of established methods to particular cases? At present one can only offer a cautious answer to this question because the data are insufficient for any firm conclusion. Until a sufficient number of applications have been filed, worked their way through the system, and endured the rigours of opposition procedure or some other form of challenge we can do little more than observe that every patent claim must be judged on the basis of the prior art and especially the documents revealed in the official search for novelty and inventive step. To genetically manipulate the production of a particular known product, using 'conventional' methods for isolating or synthesizing the gene and incorporating it into one of the well-worked plasmids and transforming cells with the hybrid plasmid, may possess novelty but be lacking in the requisite degree of inventiveness in a particular case. But one should beware of facile summary dismissals of this kind for in practice the application of these techniques may be far from straightforward and the particular tricks necessary to make them effective may well add the missing element of ingenuity. Reverting now to the scheme depicted in Figure 4 the following topics arise for consideration.

CATEGORIES OF INVENTION

1. Choice of host/vector relationship

   This is a doubtful qualifier but is mentioned on account of the possible merit there might be for reasons of safety or especial convenience in the choice of the basic system in which the manipulations are carried out. To bring together a particular plasmid and a particular host cell may have some patentable significance.

2. Isolation of plasmids

These methods are generally well known and effective and therefore it is unlikely that for this step in the technique new patentable methods will arise.

3. Enzymes for cleaving and sealing

The development of new sources of restriction endonuclease and other types of enzyme used in the successive steps of this technique could be productive of patents. There is of course a market for these agents in research work and this may be sufficient to justify the cost of patent protection. The patenting of new enzymes with favourable cleavage patterns on polynucleotide chains should follow the lines indicated previously for inventions of this kind.

4. Recombinant DNA

Hybrid plasmids are new substances and assuming that the problem of accurate definition can be overcome there appears no reason why product-*per se* claims should not be allowed for them. How a plasmid must be defined in a patent claim may eventually be the most controversial aspect of this subject. Two extreme possibilities are immediately apparent, the one being a broad definition in terms of gene function and the other being the narrow definition in which the complete nucleotide sequence is specified.

5. Transformation conditions

New methods of inducing cells to take up hybrid plasmids or to achieve this with increased efficiency could be patentable.

6. Cloning (selection)

New and especially effective methods of separating out transformed cells from a shot-gun operation, including ingenious marker systems, may also be considered. Both this topic and the transformation conditions of the previous section can obviously involve scientific ingenuity as tools of research but it may be doubted whether patents of individual practical exploitable value will derive from this kind of inventiveness.

7. New strains

This category involves probably the most usual form of claim associated with genetic engineering inventions and the one which has provoked the greatest controversy in recent years. The main battle appears now to have been won but some residual skirmishes may be ahead over subsidiary issues. The US Supreme Court's approval of the Chakrabarty product claim to:

'. . . a bacterium from the genus *Pseudomonas* containing therein at least two stable energy-generating plasmids, each of said plasmids providing a separate hydrocarbon degradative pathway . . .'

was probably well received by the bulk of the patent profession concerned and it was right that the issue was limited to the one essential question of principle. This was whether a living organism which otherwise complied with the legal requirements for patentability was nevertheless disqualified from protection merely because it was alive. But some have felt surprise at the broad scope of the claim involved in the case and the absence of any discussion of this question in the more significant argumentation and judgments throughout the entire proceedings. It is presumably to be expected, in the first crop of patents issuing on what to patent office officials is a new field, to find broad claims accepted but once the subject has become familiar to examiners there will no doubt be more critical treatment meted out to broad functional claims of this type.

The Chakrabarty claim is not typical of the form of claim envisaged for new strains produced by the methods more commonly understood as genetic engineering, of which gene splicing is an essential feature. The novelty in these claims will be largely centred on the new plasmid component so that the terminology used to define the recombinant DNA will be reflected in the claim to the organism.

8. Use of new strains to produce final products
   Process-of-use claims will be comparable in importance to organism claims because the commercial potential clearly lies in the production process and the final products (usually known products) which are produced thereby in some improved manner.

EXAMPLES OF PUBLISHED PATENTS AND APPLICATIONS

This brief analysis has drawn out of the scheme illustrated a series of categories in each of which inventions might conceivably arise. However, in dividing the subject in this way it can readily be seen that in few of the categories mentioned would there be much incentive to patent. Many of the steps in the technique are useful in research but do not have the character of continuous or batch-repeated processes of the industrial type and little useful purpose would be served in patenting them except as part of a portfolio-building patent policy in aid of a package licensing programme. In this approach it has also been taken for granted that the technique as a whole is so well-known that one has to look for improvements in any of its component steps as candidates for patentability. However, in December 1980 US Patent No. 4,237,224 was granted on the work of Professors Stanley Cohen and Herbert Boyer with the following first claim:

'A method for replicating a biologically functional DNA, which comprises:

transforming under transforming conditions compatible unicellular organisms with biologically functional DNA to form transformants; said biologically functional DNA prepared *in vitro* by the method of:

(a) cleaving a viral or circular plasmid DNA compatible with said unicellular organism to provide a first linear segment having an intact replicon and termini of a predetermined character;

(b) combining said first linear segment with a second linear DNA segment, having at least one intact gene and foreign to said unicellular organism and having termini ligatable to said termini of said first linear segment, wherein at least one of said first and second linear DNA segments has a gene for a phenotypical trait, under joining conditions where the termini of said first and second segments join to provide a functional DNA capable of replication and transcription in said unicellular organism;

growing said unicellular organisms under appropriate nutrient conditions; and

isolating said transformants from parent unicellular organisms by means of said phenotypical trait imparted by said biologically functional DNA'.

This was granted on an application which had been filed in January 1979 but which was the consummation of a series of applications deriving from a first application filed in November 1974 and linked together by the well-known and highly convenient continuation-in-part procedure of US patent practice. The utilization of this practice, whereby inventions of seminal importance have their patent rights held in abeyance for many years before issuing in surprising form, is a common feature of the patent scene in USA.

Among the patents and applications which are now beginning to appear, e.g. as early published applications in Europe a notable example is a group of European applications including 78,300,597.8 and 78,300,596.0 (equivalent to UK Patent No. 2,008,123A) on the production of peptide hormones such as somatostatin and insulin by recombinant strains of *Escherichia coli*. This example illustrates the lack of straightforwardness of the basic proposition mentioned earlier in that it is not directed simply to the incorporation of the synthetic genes for these substances into a well-known plasmid. Indeed the mere incorporation of the gene is insufficient to achieve the desired end result because even though the gene is expressed in its new habitat any resulting peptide hormone appears to be destroyed in situ. Therefore protective measures are necessary and resort is had to a system in which a larger and more resistant molecule is biosynthesized from which the wanted hormone can be ultimately chemically cleaved. The relevant claim expresses this as follows:

'A method of producing a specific polypeptide involving expression of a heterolologous structural gene therefor in a recombinant microbial cloning vehicle, wherein the structural gene is in reading phase with a DNA sequence coding for a protein other than said polypeptide so that expression yields a precursor protein comprising both the amino acid sequence of the polypeptide and additional protein containing a selective cleavage site adjacent to the desired polypeptide's amino acid sequence'.

A third example is British Application 2,003,926A which is directed to the production of single cell protein by means of microorganisms modified so as to contain the gene which enables them to assimilate ammonia by the route catalysed by glutamate dehydrogenase (GDH). The process uses *Methylophilus methylotrophus* or other organisms transformed with plasmids e.g. RP4 or phage into which the GDH-specifying gene has been inserted. The following typical claims are included:

1. A process for producing single cell protein wherein microorganisms containing genetic material specifying ammonia fixation by the GDH enzyme route are aerobically cultured.
8. Aerobically cultured microorganisms of one or more species which are capable of utilizing methanol to produce proteinaceous cell material by the GDH ammonia fixation mechanism as the result of genetic modification by plasmids or

plasmid hybrids or phage or phage hybrids each carrying DNA specifying the production of the GDH enzyme.

10. A method of making genetically modified microorganisms by incorporating into basic microorganisms one or more plasmids carrying the gene of the GDH mechanism which comprises the steps of: (a) producing from the basic microorganism a mutant deficient in genetic material specifying glutamate synthesis by the GUS mechanism; (b) preparing a plasmid hybrid consisting of plasmid DNA covalently joined to DNA specifying production of GDH enzyme; (c) introducing the plasmid hybrid into the GUS-deficient basic microorganism; (d) culturing the resulting microorganism in conditions favouring growth by the GDH mechanism; (e) selecting one or more clones of microorganisms growing by the GHD mechanism'.

The genetic manipulation procedures are described in general terms and by means of flow diagrams but without detailed experimental examples of the kind usually present in patent specifications.

REPRODUCIBILITY AND DEPOSITION

The question arises how far the written description of genetic manipulation inventions suffices as an 'enabling' disclosure. Starting from known and available plasmids and using known and available reagents it should in general be possible to write up the details of enzymatic cleavage methods, methods of extending or chewing back terminal groups, methods of ligation and so on with a degree of precision sufficient for the reader of ordinary skill to reproduce the technique and prepare the recombinant plasmid for himself. The same should apply to the subsequent stages of transformation, selection and final cultivation.

One might argue that there is no necessity to deposit either plasmids or recombinant strains in culture collections. Indeed the current form of Rule 28 of the European Patent Convention recognizes this argument in its preamble which confines its application to the case of a microorganism:

'... which is not available to the public and which cannot be described in the European patent application in such a manner as to enable the invention to be carried out by a person skilled in the art'.

The corresponding UK rule (Rule 17 of the Patents Rules, 1978) is still equivalent to the primitive form of original Rule 28 and does not contain the second limb of the saving clause mentioned above. Therefore the applicant would have to argue, if the case justified it, that the written disclosure was sufficient in itself and that therefore the legal requirement was met without application of the rule. This argument, if sustained, would dispense with the need for deposition. Plasmids are not microorganisms and this technicality can presumably be invoked to avoid all these rules but the recombinant strain cannot escape the present wording.

The present US practice favoured by the 'Manual of Patent Examining Procedure' requires deposition where the microorganism is not 'known and readily available to the public' and although this does not have the same statutory force as the British Rule 17 the practice in UK and USA will probably be the same for some time to come. In the case being postulated, i.e. where the applicant maintains that he has described a reproducible method it would be possible to argue that the US rule is not mandatory. But most applicants for US patents may not be willing to take the risk involved in not depositing the strains in the first place because in the event of an adverse ruling on the point it may well be too late then to avoid the consequences of what would be a holding of insufficient disclosure.

Chapter 9

Patenting Strategies:
Development of Patent Portfolios

The type of patent protection available in the chemical and biological sciences is such that any person or firm concerned to promote invention and marketing of new processes and products in this field must come to terms with the patent system. A patent policy of some sort cannot be avoided. This might be a negative one in the case of a manufacturer having a limited research and development base, or none at all, and content to seek entry into a patent stronghold by licence negotiation with patent-conscious firms or by making use of legally permitted compulsory licence procedure in territories where this is possible. Usually, however, wherever there is a significant research and development expenditure there will be a correspondingly positive attitude to the protection of the inventive results of this investment especially where new products emerge from it. If this positive policy has an aim and a structure we may describe it as a patenting strategy.

In general, to say that patent strategy must depend on a preceding decision to research a more or less defined area is to observe a platitude. Indeed, it may seem unnecessary to remark that patents must lie in the wake of the discoveries that actually occur rather than constitute the object of research. The scientist will know how unwise it is to attempt to forecast the outcome of research or to impose a pattern upon it in the interests of patent protection of a preconceived type. With these pre-liminaries stated, however, it is sensible in the devising and management of research programmes to pay attention to avenues which may result in potentially useful patent property. To this extent the involvement of patent advisers in some of the planning stages can be beneficial.

One obvious component of strategy is the acquisition of a patent portfolio, a group of patents stemming from a chain of research which may be straight but is more commonly branched. Again this tends to be the natural growth and outcome of decisions which are based on the goals of the research itself and the problems encountered *en route*.

Whether the innovating party is concerned with constructing a protective hedge around his commercial activities or accumulating strong cards to play in the almost inevitable licensing game with his associates or competitors he is almost certain to require a number of patents to establish a significant bargaining position.

To discuss these topics at length in the abstract is of limited value and it will be more instructive to proceed straightaway to illustrative case studies. There have been two parallel developments in the pharmaceutical field, both leading to clinical products of immense value to medicine and great commercial success for their innovators, which offer an opportunity to make a comparison of the patent structures which developed out of research partly in academic establishments and partly in industry. These are the penicillin and cephalosporin families of antibiotics.

The basic discovery of penicillin was of course much earlier than that of the first cephalosporin but the later stages in the development which gave rise to the modern generation of semi-synthetic penicillins and cephalosporins occurred as roughly contemporary events showing differences more striking than their similarities. The history of these developments from the scientific viewpoint has been written more than once by those who were close to the action and its broad outlines are well known. To follow a parallel course of the patenting history that went with it cannot be attempted in depth without considerable research and some contact with the inventive prime movers themselves or with contemporary observers. This is because there is in all developments of this kind and especially the industrial component a strong element of confidentiality which can persist for a long time after the event so that to attempt subsequently to assess what patents were of key importance is a matter of deduction rather than evidence. In the schemes now presented there is much deduction from published knowledge and the general consensus on the impact of the inventions described.

THE PENICILLINS

The scheme of these developments is given in Figure 5. It is a commonplace that the earliest observations by Fleming of the powerful antibacterial activity of a substance produced by *Penicillium notatum* were published without benefit of patent cover. The subsequent demonstrations of its chemotherapeutic power in man by the Oxford University team led by Florey also went unprotected. Much mythology has been

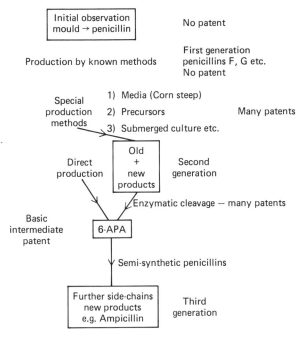

Figure 5. Penicillins

generated around these and related questions and unwarranted conclusions have been drawn as to the consequences of the failure of the academic scientists, in Britain at least, to be in the slightest degree patent-minded at that time. No critical appraisal has apparently been proposed of what kind of protection could have been achieved in the circumstances in which the discoveries were made and over the time span from initial observation to isolation of the active substance. The basic discoveries and the production methods used on a research scale which led to the first generation of products, penicillin F, G etc. do not seem to have been patented.

The transfer of the production problem to the USA and the wartime Anglo–American collaborative achievement gave rise to the first crop of important patents covering more efficient methods of producing the antibiotics in high yield and the directed biosynthesis of particular products. Notable among these are the corn steep liquor US Patent Nos. 2,442,141 and 2,476,107 (equivalent UK Patent Nos. 618,415, 618,416 and 624,411) and a group of patents covering the addition of chemically defined side-chain precursors to the fermentation medium including phenylacetic acid and its various derivatives, US Patent Nos. 2,423,873, 2,440,355, other substituted acetic, oxyacetic and thioacetic acids US Patent No. 2,479,295/6 (equivalent UK Patent No. 643,514) and phenylethylamine US Patent Nos. 2,451,853 and 2,475,920 (equivalent UK Patent No. 586,930). Examples of submerged culture methods which were patented are US Patent No. 2,443,989 (equivalent UK Patent Nos. 618,415/6) covering agitation and aeration conditions and US Patent No. 2,448,790 (equivalent UK Patent No. 600,657) on the use of molasses in association with aeration at defined pH. The development of improved strains of penicillium is less evident in the patent literature but US Patent No. 2,458,495 (equivalent UK Patent No. 691,242) on the use of *Penicillium chrysogenum* var. *brevisterigma* is one instance where patenting was thought desirable.

So far, the patents emerging from this phase of development were of the process type. The use of precursors could give rise to second-generation penicillins which were new in the sense of not being the natural products of the prior known fermentation methods, e.g. phenoxymethyl penicillin. Indeed some of the patents mentioned above are said to be 'directed to novel penicillins and to processes of producing them' but the claims are mainly directed to 'a method of producing a novel penicillin' and there is a notable absence of what are nowadays recognized as product-*per se* claims. Whether this was due in part to the insufficient knowledge then obtaining of the chemical structure of these products is not entirely clear but, except for the case of penicillin V, the product patent situation was unusual. One can have too much of a pre-occupation with product patents, however, and the substantial importance of many of these early process patents for anyone manufacturing penicillins commercially cannot be denied. Most of these patents appeared in the late 1940s.

The first development which led to a major controlling patent of the product type came in 1956/7 with the isolation and chemical identification of the penicillin nucleus 6-APA and the filing of an originating UK patent application in August 1957. This patent, UK Patent No. 870,396, which is a celebrated example of a basic dominant product patent for a key intermediate was based on direct isolation of 6-APA from a penicillin fermentation carried out in the absence of added precursors. The form of its product claim and that of the corresponding US Patent No. 3,164,604 were mentioned in Chapter 3. Although the process for producing 6-APA by direct isolation from broth was not destined to be a method of sustained industrial interest the importance of this invention in providing basis for a product claim which stood at the fountain head of the semi-synthetic penicillin industry cannot be easily over-estimated.

The development of improved methods of producing 6-APA by enzymatic cleavage of the 6-amino side-chain from penicillin was clearly the next milestone in patent terms and a number of patents duly appeared on the use of penicillin amidases from defined micro-organisms. Some quite broad claims issued on this subject, at least in UK patents, of which mention may be made of UK Patent No. 892,144 with its broad claim to the use of microbial penicillin amidases, UK Patent No. 891,173 with a wide method claim drawn to the use of mould de-acylating enzymes, and UK Patent No. 897,617 in which the claim extends to the use of a bacterium (or an enzyme obtained from it) defined by a functional test in terms of penicillin G inactivating properties. Nature has provided a wide variety of sources of enzyme for cleaving side-chains in penicillins and a selection of these were patented but it is difficult to say on the face of the documents alone whether the commercially preferred enzymes could be narrowed to any particular microbial source.

The highly efficient methods of producing the parent antibiotic and splitting out its nuclear component provided a convenient supply of 6-APA for the abundance of research which now flowed in the direction of new final products. The quantity of new penicillin patents issuing week by week has built up into a total too numerous to be counted. They tend to follow a standard pattern of construction including generic product claims to general structural formulae followed by many specific product claims to chemical sub-genera and species. Ampicillin and amoxycillin are two outstanding examples of synthetic product patent in this field which have been subject to litigation.

The patents obtained on the special production methods are com-monly said to have been held in US hands and to have effectively con-trolled post-war commercial development of penicillin technology for many years. With the grant of the 6-APA patents a restoration of the balance towards UK industry was achieved and licences were necessary to permit the marketing of semi-synthetic penicillins of clinical value promoted by other parts of the world pharmaceutical industry wherever the dominating product claim was obtained (or broad process protection for the preparation of final products by the 6-APA route). The value of the 6-APA patent was also enhanced in the UK and those British Com-monwealth territories which followed the 'saccharin doctrine', so called from the old British case in which it was established. The effect of this was that any final product made from 6-APA outside the jurisdiction of but subsequently imported into the British or Commonwealth territory where the 6-APA patent existed would be itself an infringement of the claim to 6-APA and therefore require the permission of the patentee.

THE CEPHALOSPORINS

From the isolation in Italy in 1945 of a wild strain of a species of Cephalosporium similar to *Cephalosporium acremonium* and the subsequent study of this organism and its antibiotic producing properties in Oxford University has stemmed a new family of important substances active against both gram positive and gram negative organisms. It is remarkable that exploration of the original members of this family of antibiotics, having chemical structural similarities to the penicillins, fell to the same university laboratory which had done so much on the early penicillin work and presented the university workers with the opportunity this time to achieve important patent protection from the early stages of the research.

A number of early patents were taken out on processes for the production of the variety of antibiotics first discovered in fermentation broths (cephalosporins P and N) but the first break of potential major importance came in the mid-1950s. In the course of working up the culture fluid for the production of N (shown to be a penicillin) the observation was made by Abraham and Newton of the presence of minute amounts of another substance, designated cephalosporin C, which was active against penicillinase-resistant staphylococci. Again, this and the subsequent exciting history has already been told but our patent scheme begins essentially with the patenting of cephalosporin C (UK Patent No. 810,196) as a new product, the source of future generations of antibiotics having a fused β-lactam-dihydrothiazine ring system instead of the corresponding β-lactam thiazolidine ring system in the penicillins. The respective structures are:

Penicillins   Cephalosporins

Cephalosporin C was one of the examples given in Chapter 3 to illustrate a type of product claim which was successful where the full chemical structure had not yet been established. The UK patent law at this time (1949 Patents Act) allowed product-*per se* claims whereas the previous Act (operative at the time of the Oxford workers' isolation of penicillin) had allowed only product-by-process claims.

Compared to penicillin the production of cephalosporin C by fermentation was difficult and gave low yields. Attempts to improve it by application of precursors, which had proved so successful in the case of penicillins, completely failed for the cephalosporins. It was not until 1958, after a particular mutant strain had been developed and other technical problems had been solved, that sufficient quantities could be produced for further research, structural studies, and human trials.

The potency of cephalosporin C was recognized almost from the beginning as too low to be of lasting clinical utility and therefore chemical modifications and the preparation of derivatives began quite early to generate a number of product patents many of which eventually turned out to be of minor significance. Lactonization by acid catalysed intramolecular reaction of the 3-acetoxymethyl and 4-carboxy substituents produced a compound known as cephalosporin C_C which was of low antibiotic activity. By contrast, the activity of C itself could be increased by reaction of the 3-substituent with heterocyclic bases such as pyridine to produce a group known as C_A compounds. These derivatives were still not sufficiently high in activity but the reaction itself later proved of great value in the development of subsequent compounds.

Patent strategy at this time was to protect any development that could conceivably be significant in the long term in a field which was still totally open but of uncertain future. The only brake upon this policy was in regard to territorial extent and the estimate of cost-effectiveness of the protection especially in countries where only process cover was available. Cephalosporin C, C_C and C_A compounds can be regarded as the first generation of compounds and it should be noted that none of their chemical structures had been elucidated within one year of their respective basic national filings.

The invention which clinched the decision of potential licensee industrial companies to enter the cephalosporin field came in 1959 with the investigation of acid hydrolysis breakdown products of cephalosporin C and the identification of the chemical structure of both C and its nuclear component 7-aminocephalosporanic acid (7-ACA). This led to the 7-ACA patent (UK Patent No. 953,695) and a parallel patent (UK Patent No. 966,221) for the first group of synthetic analogues of the parent substance by acylation of the free amino group of 7-ACA.

In contrast to 6-APA, 7-ACA could not be recovered directly from the fermentation broth. Its first method of production by acid hydrolysis of the parent substance resulted in very low yields in view of the large number of competitive reactions also catalysed by acid and it was recognized at the outset that it could not become the basis of commercial production of the intermediate. Some side-chain protective measures were attempted but without significant improvement in yields. The enzymatic side-chain splitting methods were applied and it has been recorded that hundreds of marine organisms, bacterial species and other microorganisms were tried without success. Some firms found these problems so daunting, i.e. the difficult fermentation and lack of a convenient route to 7-ACA, that they withdrew from the field after a short time.

The patent structure achieved by this time and its subsequent development are shown in Figure 6.

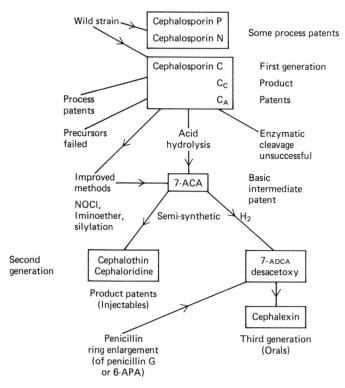

Figure 6. Cephalosporins

The 7-ACA patent now stood in relation to cephalosporin research as the 6-APA patent had done for the synthetic penicillins except that before the field could be opened up to the full extent an effective method of producing the intermediate in quantity was required. The existence of a key intermediate-product patent of this type with its promise of being crucial to new chemical routes to future cephalosporins would have justified a major investment in research into chemical methods of removing the aminoadipic acid side-chain but by the remarkable good fortune of those who had pinned their hopes to this project success came quickly. Within one year the nitrosyl chloride/formic acid method was discovered by US research workers and matured into US Patent No. 3,188,311 (equivalent UK Patent No. 948,858). This method was not a direct acid hydrolysis of the type used by the inventors of the first method mentioned earlier but depended on the intramolecular cyclization of a chemically modified side chain resulting in an intermediate product which spontaneously cleaved in acid conditions to liberate the free 7-amino group.

It was the nitrosyl chloride method which opened the way to exploration of the levels of biological activity obtainable with alternative side-chains and this led in 1961/2 to the first two semi-synthetic cephalosporins of clinical value, cephalothin (US Patent No. 3,218,318; UK Patent No. 982,252) and cephaloridine (UK Patent No. 1,028,563). Cephalothin, the 2-thienyl compound, and cephaloridine, its corresponding C_A (pyridine) derivative:

Cephalothin

Cephaloridine

were the foremost members of what can be called the second generation cephalosporins. They are active by injection and have achieved considerable hospital use against life-threatening infections and are especially valuable for the treatment of patients sensitive to penicillin.

The main thrust of the research had now moved into the industrial sector and into a highly competitive search for new final products and methods of producing 7-ACA effectively on a commercial scale. This phase of the development illustrates the falsity of the assumption that patents block progress in the biological field. One alternative to the nitrosyl chloride method for producing 7-ACA was soon provided by the iminoether method developed by Swiss workers. This involved conversion of the carbonyl portion of the 7-amido group in a cephalosporin C derivative (having protective substituents at certain parts of the molecule) first to an iminochloride and then to the iminoether which underwent mild acid hydrolysis to give a 4-carboxy protected nucleus which was readily convertible to 7-ACA itself. This process and its later improvement are to be found in UK Patent No. 1,041,985 and its patent of addition 1,119,806. Subsequently the method was improved further in other hands by the use of silylating agents to protect the free amino and carboxyl groups in the parent material and these developments were also protected by patents. A complex pattern of chemical process patenting was now forming with rights held by many of the competing companies in the field.

Meanwhile, in 1961, another discovery had occurred which passed almost unheralded at the time but later assumed significance. It was found possible both in cephalosporin C and 7-ACA to reduce the 3-acetoxymethylene group to methyl by hydrogenation over a palladium catalyst so giving rise to the deacetoxy cephalosporin system. One of the most important members of this class was to be 7-aminodeacetoxy cephalosporanic acid (7-ADCA) initially obtained directly from 7-ACA. It was recognized as an intermediate and was covered by US Patent No. 3,124,576 but the process of making it was too costly to be commercial. It also could not have been realized at the time of discovery that the 3-methyl group would be an important feature of the orally active compounds that were yet to be developed. It was not protected territorially to the same extent as 7-ACA.

The first orally active compound of major clinical significance was in fact a derivative of 7-ADCA having an α-aminobenzyl side-chain, the compound known as cephalexin:

Cephalexin

Cephalexin was introduced into medicine commercially in 1969. One method for preparing cephalexin would be by conversion of 7-ACA to 7-ADCA followed by acylation to introduce the 7-α-amino phenylacetyl group, a route which was therefore dominated by two product patents covering the intermediate nuclei. It was not a commercially acceptable method for the reason previously stated. However, it had previously been found possible to convert penicillin sulphoxides into cephalosporin compounds and this development provided the key to a practically successful method for the production of cephalexin.

The discovery that the cephalosporin ring system could be synthesized by ring expansion of penicillins opened up intriguing possibilities of altering the patent situation which until then had revolved mainly around the 7-ACA patent as the primary controlling factor in the commercial chemistry. This discovery is reflected in US Patent No. 3,275,626 which had been applied for in mid-1962 and issued in 1966 with broad claims to the conversion of penicillin sulphoxides by heating at 100–175 °C under acid conditions. This method could be applied to the sulphoxides of 6-APA and a wide range of its 6-acylated derivatives and gave rise to a 3-methyl substituent in the resulting thiazine ring, a highly convenient outcome if one wishes to produce cephalexin. Development of the method gave rise to improvement patents, e.g. UK Patent Nos. 1,204,394 and 1,204,972 directed to the use of particular solvents for the reaction and a fresh outcrop of further chemical process patents owned by different parties duly appeared which cannot be detailed here.

The US product patent for cephalexin is US Patent No. 3,507,861 which was obtained as a continuation-in-part to the basic ring expansion US Patent No. 3,275,626 mentioned above. The equivalent is UK Patent No. 1,174,335 and contains the disclosure of the two available methods of producing the product, i.e. from 7-ACA and by ring enlargement.

Cephalexin could now be prepared by a number of alternative routes starting from 6-APA or the relatively cheap starting materials penicillins G and V. Proceeding from 6-APA the cephalexin side-chain could be introduced first and the sulphoxidation and ring expansion procedure would then follow. Starting from penicillin G the sulphoxidation and ring expansion stage would produce the corresponding 3-methyl cephalosporin and a variety of alternative methods could then be carried out to convert the benzyl side-chain into α-amino benzyl.

The above exposition of the development of the penicillins and cephalosporins has of necessity been presented in a simple form to illustrate the fascinating chess board of patents that can come into existence from the interplay of chemistry and microbiology and the collaboration of academic research with that in industrial laboratories. The whole story is of course highly complex in each case and not fully known to those who have not been immersed in it continuously over many years. Consequently the conclusions that can be drawn by out-siders must be of limited scope. It is clear, however, that as the com-plexity of the patent situation grows with important advances being made by various research groups in different countries the more difficult it is for any party to maintain a monopolistic position. Indeed in both cases chosen there has been a fruitful flow of international licensing of significant technology and the function of the patent structure in all this activity has been to provide an important part of the framework or ground rules by which the game has been played out.

Chapter 10

The Enforcement of Patents

The considerable effort and expense of obtaining patent protection around the world are not undertaken lightly or without purpose. The notion that wicked industrialists will often patent valuable inventions in order to leave them quietly to accumulate dust or actively to suppress them is one of the fantasies of popular imagination which surround the subject of patents and is so far removed from reality that the patent practitioner has the greatest difficulty in accounting for its origin. The conversion of an invention into a patent results in the creation of a form of property, a right which can be utilized and must in some way be used or exploited if the investment of time and money in securing it is to produce a return.

A patent can be retained and exploited by the original owner or it can be transferred for this purpose to another person or body by assignment. In an assignment the donor is the assignor and the recipient is the assignee. A licence is not a transfer of any right of ownership but merely an immunity conferred by the licensor on the licensee. The primary purpose of obtaining protection for an invention is to obtain the legal right of exclusion and to exercise that right if necessary, and patents have historically been used more to achieve this their primary purpose than to provide the vehicle for technology transfer. Exploitation by the patentee alone therefore must be regarded as the norm applying where the patentee can supply the whole market from his own resources by direct manufacture in the home territory and by export or through the use of overseas subsidiaries. A patentee who operates in this way will sooner or later need to develop a policy with regard to exercise of the patent against imitators.

INFRINGEMENT

The unauthorized use of a patented invention is described as 'infringement' and is actionable at law in all patent systems. As a technicality it

171

does not depend on knowledge and intent (unlike the law of copyright) and the innocent or inadvertent manufacture, use, or sale of a patented invention is still infringement under the law. The use of an invention for the purposes of experiment is said not to be infringement but this statement must be clarified. The performing of an experiment on the subject of a patent in order to evaluate the invention and to test the adequacy of the patent description is about all that is clearly permitted before the act takes on the nature of an infringemet. To go further and to use the invention in connection with an experimental programme of a broader kind cannot usually escape the rights of the patentee simply on the ground that it is connected with research and not immediately with commerce. This is all the more true where the context of the research is ultimately to derive profit or material benefit of some kind. Nevertheless an owner of a right does not always exercise it and will normally consider the nature and scale of the infringing use as well as the cost of stopping it before embarking on enforcement of his patent.

Patent litigation is a civil action with the patentee as 'plaintiff' pursuing the infringer who is the 'defendant'. The plaintiff has to demonstrate to the court that the defendant's activities amount to a true infringement of the patent which the court is then asked to quell by the issuing of an injunction against further infringement and an award of damages for past infringement. The defendant will almost invariably deny that he has infringed the patent and will also counterclaim that the patent is invalid over prior art or for some other reason. Therefore before entering upon a lawsuit the patent owner will need to assure himself that his patent is likely to be held valid and enforceable. In some countries, notably UK and USA, the trial of the two separate issues of infringement and validity takes place in the same court and is heard as part of the same action whereas in others the issue of validity of the patent must be resolved in a different court from that in which the infringement trial takes place. These matters being dealt with according to the different national laws, it will be impossible here to survey the whole subject and a limited selection of examples must suffice. A broad acquaintance with the principles involved in infringement actions will enable the inventor to appreciate even more the importance of the patent claims and why it is necessary to take such trouble over these in the prosecution of the patent application.

It will be convenient to begin with the law on infringement in the United States and in Great Britain because of their similarities. These two systems exemplify the importance of the literal interpretation of the words used in the patent claims in relation to the scope of the patent and both adhere to the principle that the language must first be construed by the court to arrive at its meaning and scope. Nevertheless British and US courts are prepared to look to some extent beyond the strict literal sense of the claim (textual infringement) and to hold that infringement can occur by the substitution of equivalents for what is claimed or by the taking of what amounts to the substance of the invention or its 'pith and marrow'. Furthermore the harmonization of British and European patent law has also made a difference which the British courts must follow in the approach to the determination of the scope of a UK patent and this will undoubtedly affect the principle of literalism which has hitherto been central in the UK tradition.

In Britain it was not until 1977 that a definition or prohibition of infringement was written into the statute and the tort derived from a combination of the royal command in the words of the patent grant and the decisions of courts in case law as to what constituted forbidden acts. The express definition is of older tradition in US patent law and provides a better starting point for discussion.

Infringement in US Law

A US patent confers the 'right to exclude others from making, using, or selling the invention throughout the United States referring to the specification for the particulars thereof' (United States Code, Title 35—Patents, Section 154). Since the specification must 'conclude with one or more claims particularly pointing out and distinctly claiming the subject matter which the applicant regards as his invention' (Section 112) it is evident that infringement is decided by reference to the claims. Section 271 defines infringing acts as follows:

'(a) Except as otherwise provided in this title, whoever without authority makes, uses or sells any patented invention, within the United States during the term of the patent therefor, infringes the patent.

'(b) Whoever actively induces infringement of a patent shall be liable as an infringer.

'(c) Whoever sells a component of a patented machine, manufacture, combination or composition, or a material or apparatus for use in practicing a patented process, constituting a material part of the invention, knowing the same to be especially made or especially adapted for use in an infringement of such patent, and not a staple article or commodity of commerce suitable for substantial non-infringing use, shall be liable as a contributory infringer.

'(d) No patent owner otherwise entitled to relief for infringement or contributory infringement of a patent shall be denied relief or deemed guilty of misuse or illegal extension of the patent right by reason of his having done one or more of the following: (1) derived revenue from acts which if performed by another without his consent would constitute contributory infringement of the patent; (2) licensed or authorized another to perform acts which if performed without his consent would constitute contributory infringement of the patent; (3) sought to enforce his patent rights against infringement or contributory infringement'.

These sections (a), (b) and (c) may be described respectively as direct infringement, inducement to infringe and contributory infringement.

Direct infringement is a relatively straightforward matter once the court has made up its mind as to the scope of the claim and the nature of the defendant's product or process has been established in evidence. The court will interpret the claim and not attempt to amend or re-work it from the disclosure and it will take into account anything the patentee has relied on during the prosecution of the application insofar as it has a bearing on this investigation. The patentee cannot stretch his claim in court beyond his posture in prosecution; he is prevented from doing so by what is known as 'file-wrapper estoppel'! The following quotation from the great lawyer Judge Hand will, however, encourage the inventor in his struggle with the limitations of language:

'Courts do indeed treat the language of claims plastically, now stretching to save the whole scope of the invention, now squeezing to limit the claim so that it can survive. There are no absolutes; when justice requires, it is a question of filling the language as full as it will bear without bursting, or of pressing it so long as it will not quite break, though of course the words have their limits . . . were this not true, any ingenious mechanic might pick an inventor's brains at pleasure'.

The protection given by the claim extends also to the making of products for export even though actual sale is outside the USA. As to importation into the USA there is an important difference between product and process claims. A product claim is infringed by importation but a process claim will not itself prevent importation of a product made by that process outside the country. It is important therefore to obtain a product claim of some kind, if at all possible, to control the situation by means of the patent law. A product-by-process claim may be effective in this connection but such claims are usually difficult to obtain especially where the product is not a new substance *per se*.

The contributory infringement provision of Section 271 (c) and its corollary (d) codify a long and intricate historical development of US case law. This provision has always been of great importance and benefit to patentees and one which the patent law of many other major countries has at last begun to emulate. Its main impact has applied to the discovery of new properties and new uses for old chemical compounds and other substances which by definition could not be patented as products and perhaps could not be effectively protected as compositions or special formulations. It has meant that such inventions could be patented as processes or methods in the knowledge that sale of the compound or material would be covered by the patent and could be controlled by licensing or otherwise. It was not necessary therefore to pursue every user small or large in order to reap a benefit from such a patent. The application of the contributory infringement doctrine is limited, as stated, to non-staple articles and those which do not have a substantial use other than that of the patented use. This proviso reflects the chequered legal history of the doctrine in the light of an established principle of US anti-trust law condemning monopolization of anything other than the subject of the patent itself. There seems not to be a controlling definition of what is meant by a 'staple article' and it is not entirely clear that it must be something of a distinct kind from the commodity referred to in the ensuing words of the sub-section. It probably means a generally available raw material or commercial commodity and especially one that is perishable or consumable in the course of use according to the patent. On such an important point of law one would require specialist advice in a particular case.

Most contributory infringement cases arising in the US courts over a period of almost a century have revolved around the sale of unpatentable disposable items used as components of patented combination devices and systems, or unpatented materials used in patented processes, e.g. paper and ink in a printing mechanism, dry ice in a refrigeration package, and salt tablets for a dispenser, Having been decided before the present law of 1952 was enacted, most cases refused to support the doctrine under consideration and therefore the 1952 statute can be regarded as corrective legislation to restore a limited doctrine of contributory infringement. The Supreme Court has recently confirmed the state of the law in the important case of Rohm and Haas Co. *v.* Dawson Chemical Co. involving the sale of the compound propanil as a herbicide for use in a patented method of treatment of rice crops (the claim is set out in Chapter 3 as an example of method of treatment patents). The court held that:

> 'Section 271 (c) identifies the basic dividing line between contributory infringement and patent misuse and adopts a restrictive definition of contributory infringement that distinguishes between staple and non-staple articles of commerce'.

The compound propanil was not itself the subject of a product claim and in fact the patentees of the method of use patent had succeeded in other proceedings in preventing the grant of a product claim for propanil to another party. The issue was fairly drawn therefore to the legality of a method of use patent being applied to control the sale of an unpatentable substance used as an essential element of the method. Propanil being a non-staple substance and indeed one which had no other practical use this was a clear case for the application of Section 271 (c) and the patentee won though by the narrowest majority. The patent misuse argument used by the defendant will be outlined in the next chapter because of its closer connection with the subject of patent licensing.

Equivalency in US law

The doctrine of equivalents in US law encompasses a vast quantity of case law much of which is concerned with invention in the mechanical arts. The leading principle is whether 'the two devices do the same work in substantially the same way, and accomplish substantially the same result'. The extent to which it applies depends on whether in the assessment of the court the invention is pioneer, a marked improvement over prior art, or only a narrow improvement and the range of application extends from allowing a broad range of equivalents to virtually none at all.

In the leading case on the subject (Supreme Court, 1950) a claim calling for the use of an alkaline earth metal silicate in a welding flux was held infringed by the use of manganese silicate, it being clear from the prior art that this was a known equivalent to magnesium silicate (used in the patentee's composition). Because the question of what constitutes equivalence depends on all the circumstances of the case it remains a matter of uncertainty and weakens the case of the patentee in licence negotiations and other dealings outside litigation. The burden is upon him to convince the other party that the doctrine would apply in his favour. There is no substitute for claims which are broad enough to 'read on' what the other party actually makes or does.

The patentee's argument that what is being done is an obvious equivalent of what is claimed will provoke the question why, therefore, was it not clearly included within the scope of the claims when these were formulated. The real answer sometimes is that clever thought has been given by the other party to 'designing around' the words of the claim but often it is because the examiner has insisted on a particular claim formulation during prosecution and the hard-pressed applicant, faced with the alternative of a costly appeal, has taken what was on offer without deeply considering how evasion of literal infringement might ultimately be contrived. In the manganese silicate case mentioned above there were other claims in the patent which would have covered the use of the substituted material but these had been held invalid by the court. It was a sort of rough justice therefore for the court to support the patentee on the point of equivalence in relation to the more narrowly worded claims.

Product-*per se* claims to organic compounds present an open field for debate as to the application of the doctrine of equivalence. One opinion is that there is less room for the principle to operate here than in the case of multiple component compositions in which one component is substituted by another substance. For composition claims there is already precedent for extending the scope of the numerical range of proportions of specified ingredients e.g. (1) 13% held to infringe a claim reciting a 1–10% range of the particular component and (2) a minimum requirement of 0.04% magnesium in an alloy held infringed by 0.02%. But *per se* claims to individual new compounds have been held to cover related material where the court has been impressed with the merit of the invention. A claim to the α-DL form of an analgesic compound was held infringed by the α-D isomer because the invention was rated as pioneer and the α-D compound performed substantially the same function in substantially the same way. Similar reasoning could be applied to the case of an important intermediate compound intended for conversion into a biologically active final product in which a functional derivative of the compound (synthesized indirectly) is substituted for the claimed intermediate. In the microbiological field, the doctrine might reasonably be expected to extend to the substitution of closely related strains of microorganism where the differences between the two entities are smaller and more difficult to visualize than in the case of organic compounds of known structure.

Because equivalence is a matter of the court's discretion and depends on the significance of the invention it can never be taken for granted by inventors and patent attorneys in the early stages of creative drafting of the application. It must always be openly considered in the process of drawing up the first specification and will often point to the need for further experimental work before filing is undertaken.

Finally, brief mention must be made of procedural matters. US patent infringement cases are heard in the Federal Courts. The choice of District Court in which to sue is governed in part by the venue rules applicable to domestic or foreign parties to the action and to a significant extent by the varying attitudes to patent validity and infringement shown by the different courts and especially the corresponding Courts of Appeal. The latter consideration is popularly referred to as 'forum shopping'. Leave to appeal to the Supreme Court can sometimes be granted. Duration and costs of infringement actions are like the proverbial piece of string but can be anything up to ten years and a million dollars depending partly in the issues involved but more upon the tenacity and depth of purse of the combatants.

Infringement in British Law

Before the 1977 Patents Act the principles of the law of infringement were derived from a study of the cases. As in USA the decisions of the British courts contain the same two streams of tradition, the one stressing the controlling effect of the words of the claim the other moderating the severity of pure literalism by appealing to the concept of an infringement of the 'substance' of the claim or its 'pith and marrow'. So we have the classic quotation from the High Court in 1894 that:

'In order to make out infringement it must be established that the alleged infringer, dealing with what he is doing as a matter of substance, is taking the invention claimed in the patent: not the invention which the patentee might have claimed if he had been well advised or bolder, but that which he has in fact and substance claimed on a fair construction of the specification'.

It will be noticed that even this strong statement, which patentees frequently rely on in infringement actions, is tempered by the notion of 'substance'. In 1911 the High Court introduced the distinction between 'essential' and 'non-essential' integers in relation to the specifically recited components of the claim. The following is an extract from the famous passage of the judgment.

'It is a well-known rule of patent law that no one who borrows the substance of a patented invention can escape the consequences of infringement by making immaterial variations. . . . Again, where the patent is for a combination of parts or a process, and the combination or process, besides being itself new, produces new and useful results, everyone who produces the same results by using the essential parts of the combination or process is an infringer, even though he has, in fact, altered the combination or process by omitting some unessential part or step and substituting another part or step, which is, in fact, equivalent to the part or step he has omitted. The question here, again, is a question of the essential features of the invention said to have been infringed. If that part of the combination, or that step in the process for which an equivalent has been substituted, be the essential feature, or one of the essential features, then there is no room for the doctrine of equivalents, and, to ascertain the essential features of an invention, the specification must be read and interpreted by the light of what was generally known at the date of the patent.'

In view of the age of some of the leading cases on pith and marrow or equivalents there has been a tendency for lawyers acting for defendants in modern times to propose to the courts that the doctrine is dead as a result of the increasing emphasis placed on the role of the claims in patent law. The courts have refused to make this pronouncement and have reserved their right to apply the doctrine in suitable cases. A celebrated recent case in which the argument again arose was the infringement action brought on the ampicillin patent against importation of the defendants product hetacillin. The relevant structures are as shown.

Ampicillin

Hetacillin

The broad product claim of the ampicillin patent, UK Patent No. 873,049 (see Chapter 3), specified a free amino group in the α-position in the side-chain. Hetacillin being the reaction product of ampicillin with acetone does not contain such a free amino group and therefore does not itself fall within the strict literal wording of the claim. The preparation of hetacillin from ampicillin is an infringement of the claim to the latter compound but in this case the process was carried out outside the UK and therefore beyond the jurisdiction of the British court. The defendants were destined to fail because of a particular precedent in the English law of infringement by importation (known as the saccharin doctrine). However, on the point of textual infringement and the issue of pith and marrow they succeeded in the first court. On the latter point they failed in both the Court of Appeal and in the House of Lords which held hetacillin to be ampicillin 'albeit temporarily masked' and a clear case for the application of the pith and marrow doctrine.

The hetacillin case was one where the precision of chemical language allowed a relatively clear answer to be given on the question of textual infringement and this is normally the case where a structural formula is used in the claim. Sometimes the meaning of a single chemical term can prove more troublesome as in a more recent case where in a hearing lasting 103 days a good deal of the time was taken up in arguing the meaning of the term 'a polyhydroxyacetic ester'. The claim was to a surgical suture made from this material. The defendants argued that the claim was limited to the use of a homopolymer produced from hydroxy-acetic acid or its dimer glycollide which would therefore have a simple straight chain backbone. If so the claim would not then cover the defendant's product which was made of a 90/10 glycollide lactide co-polymer which contained a small proportion of methyl groups attached to the main carbon to carbon chain. This was not a pith and marrow case though it sounds like one in the final outcome. The whole of the infringement aspect was concerned with how the claim was to be construed. In the end it was held not to be limited to homopolymers but to embrace the possibility of some co-monomer units provided the amount of these was not so great as to prevent expression of the essential qualities of the homopolymer.

This last case was one in which the role of the expert witness in patent cases received a modern airing. It is a time-honoured principle in British patent lawsuits that the scientific experts brought by one or both sides to the dispute are there to assist the court on the state of the art, the meaning of technical terms, and the common general understanding of skilled workers in a particular field at a particular time. Of course the experts are acting for one of the protagonists and this is given due weight but as scientists of integrity they must give an objective account of the technological background. They must in no way appear to pre-empt the decision of the court in matters of law or findings of fact but simply restrict themselves to giving the evidence from which the judge will draw the necessary conclusion. The traditional role of the expert in relation to the meaning of individual technical terms was extended in this case to sentences and paragraphs in the patent specification which are 'technical in flavour and connotation' and on which they can properly be asked what these mean to them. Furthermore they could be asked about terms or phrases even when these were part of the claims, the hitherto guarded stronghold of the lawyers alone.

British statutory definition

Section 60 of the 1977 Act states that a person infringes a patent if:

'(a) where the invention is a product, he makes, disposes of, offers to dispose of, uses or imports the product or keeps it whether for disposal or otherwise;

'(b) where the invention is a process, he uses the process or offers it for use in the United Kingdom when he knows, or it is obvious to a reasonable person in the circumstances, that its use there without the consent of the proprietor would be an infringement of the patent;

'(c)   where the invention is a process, he disposes of, offers to dispose of, uses or imports any product obtained directly by means of that process or keeps any such product whether for disposal or otherwise'.

This may be described as direct infringement and broadly codifies the previous law. It does not refer to the patent claims but it is always understood that the invention is defined by the claims.

Among certain acts which are exempted from the definition of infringement are those done 'privately and for purposes which are not commercial'. This phrase has not yet been interpreted but it probably applies to acts done by persons in their capacity as private individuals where no element of trading is present. It should not be confused with acts performed in the privacy of industrial research laboratories.

Another aspect of infringement which has a long history of controversy about it has been settled by the 1977 Act, namely, the indulging in activities which fall short of taking the whole of the invention defined in the claims but which have the character of contributory infringement or inducing infringement. Section 60 (2) also defines as infringement the act of one who:

'. . . supplies or offers to supply in the United Kingdom a person other than a licensee or other person entitled to work the invention with any of the means, relating to an essential element of the invention, for putting the invention into effect when he knows, or it is obvious to a reasonable person in the circumstances, that those means are suitable for putting, and are intended to put, the invention into effect in the United Kingdom'.

This provision could prove of great practical importance. For the purposes of satisfying the examiner that the applicant is claiming a patentable combination of features, or a fully operative combination, it is often necessary to include in the claim an item which can be supplied separately, especially a consumable or disposable element of the combination. In the past, a loophole to easy avoidance of the patent by omission of this particular item was offered by a law which did not recognize the 'aiding and abetting' of infringement as wrongful. This provision is also relevant to process claims directed to a new use of a known compound. However, the sub-section does not apply to the supply of a staple commercial product unless made for the purpose of inducing infringement.

Infringement by importation (saccharin doctrine)

It is a general rule that to import into any country a product falling within the terms of a valid product claim subsisting in that country is an infringement. Where the invention is a process and there is no product claim as such in the patent in the country into which the product is imported, a more qualified answer has to be given to the question of infringement. It is the law of many countries that the protection given by a process claim extends also to the direct product of that process in which case importation of that product will be an infringement. This was the national law of many European countries before the European patent was instituted and it is now explicitly stated in EPC Article 64(2).

The British law was even more generous to the patentee in the matter of infringing importation as applied to process patents and the saccharin case decided in 1900 was the prototype decision. The process patent in that case was for the preparation of the *o*-toluene sulphonyl chloride intermediate which required two further chemical steps before saccharin was itself produced. The importation of the final product was therefore not an activity caught by the above mentioned rules since there was no relevant product claim and the imported product was not the direct product of the process claimed. Nevertheless the strong sense of equity in British law again prevailed to protect the patentee from being so easily by-passed by another party who would still derive profit and advantage in the UK from the patented invention through the technicality of territorial jurisdiction. The importer was held to be infringing by 'indirectly making use of the invention'. It was decided in 1925 that the saccharin doctrine has to be qualified by the proviso that the process carried out abroad 'must have played more than an unimportant or trifling part in the manufacture abroad of the product, each case depending in its own merits'. Both these factors were present in the ampicillin case and the plaintiff's success is clear proof that the saccharin doctrine was good law up until the enactment of the Patents Act of 1977. This Act now includes a definition of infringement and Section 60(c) deals explicitly with importation in relation to process inventions. The clause refers to importation of 'any product obtained directly by means of that process'. It remains to be seen whether this limitation, which is in harmony with EPC principles, will override the more extensive common law tradition of the British courts.

Infringement of European Patents

The European Patent Convention does not deal with the question of infringement. This is because the European patent, as an object of property, is of ephemeral existence only. Once the patent is formally granted by the European Patent Office it enters into the so-called national phase in which its separate registration in the designated territories must take place. Thus the European patent stratifies into a bundle consisting of a European patent (UK), a European patent (France), and so on. Infringement then becomes a matter of national law under the relevant patent in the national court of the country where it occurs. There is a period of nine months in which the European patent is open to central attack in formal opposition proceedings but after that period has expired a potential or actual infringer who wishes to clear the ground must seek to invalidate the patent, or risk being sued for infringement, territory by territory.

The convention does touch, however, on a point affecting infringement in that it has something to say on the interpretation of patent claims. It includes a protocol which states that the protection of the patent is not defined by 'the strict literal meaning of the wording used in the claims' but neither do the claims 'serve only as a guideline'; the position is 'between these extremes'.

The other form of European patent, i.e. the Community patent which is provided for by the Community Patent Convention will exist as a single indivisible property right from the moment of grant and will be effective for the territory of the Community as a whole. It will be recalled that this convention awaits ratification and therefore no such patents yet exist. Unlike EPC, however, CPC does define the right a Community patent confers on its proprietor. Articles 29 and 30 define infringement by direct use and indirect use respectively, and in terms which are broadly similar to those already discussed in relation to national laws on direct infringement and contributory infringement.

Problems of timescale

The non-lawyer is naturally impatient at the law's delay. The inventor who feels that his invention is particularly meritorious will not highly rate a system that keeps him waiting year after year before the fact is recognized. Even after the examiner has been persuaded to allow the application to proceed to publication and/or grant there will be an opportunity for third parties to institute formal opposition or revocation proceedings so that the eventual outcome is further suspended. The result is that should an 'infringer' appear in the scene it will be difficult to apply any immediate effective restraint. The USA is a notable exception to the general rule that the term of a patent runs from the date of application and in a controversial case up to about half of this can be taken up in the process of procuring the patent. A significant further portion of the term will run out before an infringement and validity trial reaches a final conclusion. The existence of appeal proceedings in relation to all these stages of prosecution and enforcement of rights contributes towards the protracted nature of the whole exercise. Of course the infringer is taking the risk that the patent will ultimately be found valid and that he will have to pay for past infringement committed after the patent application was first published. Furthermore a patent can be sued on after it has expired, subject to any statute of limitations in the local law.

Where the parties to an infringement action are competitors between whom there is little dialogue the action will be brought speedily after the essential preliminaries. The patentee may notify the infringer of the existence of the patent, obtain evidence of commercial sale, produce proof that the product is an infringement, e.g. by chemical analysis, and then serve the writ. Proof of infringement may be difficult to provide especially in the case of a process patent and indeed it may be practically impossible to proceed at all without a *prima facie* case that infringement has occurred. To inspect the infringer's process in order to confirm the fact of infringement requires a court order for 'discovery' and this cannot be obtained until the action has reached a later stage. In granting such an order the court will strictly limit the number of observers and will ensure that the defendant's legitimate commercial secrets are protected.

As a partial solution to the time problem it is possible for a patentee to obtain a preliminary injunction (also called an interim or interlocutory injunction) as soon as the defendant's product appears on the market. This is not a full trial of the issues but an attempt by the patentee to freeze the defendant's commercial activities until the full trial can be heard. The patentee must establish a *prima facie* case of infringement and show that in the circumstances a temporary hold is a fair balance of the interests of both parties.

Chapter 11

The Exploitation of Patented Inventions

This chapter is concerned with the exploitation of inventions by means of a transfer or sharing of patent rights. This method of exploitation contrasts with the policy of exploitation exclusively by the original inventor or owner of the rights which, as we saw in Chapter 10, may involve the problem of enforcement to maintain that privileged position. A complete transfer of ownership in a patent is an assignment executed by means of a document of the same name which can be recorded on the official register of the relevant patent office and usually must be so registered before the new owner can exercise, i.e. enforce, the patent on his own behalf. A licence confers the right to operate under the patent and this may also be registered if desired. Assignments and licences (or agreements to license) can be effected while the application is pending.

THE ASSIGNMENT OF PATENTS

Where the original inventor or applicant lacks the resources necessary for development or exploitation of an invention on a significant commercial scale it may be desirable to seek a suitable body, be it an industrial company or other corporate body, in which to vest ownership and responsibility for exploitation. The private inventor or small company which has an invention beyond its market power to exploit fully can enter into an agreement with the larger or more effective body either to exploit the invention directly itself or to license it to others. Assignment may be effected for a lump sum or for a continuing royalty or for a combination of payments of this kind.

Safeguards which the original inventor or owner of the rights will wish to include in the assignment agreement will include the following:

1. A commitment of the assignee to use its 'best endeavours' to exploit the invention. It will be difficult to define a precise criterion under this heading and the assignee will not usually accept more than an 'in good faith' undertaking and certainly not one that requires a

reassignment of the rights if performance does not measure up to expectation.

2. An undertaking to meet the costs of patenting including the inventor's costs of assisting in the patenting and/or exploitation process.
3. A regular accounting for income derived from exploitation and a sharing of revenue if appropriate.
4. An offer of reassignment of patent applications or patents in any country in which the assignee is unwilling to maintain them.

In turn the assignee will require the following:

1. The right of decision as to the best mode of exploitation and the power to execute the decision without reference back.
2. The right of call upon technical assistance from the inventive source including know-how and technical data in their possession and collaboration in all patent matters.
3. Full discretion over the territorial extent of patenting undertaken at its own expense.
4. Assignment of, or at least access to, further inventions and improvements related to the original invention(s).
5. Consultation in regard to publication by the inventors and the timing of these in relation to patent applications.

These items are the basic minimum of patent aspects of assignment agreements and they are usually supplemented by other provisions depending on the circumstances. For example where the assignee is to exploit the invention by direct use it should be made clear where responsibility lies for obtaining clearance of the product from public health authorities.

In assigning inventions in this way the individual inventor or group of research workers has to take a great deal on trust from the assignee and must therefore have confidence in the body selected to handle exploitation. It is clearly inadvisable to enter into agreements which are open-ended especially about financial matters. One should look very closely at gentleman's agreement clauses which provide loosely for some form of payment at some unspecified time at some notional royalty rate depending on the circumstances and the extent to which the assignee company has itself contributed to the commercial success of the invention such to be determined at the assignee's sole discretion. Another pitfall is to enter unwarily into blanket agreements to assign all inventions of the particular research group arising in a broadly defined field. There may of course be circumstances in which the inducement to accept provisions of this kind is strong. For example the assignee may contribute substantial financial support to the development of the research and may offer the inventive source an unrivalled opportunity for collaboration in a field in which the assignee has special expertise, test facilities and other technical attractions. Moreover, the assignee must have reasonable protection for the future in a high-risk venture of this kind. The rule of reason must prevail here as in all other contracts and a willingness on both sides to debate these issues at the outset with some showing of flexibility is a good omen for the future relationship.

THE LICENSING OF PATENTS

Licensing is the most common form of shared exploitation where the licensor and licensee are comparable in size, have complementary expertise, wish to avoid duplication of research and development effort, and perhaps require cross-licensing in process technology or across a product field.

1. A *plain* licence is *non-exclusive* and any number can be granted.
2. A *sole* licence implies that exploitation is shared between the patentee and one licensee only.
3. An *exclusive* licence places exploitation in the hands of only one licensee and excludes the patentee.

Although there are commonly recurring factors of licensing practice and licence agreements follow a standard ground plan each situation has its own individual character depending on the participants and all the other ingredients of the mixture.

The licence itself is usually a brief formal document of standard type which can be registered in the patent office to provide a public record of the licensee's position.

The licence agreement is the normal place for the detailed terms settled between the parties, and these can vary considerably in complexity. One expects to find the following items covered:

1. Identification of parties.
2. Preamble and recitals—business background and desire for relationship.
3. Definition of keywords—e.g. basic technology, patent, technical information, know-how, improvements, developments, field of use, subsidiary company.
4. Scope of licence—identification of field and technology, manufacturing and/or selling rights.
5. Territorial extent.
6. Exclusive or non-exclusive—period of exclusivity.

7. Down-payments—if any.
8. Royalty rate and royalty base—volume of production, gross or net selling price.
9. Guaranteed minimum royalty—or break clause.
10. Most favoured nation.
11. Infringement provisions.
12. Compulsory licence provisions.
13. Duration and termination conditions.
14. Settlement of disputes.

The negotiating team for each party will normally comprise someone at or close to board level in charge of policy but the key member may often be a licensing executive whose main qualifications are sound knowledge of the technology and ability to evaluate its worth to licensor and licensee, negotiating skill, and at least some general legal and patent law knowledge. The team will frequently include a lawyer responsible for drafting the agreement and a patent agent with a thorough grasp of the total patent position.

It is common practice for a potential licensor and licensee to enter into an option agreement before concluding the main licence agreement. This gives the licensee a limited period of time in which to evaluate the technology to be licensed. The option will define the patent rights to be licensed and the technical information to be transferred and will delineate the scope of the option and the nature of the intended licence (exclusive or non-exclusive, worldwide or restricted territorially). It will provide the time period during which the option may be exercised and will state exactly how the option may be exercised to bring the licence agreement into effect.

Although the straight patent licence is still in use most companies prefer the mixed agreement covering both patent rights and know-how because this gives the parties greater flexibility in the terms of the agreement and the agreement will still survive even though the patent rights undergo alteration or are lost altogether. Bearing in mind that all such agreements have to contend with the brooding omnipresence of anti-trust laws it is very useful in the opening recitals of the agreement to state the intentions of the parties and what they are seeking from each other freely and in good faith as a mutual declaration of the non-restrictive non-coercive nature of the agreement.

The grant clause sets out in broad terms the rights that are being granted and typically includes the following provisions:

1. Whether the licence is exclusive or non-exclusive.
2. A licence to manufacture, and the area or territory in which this licence may be exercised, together with any reservations of rights that may be made by the licensor.

3. A licence to use and sell, and a demarcation of the territory throughout which the licence is granted.
4. A right to sub-license may frequently be given particularly where the grant is of an exclusive licence.

Where the technology can be used in more than one field it is common to grant field of use licences and these can be exclusive in defined fields if necessary.

Provisions for the payment of royalties will include a definition of the royalty base, i.e. the item used as the base against which the percentage royalty rate is applied to determine the royalty due. The royalty base must be reasonably related to the licensed technology. Royalties are often calculated as a percentage of the net selling price of the licensed products and a graduated scale may be used. Frequently there will be provision for a minimum annual royalty regardless of the amount of use especially where the licence is exclusive.

Most agreements provide for an initial transfer of a substantial body of know-how and information. For a chemical process this would include, for example, a detailed description of the process, a flow sheet showing major items of equipment, operating parameters, material balances, raw material and product specifications, analytical procedures and so forth. There will also be provision for technical assistance between the parties, exchange visits and continuing access to improvements to the process made by either side.

As to the patent aspects of licence agreements it is important to provide for the conduct of prosecution of patent applications, for a situation in which patents fail to issue or are held invalid, and for responsibilities as regards infringement by third parties.

One might suppose that the terms of the agreement would be left entirely for settlement between a willing licensor and a willing licensee. There is, however, a third dimension, that of public policy, in the form of laws designed to safeguard free and fair competition such as the anti-trust laws and laws on restrictive practices. Many countries have national laws of this kind as in USA where Federal laws, including the Sherman Act of 1890, the Clayton Act of 1914 and others, have created a domain for the specialist anti-trust lawyer in which ordinary mortals tread with great uncertainty. The Federal structure of USA and the importance of unhindered trade between the separate States have provided the model for similar legal concepts in the Treaty of Rome establishing the European Economic Community. The principle of free circulation of goods within the community has repeatedly clashed with the principle of the legitimate exercise of national rights of industrial property and has produced much case law.

Anti-trust in USA

These laws are directed primarily against commercial practices which give rise to monopoly and restraints on competition, as can be seen from the following.

Sherman Act

1. Every contract, combination in the form of trust or otherwise, or conspiracy, in restraint of trade or commerce among the several States, or with foreign nations, is declared to be illegal . . .
2. Every person who shall monopolize, or attempt to monopolize, or combine or conspire with any other person or persons, to monopolize any part of the trade or commerce among the several States, or with foreign nations, shall be deemed guilty of a misdemeanor . . .

Clayton Act

It shall be unlawful for any person engaged in commerce, in the course of such commerce, to lease or make a sale or contract for sale of goods, wares, merchandise, machinery, supplies, or other commodities, whether patented or unpatented, for use, consumption, or resale within the United States . . . or fix a price charged therefor, or discount from, or rebate upon, such price, on the condition, agreement, or understanding that the lessee or purchaser thereof shall not use or deal in the goods, wares, merchandise, machinery, supplies, or other commodities of a competitor or competitors of the lessor or seller, where the effect of such lease, sale, or contract for sale or such condition, agreement, or understanding may be to substantially lessen competition or tend to create a monopoly in any line of commerce.

The Clayton Act also condemns price discrimination, acquisitions of competing companies, and interlocking directorates.

Patents and patent licensing practices come within the purview of anti-trust to the extent that they conflict with the broad aims of the law in that field. The patent law authorizes the creation of individual monopolies limited in subject matter, duration and geographical extent. There is therefore inevitably an interface and sometimes a collision between the patent system and anti-trust and the guardians of anti-trust philosophy, the US Department of Justice.

The anti-trust division of the DOJ outlined in 1972 certain specific patent licensing practices considered by them to be illegal *per se* but since that time has made it clear that it can never provide a for-all-time exhaustive guide for the businessman. The following list of items to be avoided or at least considered carefully derives from US anti-trust law but most of them have relevance to international licensing in general. Some are intrinsically bad (*per se* violations) whereas others have to be judged according to circumstances.

The tie-in

As a condition of securing a licence, the licensee is required to purchase or otherwise obtain goods or services from the licensor which are outside the scope of his patent protection.

The tie-out

A restriction placed on the licensee's freedom to purchase or otherwise deal in the products of the licensor's competitors.

Mandatory package licensing

Package licensing is legitimate, convenient and often necessary where the licensor holds many patents covering the licensed technology. It should not, however, be a condition of granting a licence on the relevant patents that the licensee must take the whole package.

Excessive royalties

It is often convenient and acceptable to both parties to measure royalties on some basis other than the exact coverage of the claims of the licensed patents and freely-entered commitments of this kind are probably safe. However, any element of coercion of the licensee to pay royalties on its total sales regardless of whether the products fall within the claims of the licensed patents constitutes a *per se* violation of the anti-trust laws. Another example of excess under this heading is the requirement to pay royalties after expiration of relevant patents.

Restrictions on re-sale

The first authorized sale exhausts a patent monopoly and further restrictions may not be imposed upon a purchaser by the licensor. This was once considered to be a *per se* violation but the law is now said to be less clear on the point.

Specific DOJ targets

The Department of Justice has indicated that it will seek court decisions branding the following restrictions as illegal: price fixing, licensee right of veto on further licences, exclusive grant back provisions (assignment or exclusive licence), quantity restrictions.

The rule of reason

The topics listed above have been declared *per se* violations by court decision or have been alleged to be such by the DOJ. Many other categories of restriction exist which commend themselves from time to time to businessmen for inclusion in licence agreements. These can either attract or be free of anti-trust objections depending on the circumstances. Thus field of use restrictions can often be justified in the public interest. Field of use restrictions are legal if truly based on technological distinctions but not when they amount in reality to marketing restrictions or the division of markets between companies that would otherwise be competitors. Similarly the US patent law authorizes licensing for specific parts of the USA and therefore territorial restrictions of this kind are acceptable. Division of world markets clearly runs foul of the Sherman Act. The non-exclusive grant back of improvements developed by a licensee is acceptable under the rule of reason. Cross-licensing of patents is permissible so long as it does not take on the character of patent pooling by a group with the aim of forming an exclusive club. Finally under this heading it is important to note that nothing in United States law, statutory or court made, suggests any intrinsic wickedness in an exclusive licence.

The patent–anti-trust interface

Related to anti-trust philosophy, though not formally part of it, is the doctrine of patent misuse largely developed by the judiciary as a possible defence in a patent infringement action. Its basic idea is that objectionable commercial behaviour of the patentee causes a taint on the patent itself rendering it unenforceable ('unclean hands'). From the mid-1960s, however, one aspect of patent misuse has by court-made law also become an anti-trust matter; fraudulent procurement and enforcement of the patent has been held to provide basis for a treble damage anti-trust claim. For the inventor and patent practitioner today the issue of 'fraud on the patent office' has become a dominant theme in the prosecution of US patent applications and in the assessment of the validity and enforceability of any US patent.

In the recent case of Rohm and Haas *v.* Dawson Chemical the patent was for a process for retarding weed growth in a rice field by applying the selective herbicide propanil. There was no product claim to propanil itself and therefore the sale of this substance would not be a direct infringement under Section 271(a) but anyone selling it with instructions on how to use it according to the patented process would infringe under Section 271(c). Propanil has no other use and is quite material to the invention claimed. Although unauthorized sale of propanil would seem to be a straightforward instance of contributory infringement the case went to the Supreme Court and was decided in favour of the patentee by a close margin (five to four). The defendant had succeeded in giving a good run to the argument of 'patent misuse'. Although patent misuse is not strictly an anti-trust doctrine it is clearly inspired by anti-trust principles and objectives and closely follows anti-trust criteria. Moreover, the defendants' argument here was that the patentees were guilty of a tie-in because licences were in effect granted by the patentee only to purchasers of their unpatented product. The argument was ingenious because no express licence by the patentees to their customers existed; there was merely an implied licence to retailers and farmers to use the product sold to them. The only explicit licence in the whole case was the one requested from the patentees by the defendant, which was refused.

The Supreme Court decided that Section 271(c) identified the dividing line between the proper use by the patentee of the contributory infringement provision and the patent-misuse doctrine; the distinction between staple and non-staple articles of commerce is the key. The patentees here were not seeking any degree of control over unpatented materials beyond what Section 271(d) already allows.

Licensing in the EEC

Licensing activity in Europe has had to contend with a conflict of laws arising, on the one hand, from the Treaty of Rome basic conception of a unitary market transcending national barriers and, on the other, the strict national character of our historical systems of industrial property right. Patent owners who have positive licensing policies and the desire to maximize income from this kind of exploitation have very soon discovered the obstacles against effective partitioning of their licensing power, e.g. exclusive rights for France to a French company and similar rights for Germany to a German company, and so on. The principal constraints arise from the application of the principle of free movement of goods in the community. Article 36 of the treaty allows export/import restrictions designed to protect industrial property provided they do not amount to arbitrary discrimination or a disguised restriction on trade between member states. Article 85(i) prohibits agreements which restrict competition within the Common Market and Article 86 condemns the abuse of a dominant position.

Article 85(i)

'The following shall be prohibited as incompatible with the common market: all agreements between undertakings, decisions by associations of undertakings and concerted practices which may affect trade between Member States and which have as their object or effect the prevention, restriction or distortion of competition within the common market, and in particular those which:

(a) directly or indirectly fix purchase or selling prices or any other trading conditions;
(b) limit or control production, markets, technical development, or investment;
(c) share markets or sources of supply;
(d) apply dissimilar conditions to equivalent transactions with other trading parties, thereby placing them at a competitive disadvantage;

(e) make the conclusion of contracts subject to acceptance by the other parties of supplementary obligations which, by their nature or according to commercial usage, have no connection with the subject to such contracts.'

Many cases have come before the commission and the European Court of Justice on the application of these ideas to agreements relating to patents, trademarks and copyright. The commission has consistently fought for the view that once a product is lawfully marketed in one state the free circulation principle must allow export to another state even though national law was against it. The court has in recent years restored the balance in favour of reasonable use of national property rights where their exercise does not stem from an agreement or concerted practice aimed at the partitioning or isolation of the Common Market. National patent systems will continue even after the Community patent system has been ratified and enters into force and the Community Patent Convention contains the following exposition of the principle of exhaustion of rights.

Article 81

'A. The rights conferred by a National patent in a contracting state shall not extend to acts concerning a product covered by that patent which are done within the territory of that contracting state after that product has been put on the market in any contracting state by the proprietor of the patent or with his express consent, unless there are grounds which under Community law would justify the extension to such acts of the rights conferred by the patent.

'B. Paragraph A shall also apply with regard to a product put on the market by the proprietor of a national patent granted for the same invention in another contracting state who has economic connections with the proprietor of the patent referred to in paragraph A. For the purpose of this paragraph two persons shall be deemed to have economic connections when one of them is in a position to exert a decisive influence on the other, directly or indirectly, with regard to the exploitation of a patent, or where a third party is in a position to exercise such an influence on both persons.

'C. The preceding paragraphs shall not apply in the case of a product put on the market under a compulsory licence.'

The legality under Article 85 of exclusive licences and other types of agreement has been the major topic in unending debate in the industrial property field between European industry and the Brussels Commission. The commission have produced guidelines for the exemption of certain agreements from the effect of Article 85 ('Proposed Block Exemption Regulation').

European Patent Convention

ARTICLE 52

Patentable Inventions

1. European patents shall be granted for any inventions which are susceptible of industrial application, which are new and which involve an inventive step.
2. The following in particular shall not be regarded as inventions within the meaning of paragraph 1:
   (a) discoveries, scientific theories and mathematical methods;
   (b) aesthetic creations;
   (c) schemes, rules and methods for performing mental acts, playing games or doing business, and programs for computers;
   (d) presentations of information.
3. The provisions of paragraph 2 shall exclude patentability of the subject-matter of activities referred to in that provision only to the extent to which a European patent application or European patent releates to such subject-matter or activities as such.
4. Methods for treatment of the human or animal body by surgery or therapy and diagnostic methods practised on the human or animal body shall not be regarded as inventions which are susceptible of industrial application within the meaning of paragraph 1. This provision shall not apply to products, in particular substances or compositions, for use in any of these methods.

ARTICLE 53

Exceptions to Patentability

European patents shall not be granted in respect of:
   (a) inventions the publication or exploitation of which would be contrary to 'ordre public' or morality, provided that the exploitation

shall not be deemed to be so contrary merely because it is prohibited by law or regulation in some or all of the Contracting States;

(b) plant or animal varieties or essentially biological processes for the production of plants or animals; this provision does not apply to microbiological processes or the products thereof.

ARTICLE 54

Novelty

1. An invention shall be considered to be new if it does not form part of the state of the art.
2. The state of the art shall be held to comprise everything made available to the public by means of a written or oral description, by use, or in any other way, before the date of filing of the European patent application.
3. Additionally, the content of European patent applications as filed, of which the dates of filing are prior to the date referred to in paragraph 2 and which were published under Article 93 on or after that date, shall be considered as comprised in the state of the art.
4. Paragraph 3 shall be applied only in so far as a Contracting State designated in respect of the later application, was also designated in respect of the earlier application as published.
5. The provisions of paragraphs 1 to 4 shall not exclude the patentability of any substance or composition, comprised in the state of the art, for use in a method referred to in Article 52, paragraph 4, provided that its use for any method referred to in that paragraph is not comprised in the state of the art.

ARTICLE 55

Non-prejudicial Disclosures

1. For the application of Article 54 a disclosure of the invention shall not be taken into consideration if it occurred no earlier than six months preceding the filing of the European patent application and if it was due to, or in consequence of:
   (a) an evident abuse in relation to the applicant or his legal predecessor, or

(b) the fact that the applicant or his legal predecessor has displayed the invention at an official, or officially recognized, international exhibition falling within the terms of the Convention on international exhibitions signed at Paris on 22 November 1928 and last revised on 30 November 1972.

2. In the case of paragraph 1(b), paragraph 1 shall apply only if the applicant states, when filing the European patent application, that the invention has been so displayed and files a supporting certificate within the period and under the conditions laid down in the Implementing Regulations.

ARTICLE 56

Inventive Step

An invention shall be considered as involving an inventive step if, having regard to the state of the art, it is not obvious to a person skilled in the art. If the state of the art also includes documents within the meaning of Article 54, paragraph 3, these documents are not to be considered in deciding whether there has been an inventive step.

ARTICLE 57

Industrial Application

An invention shall be considered as susceptible of industrial application if it can be made or used in any kind of industry, including agriculture.

Extract from United States Code Title 35—Patents

SECTION 100   DEFINITIONS

When used in this title unless the context otherwise indicates—

(a) The term 'invention' means invention or discovery.

(b) The term 'process' means process, art or method, and includes a new use of a known process, machine, manufacture, composition of matter, or material.

(c) The terms 'United States' and 'this country' means the United States of America, its territories and possessions.

(d) The word 'patentee' includes not only the patentee to whom the patent was issued but also the successors in title to the patentee.

SECTION 101   INVENTIONS PATENTABLE

Whoever invents or discovers any new and useful process, machine, manufacture, or composition of matter, or any new and useful improvement thereof, may obtain a patent therefor, subject to the conditions and requirements of this title.

SECTION 102   CONDITIONS FOR PATENTABILITY; NOVELTY AND LOSS OF RIGHT TO PATENT

A person shall be entitled to a patent unless:

(a) the invention was known or used by others in this country, or patented or described in a printed publication in this or a foreign country, before the invention thereof by the applicant for patent, or

(b) the invention was patented or described in a printed publication in this or a foreign country or in public use or on sale in this country, more than one year prior to the date of the application for patent in the United States, or

(c) he has abandoned the invention, or

(d) the invention was first patented or caused to be patented, or was the subject of an inventor's certificate, by the applicant or his legal representatives or assigns in a foreign country prior to the date of the application for patent in this country on an application for patent or inventor's certificate filed more than twelve months before the filing of the application in the United States, or

(e) the invention was described in a patent granted on an application for patent by another filed in the United States before the invention thereof by the applicant for patent, or on an international application by another who has fulfilled the requirements of paragraphs (1), (2), and (4) of section 371(c) of this title before the invention thereof by the applicant for patent, or

(f) he did not himself invent the subject matter sought to be patented, or

(g) before the applicant's invention thereof the invention was made in this country by another who had not abandoned, suppressed, or concealed it. In determining priority of invention there shall be considered not only the respective dates of conception and reduction to practice of the invention, but also the reasonable diligence of one who was first to conceive and last to reduce to practice, from a time prior to conception by the other.

SECTION 103   CONDITIONS FOR PATENTABILITY; NON-OBVIOUS SUBJECT MATTER

A patent may not be obtained though the invention is not identically disclosed or described as set forth in section 102 of this title, if the differences between the subject matter sought to be patented and the prior art are such that the subject matter as a whole would have been obvious at the time the invention was made to a person having ordinary skill in the art to which said subject matter pertains. Patentability shall not be negatived by the manner in which the invention was made.

New Rule 28 (EPC)

ARTICLE 1

The following text shall be substituted for Rule 28 of the Implementing Regulations:

Rule 28

Requirements of European patent applications relating to micro-organisms

1. If an invention concerns a microbiological process or the product thereof and involves the use of a micro-organism which is not available to the public and which cannot be described in the European patent application in such a manner as to enable the invention to be carried out by a person skilled in the art, the invention shall only be regarded as being disclosed as prescribed in Article 83 if:

    (a) a culture of the micro-organism has been deposited with a recognized depositary institution not later than the date of filing of the application;

    (b) the application as filed gives such relevant information as is available to the applicant on the characteristics of the micro-organism;

    (c) the depositary institution and the file number of the culture deposit are stated in the application.

2. The information referred to in paragraph 1(c) may be submitted:

    (a) within a period of 16 months after the date of filing of the application or, if priority is claimed, after the priority date;

    (b) up to the date of submission of a request for early publication of the application;

    (c) within one month after the European Patent Office has communicated to the applicant that a right to inspection of the files, pursuant to Article 128, paragraph 2, exists.

    The ruling period shall be the one which is the first to expire. The communication of this information shall be considered as constituting the unreserved and irrevocable consent of the applicant to the deposited culture being made available to the public in accordance with this Rule.

3. The deposited culture shall be available upon request to any person from the date of publication of the European patent application and to any person having the right to inspect the files under the provisions of Article 128, paragraph 2, prior to that date. Subject to the provisions of paragraph 4, such availability shall be effected by the issue of a sample of the micro-organism to the person making the request (hereinafter referred to as the 'requester'). Said issue shall be made only if the requester has undertaken *vis-à-vis* the applicant for or proprietor of the patent:

   (a) not to make the deposited culture or any culture derived therefrom available to any third party before the application has been refused or withdrawn or is deemed to be withdrawn or, if a patent is granted, before the expiry of the patent in the designated State in which it last expires;

   (b) to use the deposited culture or any culture derived therefrom for experimental purposes only, until such time as the patent application is refused or withdrawn or is deemed to be withdrawn, or up to the date of publication of the mention of the grant of the European patent. This provision shall not apply insofar as the requester is using the culture under a compulsory licence. The term 'compulsory licence' shall be construed as including *ex officio* licences and the right to use patented inventions in the public interest.

4. Until the date on which the technical preparations for publication of the application are deemed to have been completed, the applicant may inform the European Patent Office that, until the publication of the mention of the grant of the European patent or until the date on which the application has been refused or withdrawn or is deemed to be withdrawn, the availability referred to in paragraph 3 shall be effected only by the issue of a sample to an expert nominated by the requester.

5. The following may be nominated as an expert:

   (a) any natural person provided that the requester furnishes evidence, when filing the request, that the nomination has the approval of the applicant;

   (b) any natural person recognized as an expert by the President of the European Patent Office. The nomination shall be accompanied by an undertaking from the expert *vis-à-vis* the applicant: paragraph 3 (a) and (b) shall apply, the requester being regarded as a third party.

6. For the purposes of paragraph 3, a derived culture is deemed to be any culture of the micro-organism which still exhibits those characteristics of the deposited culture which are essential to carrying out the invention. The undertaking referred to in paragraph 3 shall not impede a deposit of a derived culture, necessary for the purpose of patent procedure.

7. The request provided for in paragraph 3 shall be submitted to the European Patent Office on a form recognized by that Office. The European Patent Office shall certify on the form that a European patent application referring to the deposit of the micro-organism has been filed, and that the requester or the expert nominated by him is entitled to the issue of a sample of the micro-organism.

8. The European Patent Office shall transmit a copy of the request, with the certification provided for in paragraph 7, to the depositary institution as well as to the applicant for or the proprietor of the patent.

9. The President of the European Patent Office shall publish in the Official Journal of the European Patent office the list of depositary institutions and experts recognized for the purpose of this Rule.

ARTICLE 2

The following Rule 28a shall be inserted in the Implementing Regulations:

Rule 28a

New deposit of a micro-organism

1. If a micro-organism deposited in accordance with Rule 28, paragraph 1, ceases to be available from the institution with which it was deposited because:
   (a) the micro-organism is no longer viable, or
   (b) for any other reason the depositary institution is unable to supply samples,
   and if the micro-organism has not been transferred to another depositary institution recognized for the purposes of Rule 28, from which it continues to be available, an interruption in availability shall be deemed not to have occurred if a new deposit of the micro-

organism originally deposited is made within a period of three months from the date on which the depositor was notified of the interruption by the depositary institution and if a copy of the receipt of the deposit issued by the institution is forwarded to the European Patent Office within four months from the date of the new deposit stating the number of the application or of the European patent.

2. In the case provided for in paragraph 1(a), the new deposit shall be made with the depositary institution with which the original deposit was made; in the cases provided for in paragraph 1(b), it may be made with another depositary institution recognized for the purposes of Rule 28.

3. Where the institution with which the original deposit was made ceases to be recognized for the purposes of the application of Rule 28, either entirely or for the kind of micro-organism to which the deposited micro-organism belongs, or where that institution discontinues, temporarily or definitively, the performance of its functions as regards deposited micro-organisms, and the notification referred to in paragraph 1 from the depositary institution is not received within six months from the date of such event, the three-month period referred to in paragraph 1 shall begin on the date on which this event is announced in the Official Journal of the European Patent Office.

4. Any new deposit shall be accompanied by a statement signed by the depositor alleging that the newly deposited micro-organism is the same as that originally deposited.

5. If the new deposit provided for in the present Rule has been made under the provisions of the Budapest Treaty on the International Recognition of the Deposit of Microorganisms for the Purposes of Patent Procedure of 28 April 1977, the provisions of that Treaty shall prevail in case of conflict.

Extract from the Budapest Convention

RULE 11—FURNISHING OF SAMPLES

3. Furnishing of samples to parties legally entitled
   (a) Any international depository authority shall furnish a sample of any deposited micro-organism to any authority, natural person or legal entity (hereinafter referred to as 'the certified party'), on the request of such party, provided that the request is made on a form whose contents are fixed by the Assembly and that on the said form the industrial property office certifies:
      (i) that an application referring to the deposit of that micro-organism has been filed with that office for the grant of a patent and that the subject matter of that application involves the said micro-organism or the use thereof:
      (ii) that, except where the second phrase of (iii) applies publication for the purposes of patent procedure has been effected by that office;
      (iii) *either* that the certified party has a right to a sample of the micro-organism under the law governing patent procedure before that office and, where the said law makes the said right dependent on the fulfilment of certain conditions, that that office is satisfied that such conditions have actually been fulfilled *or* that the certified party has affixed his signature on a form before that office and that, as a consequence of the signature of the said form, the conditions for furnishing a sample to the certified party are deemed to be fulfilled in accordance with the law governing patent procedure before that office; where the certified party has the said right under the said law prior to publication for the purposes of patent procedure by the said office and such publication has not yet been effected, the certification shall

expressly state so and shall indicate, by citing it in the customary manner, the applicable provision of the said law, including any court decision.

(b) In respect of patents granted and published by any industrial property office, such office may from time to time communicate to any international depository authority lists of the accession numbers given by that authority to the deposits of the micro-organisms referred to in the said patents. The international depository authority shall, on the request of any authority, natural person or legal entity (hereinafter referred to as 'the requesting party'), furnish to it a sample of any micro-organism where the accession number has been so communicated. In respect of deposited micro-organisms whose accession numbers have been so communicated, the said office shall not be required to provide the certification referred to in Rule 11(3)(a).

Index